POLITICS & LANGUAGE

A CASE STUDY OF GOA

POLITICS & LANGUAGE

A CASE STUDY OF GOA

PRADIP NARAYAN MASKE

KALPAZ

Published by

Kalpaz Publications
C-30, Satyawati Nagar,
Delhi – 110052
Ph.: 011-47034999, 9811692060
www.kalpazpublications.com
E-mail: kalpaz@hotmail.com

Distribution Network
gyanbooks.com
India, USA, Canada, UK, Australia, France

ISBN: 978-93-5722-693-6 (HB)
First Published, 2025

Printed at: Gyan Press, Delhi.

POLITICS & LANGUAGE
Author : PRADIP NARAYAN MASKE

Contents

Foreword

Tiny territory of Hindusthan was and is victim of machinations of colonialists and their indigenous collaborators. Real name of this territory is Gomantak. Not only its real name is tarnished but also names of many places within it are soiled. Gomantak is named Goa and names such as Salvador de Mundo, St. Inez, Santa Estevo, Santa Jose de Areal, Soccoro, Dona Paula, Campal, Penha de Franca, Reis Magos, Vasco da Gama are imposed.

When their attempts to destroy Konkani, the original language of people, failed, Christians tore its script. Devanagari script was replaced by Roman script. Their cherished goal is to make Gomantak forever Rome of the East under tutelage of Pope. If total area of Sovereign State of Pope can be just 108.7 acres of Rome, the Capital of Italy, why Gomantak cannot be Rome of the East within the State of Hindusthan? Such was their logic. Their means were brutish and boorish. Their Inquisitions are specimen of disgraceful and notorious events in world history.

Reality tells that Reorganisation of Nation's territories on the basis of languages has done more harm than good. It has weakened Unity of Nation and strengthened Anti-Nationalist forces. In Gomantak, Konkani Language has become valuable weapon for perpetual preservation of Christian culture in Hindusthan.

Author has concentrated on the exposition of the nefarious activities of Divisive forces using Konkani Language. His book is a notable contribution towards Truth-based Knowledge.

Maruti Jagannath Audi

(*Retired-Reader, Department of Political Science,*
Goa University, Taleigao Plateau, Goa)

Preface

The work is an outcome of the thesis submitted for the award of a doctoral degree in 2001 by the Nehru Institute of Social Sciences, Tilak Maharashtra Vidyapeeth, Pune, India. It is a historical-cum-analytical, descriptive, and explorative study. It aims at in-depth and comprehensive analysis of linkages between politics and language. The period of study ranges from the genesis of linguistic controversy in the pre-Liberation period to the revival of language controversy in 1985-87 and its revival after the judgement of the Panaji Bench of the Mumbai High Court on March 30, 2000, in the Marathi Rajya Bhasha Prasthapan Samiti and Gomantak Marathi Akademy V/s State of Goa case.

India is facing a twin issue of nation-building on the one hand and state-building on the other. Instead of erosion of primordial loyalties, India is witnessing its revival for economic gain and political power. Language is a uniting as well as a disuniting force. It affects the integration of the political community. The parochial loyalties are often expressed in cultural terms. The elevation of parochial loyalties at the political plane work against public interest, thereby leading to socio-political tensions. The sub-national sentiments and sub-national competition at the periphery works against the national unity.

The volume and scale of conflicts between integration and anti-integration groups increased soon after the Liberation of Goa. The anti-integration groups stressed the separate identity of Goa. The integration groups identified with the cause of Marathi language and literature. They refuted the claim that the territory has had a separate linguistic identity. They supported the cause of merger with Marathi-speaking areas of Maharashtra to counter the forces that were pitted against the integration of Goa with India. The advocates of Konkani groups succeeded in mobilizing public opinion in favour of the status quo over the future of the territory in 1967. It temporarily affected the cause of Marathi. The anti-integration groups claimed that the statehood in 1987 gave a permanent burial to the ghost of merger. The Konkani language movement has turned to be a symbol of self-pride, whereas the Marathi language movement evoked national pride.

The attempts were made by the Bharatiya Janata Party to amend the Goa, Daman & Diu Official Language Act, 1987, to give equal status to the Marathi language for its use for all the official purposes for which Konkani language is used for the official purposes of the State of Goa. The High Court of Bombay at Goa in its judgement dated 30-03-2000 passed in Writ Petition No. 286/96 has held that both, the Konkani and Marathi languages do not enjoy the equal status. The present Bill, the BJP claimed, is being introduced to remove said lacunae and to achieve and give effect to the original intention as referred to above so to make it express and explicit. The Bill also seeks to encourage the people to use the Konkani and Marathi languages for the official purposes of the state of Goa. The statehood of Goa has diluted rather than strengthened the separate identity of Goa. The question is raised which way and how should Goa go in the changing socio-political and demographic scenario. The language controversy continues to raise its head in the fragile political set-up. The state government has not adopted a clear-cut language policy. The Roman Catholic Church is in favour of use of the Roman script for official purpose. The Study is carried out in the light of integration theory and focuses on the interaction between language and political process. This is first of its kind.

Acknowledgement

I am indebted to Dr. S. R. Kakade for his guidance, encouragement, and inspiration in this unique, challenging, and interesting study. I express my gratitude to late Shashikala Kakodkar, former Chief Minister of Goa, Daman & Diu; Pratapsing Raoji Rane, former Chief Minister of Goa and Speaker, Goa Legislative Assembly; late Jayantrao Tilak, former Speaker of Maharashtra Legislative Council; P. P. Shirodkar, first Speaker of the Legislative Assembly of Goa Daman & Diu; Adv. Ramakant Khalap, former Union Minister for Law & Judiciary; late Dr. Kashinath Jalmi, former Minister for Law; late Ravindra Kelekar, freedom fighter, Gandhian thinker and writer; Uday Bhembre, ex-editor of Konkani daily Sunaprant and ex-MLA; Naguesh Karmali, freedom fighter and Konkani writer; Dr. Tanaji Halarnkar, ex-editor, Konkani Encyclopaedia; Pundalik Naik, Konkani writer and former Convenor of Konkani Porjeacho Awaz; N. Shivdas, eminent Konkani writer; late Principal Gopalrao Mayenkar, President, Gomantak Marathi Akademy; Bhiku Pai Angle, Marathi writer and educationist; Jaisingrao Abasaheb Rane Sardessai, Marathi writer and freedom fighter; and the members of Goa Legislative Assembly for sharing their views, comments and suggestions in this academic exercise.

I acknowledge the financial assistance of INR 15,000/- provided by the University Grants Commission, New Delhi, under the Minor Research Project in 2003 for the completion of the research study. I thank the director and staff of the Nehru Institute of Social Sciences, Tilak Maharashtra Vidyapeeth, Pune, Goa University, and the management, principal, and staff of the G.V.M's G.G.P.R. College of Commerce & Economics for their encouragement and cooperation in this fruitful exercise. I am grateful to the Directorate of Higher Education, Government of Goa, for sanctioning my earned leave from December 9, 2024 to April 30, 2025 for writing this book.

In Goa, the following institutions provided me library material— the Central Library; Xavier Centre of Historical Research; S. P. Chowgule College of Arts & Science; Government College of Arts, Commerce & Science; PES's SRSN College of Arts & Science; and the library units of dailies—The Navhind Times; and Gomantak and Goa Legislature

Secretariat; Department of Information & Publicity; Department of Statistics, Planning & Evaluation; Directorate of Education; and Directorate of Official Language & Public Grievances, Government of Goa. In Pune, Jayakar Library and Centre of Advanced Studies in Sanskrit of University of Pune and Marathi dailies—*Sakal* and *Kesari* provided me the facility for the library reference work.

I dedicate this book in memory of my late mother Suhasini Narayan Maske and father Narayan Baburao Maske.

Chapter–I

INTRODUCTION

A language that a person speaks is next to his or her heart. It has an emotive appeal. It is not a process or product. It is primarily a thought itself. The social necessity of various communities, in the past, resulted into separation, isolation, and interaction leading to the development of different speech communities that hitherto belonged to common parent language. 'Language was not a major symbol of identity in the pre-modern societies' (Rahman, 1998: 17). Language has an impact beyond words and literature. A common language is a bond that unites the people. Also, separate others. It is an icon. It possesses power to alter history. It moves the masses at political plane. A language is not like an umbrella or over-coat that can be borrowed by unconscious or deliberate mistake. It is like a living skin itself.

Language, at no point of history, formed the basis for nationhood in Indian psyche. 'The concept of nation-state in the West is built on unitary symbols. It is presumed that each nation has one language, one religion and one culture. Therefore, it is nationally integrated' (Bayer, 1986: 69). Rousseau argued in his essay on the Origin of Languages that 'language must develop before politics is possible and that language originally distinguished nations from one another' (*Op. Cit.* King, 1997: 24). 'In the heyday of European nationalism from 1848 to 1919, language was more frequently invoked than any other criterion to assert nationality' (Rustow, 1967: 47). 'The belief that political boundaries should coincide with linguistic boundaries had emerged recently on the world scene. It was the product of nineteenth century nationalism' (King 1997: 25).

For the outside world, India is a babel or laboratory of multi-lingualism. In 1886, the World Congress of Orientalists asked for systematic and thorough study, which produced Sir George Grierson's Linguistic Survey of India (1894-1927). The Linguistic Survey of India (1901) enumerated 179 languages and 544 dialects. The Census of 1951 enumerated 845 so-called mother tongues, including local dialects. However, perfect, definitive and unquestionable classifications though desirable, are not available anywhere in the world. The Census of 1991, recorded 1652 mother tongues including 63 non-Indian spoken languages (Basu, 2000; 387). Out of which people speak 33 over a lakh of the population.

There are 22 languages included in the Eighth Schedule of the Constitution of India till date. There is demand for inclusion of more languages in the Eighth Schedule to the Constitution of India. Interestingly, there is no standard for inclusion of the languages in the Eighth Schedule. These are national languages. Marathi is elevated to the states of classical language in 2024. The National Education Policy 2020 aims at promotion of Indian languages in the colleges and universities in India. The linguistic identification and administrative decisions behind offering official status to the languages may disagree with the sentiments of the people, today.

In the past, the multiplicity of languages did not threaten the unity of India. Many languages are presently seen as linguistic confusion and local nationalism a counter-force of nation-wide nationalism. In 19th century, Lokmanya Bal Gangadhar Tilak stated 'the existence of multiplicity of languages does not give rise to different nationalities. It only reflects unhealthy and incomplete signs of nationality' (*Kesari*: 09-09-1890). 'We can appeal to our people better through vernaculars than through English. English can never hope to become the language of the people. We must appeal to them through vernaculars' (*Op. Cit.* Sathe, 1994: 113). Socio-linguists argue that many languages in a country are not always an index of barrier of communication in that country. A multi-lingual country should not be treated as mere juxtaposition of a number of monolingual territories. In a large multi-lingual country like, India, continuous movement of people and ideas over long period has resulted in diffusion of linguistic features across language families. Nonetheless, history of India is the history of migration. One of the significant features of multi-lingualism in India is existence of stable bi-lingual or multi-lingual communities. For that matter, the linguistic nationalism is alien to Indian tradition, people and psyche.

'In Indian tradition, both oral and literate cultures have played a vital role. The plural heritage rejects the supremacy of one over the other' (Khubchandani 1992: 24). A language flourishes at the socio-cultural plane. It cannot be imposed from out side. All languages have inherent limitations and they have to work within those limitations. Nonetheless, language has turned out to be a tool to mobilise people politically in the modern period of history. Language became a marker of sub-nation or local identity. It has sapped our ability to reinforce national integration. Language represents particular interest, *per se*. It overrides public interest. It wields covert ideological power. 'Linguism elevates language as a basis of group sentiments seeking expression in terms of power politics. It is identified with culture and equated culture with political boundaries of the province', according to K. M. Munshi (*Op Cit*. Phadke 1973: 12).

In the past, oral and literate culture represented by regional languages— Konkani and Marathi simultaneously flourished in Konkan region of which Goa is a part. A minuscule and articulate minority whipped up the linguistic sentiments for political and economic gain in the post-Liberation era. The language issue engulfed Goa soon after Liberation in 1961. It surfaced caste, regional, and communal loyalties during the Opinion Poll in 1967 and language agitation in 1985-1986. On May 30, 1987, Goa became a full-fledged state. It gave a separate political and linguistic identity. The language controversy again surfaced after the judgement of the Panaji Bench of Bombay High Court on March 30, 2000 in the State. The Bench interpreted that the Konkani and Marathi languages do not enjoy equal status under the Goa, Daman & Diu Official Language Act, 1987. The Act of 1987 was in fact a compromise formula that did not satisfy the Roman Catholic Church in Goa which favoured the Roman script for Konkani instead of the Devanagari script. Konkani is accorded the sole official status with Devanagari script. The demand for Roman script for Konkani not entirely extinct after 38 years of the enactment of the Goa, Daman & Diu Official Language Act, 1987.

Linguistic Nationalism Versus Cultural Nationalism

Goa was liberated 14 years after Independence of India in December 1961. There are 47 banks with 787 branches and covering average population of 1807 as on 31/03/2020. A strong, reliable and robust banking sector aids poverty eradication programmes undertaken by the state and non-state agencies. The work to eradicate extreme poverty by 2030 has begun and 45564 persons have exited multi-dimensional poverty in Goa, according to the national multidimensional poverty index report of the Institution for Transforming India (NITI) Aayog Report in 2023. Kerala and Goa are the two states with less than 1% population living in multidimensional poverty index in 2023.

Language is a uniting as well as a disuniting force. The map of India was drawn and redrawn on the linguistic basis in India, That Is Bharat. There are 28 states and 8 union territories in Union of India, today. Language is not a marker of identity. More than one language flourished in a province before the occupation of Hindusthan by foreign powers. Goa was part of Konkan Kshetra from the Vedic period. The native people nursed the territory spiritually and materially. The oral and written languages flourished in Goa in the past.

The Portuguese occupied the Islands of Tiswadi 1510 ACE, and Bardez and Salcete in 1543 ACE. The remaining areas of territory came under the Portuguese occupation in 1788 ACE. The Jesuit priests authored the Holy Inquisition for suppression of heresy and punishment of heretics in 1545 ACE to the king of Portugal. Portugal extended the Inquisition to Goa in 1560. The Inquisition was finally abolished in 1812. In terms of the Portuguese language and their religion, the native languages and religion were far superior to the Europeans. They came to know that the learned class were well-versed in Sanskrit and they failed to convince the benefits of conversion to Christianity. And chose the Inquisition to foist their religion, language on the native people by force fraud and inducement. Portuguese inflicted the worst atrocities on the native people under the Institution of Inquisition. The Konkani speakers migrated to neighbouring states to save life, honour, and religious freedom and others lived a life of second class citizens in Goa. The colonial rulers failed to impose the Portuguese language on the native people, despite 450 years of their occupation. Less than two per cent people could hardly speak Portuguese at the fag end of Liberation of Goa in 1961. Interestingly, Portugal remained as the illiterate country of the Europe and 56 per cent of country's population could only read, count and write in 1950.

The native tongue was despised by colonial rulers and rich and influential converted class to christianity as a 'kitchen language.' Konkani originated in Konkan, as the name suggests. Marathi was used as a written medium of expression by Hindus in Goa. Portuguese stunted the growth of native languages and exploited the people materially and spiritually.

The Maharashtrawadi Gomantak Party championed the cause of Marathi and merger with Maharashtra soon after the Liberation of Goa in 1961. The United Goans Party opposed the merger and identified itself with the Konkani language. Mysore (now Karnataka) laid claim over the union territory of Goa, Daman and Diu because of its rich iron ore deposits, historical links, and geographical contiguity. Maharashtra justified the merger on grounds of linguistic and cultural affinity. The supporters of Vidarbha region, however, did not favour the merger of Goa with Maharashtra. The Opinion Poll in 1967 put to rest the merger issue.

The Official Language Act, 1987 provides that Konkani shall be the official language and Marathi shall be used for all or any of the official purposes. Konkani has evolved as a modern literary language. Devanagari script is a popular, distinct, and natural script of Konkani. The official status given to any language need not reflect its literary merit, but it paves the way for growth of national languages in the mainstream of the country. Goa has merged with the mainstream of the country, today. The official status to Konkani with Devanagari script was a compromise formula to pacify both communities—Hindus and Christians in Goa.

The anti-integration forces that were opposed to the integration of Goa with the mainstream of India are not entirely extinct. They try to justify their vested interests as freedom of expression by resorting to non-violent to violent tactics in a nascent democracy. Nonetheless, the nation comes first. All other things are secondary. Lokmanya Bal Gangadhar Tilak wrote in 'Kesari' on 09/09/1890 'the existence of multiplicity of languages does not give rise to different nationalities. It only reflects unhealthy and incomplete signs of nationality'.

The new mantra is Viksit Bharat@2047' to transform India, that is, Bharat into a developed nation by striking harmony, balance, and equilibrium between development and heritage. India is not merely a Union of 28 states and eight union territories, but a living civilization.

Locale of the Study

Goa, the tiniest State of Union of India, is the land of scenic beauty and hospitable people. It is situated at 14-53 N and 15-40 N latitude and 73-40 E and 74-21E longitudes. The Union territory of Goa, Daman and Diu was liberated from Portuguese rulers on December 19, 1961. Goa emerged on the map of India as a full-fledged State on May 30, 1987. It is administratively divided into two districts— North Goa and South Goa, seven sub-divisions and 12 talukas. There are 44 towns— 14 municipal and 359 revenue villages in 2001. Goa is 105 kms long and 62 kms wide. It covers geographical area of 3,702 sq. kms. The State of Maharashtra bound it to the North, State of Karnataka lies at its East and South and the Arabian Sea in the West. The river Tiracol runs along the northern boundary and the Sahyadri Range separates the eastern boundary. The 111 metre high peak at Polle in Canacona bounds southern section of the State.

Geologically, most part of the State belongs to Chitradurga group of rocks of Archaean to lower Proterozoic period. It comprises of coastal region, plateau region, Sahyadri range, and forest areas. The coastal region covering Salcete, Tiswadi, Bardez, Mormugao and parts of Perne, Ponda, Bicholi and Canacona. It comprises of 36.06 per cent of total geographical area of the State. The Plateau region (31.74%) covers talukas of Quepe, Perne, Bicholi, Ponda, Sattari, and Sangue. The Sahyadri hills (24.24%) cover Sattari, Sangue, and Canacona talukas. The Chauri forested areas

(7.61%) include Quepe, Canacona and Anjadip Island of Canacona, which is situated off-Karwar coast, according to Census of 1981.

The intersection of rivers has given rise to many islands. The principal islands are - Tiswadi, Chorao, Divar, Cumbharjuve, Dongri, Queloshi and Khorjuve. The economic life depended on the rivers. Goa's external trade flourished in the river basin. Traditionally, Goa was well-known water harvesting territory of the Konkan Kshetra. The inland river system with natural harbour has contributed for cheap, easy and speedy transportation of mineral ore from hinterland to coastal basin. The main rivers of Goa are - Mandovi, Zuari, Chapora, Tiracol, Galgibag, Sal, and Talpon. 'The total navigability for small country craft is approximately 371 kms whereas for large craftmine it is 253 kms. The soil is predominantly laterite and covers three zones, laterite, middle, and hinterland. The climate is warm and humid. The annual rainfall ranging between 280 to 350 cms.

Goa recorded 4,75,513 population in 1900; 4,86,752 in 1910; 4,69,494 in 1921; 5,05,281in 1930; 5,40,925 in 1940; 5,47,448 in 1950; 5,89,997 in 1960; 7,95,120 in 1971; 10,07,749 in 1981; 11,69,793 in 1991; and 13,43,998 in 2001, 14,58,545 in 2011, respectively (Census of India, 2011). The projected population in 2025 is 15.90 lakhs. In 1960-71, Goa registered a spurt in the population with 34.77 growth rate— due to changes in the social, political and economic situation and large-scale development programmes undertaken by the government, which attracted labour from the other states. The percentage of rural population to the total population was 37.83 and that of urban population was 62.17 in 2011. The percentage of literate population 79.90 per cent in 2011. Goa's forest cover is 2265.72 sq. km. out of total geographical area of 3702 sq. km. in 2023. The Census of India 2021 is postponed to 2025.

Portuguese interfered with Gaokary system (communidades) which were autonomous, powerful, self-sufficient bodies in the entire Konkan region of India. The members of Gaokary system managed agricultural land and simultaneously were vested with municipal, judicial, fiscal functions and discharged public welfare activities. 'The Gaokars were the earliest settlers of Goa and included, Gauda, Kunbi and Jalmi communities. They nursed 'Gaokary system and were Mahajans (Mazanias), which existed before 1054 BCE in Goa' (Pereira, 1978:2).

In 2003, Gawda, Kunbi and Velip communities were included in the scheduled tribes category. As per Census of 2011, population of scheduled tribes constitute 10.23% in Goa. There is no political reservation extended to the to these tribal communities. Besides, Dhangar community which constitute population of 20000 have demanded for inclusion of their community in the scheduled tribe category. The demand is yet to be realised in Goa. Political reservations for the vulnerable sections of the society also helps to escape the extreme poverty net in India. The Readjustment of Representation of Scheduled Tribes in Assembly Constituencies of the State of Goa Bill introduced in Parliament on August 5, 2024 would enable to seek reservations to these communities under Article 332 of Indian Constitution in 2027.

This book is an exposition on the linguistic affairs of Goa. It throws light on dynamics of reorganisation of states in India and linguistic affairs of Goa from pre-liberation to statehood phase. It is a historical, analytical, descriptive and explorative study of the smallest state of Union of India. It is study of its kind after 64 years of the liberation of the Union Territory of Goa, Daman and Diu and 38 years of statehood of Goa.

Chapter Scheme

The present study, firstly, aims at tracing the genesis of linguistic conflict in Goa. Secondly, to examine the position taken by the advocates of Konkani and Marathi over the status of Konkani. Thirdly, to examine the basis for elevation of the status of Konkani. Lastly, to highlight upon areas of linguistic conflict in the political community and areas of co-operation amongst the masses. The present study is divided into six chapters. The first chapter deals with Introduction. The second chapter titled Dynamics of Reorganisation of States in India highlights upon linguistic demands in India and thinking on regional languages. The third chapter entitled Linguistic Affairs of Goa— The Pre-Liberation Phase covers linguistic persecution in Goa; language & identity in Goa; and script controversy in Goa. The fourth chapter titled Linguistic Affairs of Goa—The Opinion Poll Phase highlights upon the controversy over status of Konkani in Goa; impact of neighbouring states on Goa; and pressure groups & merger issue in Goa. The fifth chapter entitled Linguistic Affairs of Goa— The Statehood Phase covers elevation of status of regional languages in Goa; language & statehood of Goa; and official language policy in Goa. The last chapter deals with Conclusion.

Chapter–II

DYNAMICS OF REORGANISATION OF STATES IN INDIA

Although Indian nationalism is not based on the language, the demand for linguistic reorganisation of states in the country dates back to the pre-Independence era. The political expediency marked the reorganisation of the states. It sacrificed the vital component of economic viability, administrative convenience, and linguistic principle giving rise to illogical, artificial and haphazard political boundaries. The political, military and strategic considerations formed the basis for the provincial reorganisation during the British rule. The imperial policy aimed at consolidation of political power and weakening of the nationalist forces. The colonial rulers encouraged the native languages so that each linguistic group would think in terms of separate nationalities.

LINGUISTIC DEMANDS IN INDIA

Linguistic Demands before 1947

There were eleven governor's provinces, and five chief commissioner's provinces under the umbrella of the British Crown. 'The lack of any natural frontiers between States and British India reflected in the character of their respective peoples. The inhabitants of the States all spring from the same race, speak same language, profess the same religion as their neighbours over the borders' (Meherwade, 1973: 14). In 1876, the Oriya-speaking in people raised the demand for a separate province followed by Bihar in 1896.

Lokmanya B. G. Tilak wrote: "*The present administrative division of India is the result of certain historical process and in some cases is exclusively the result of chance circumstances... If it is replaced by a system of administrative units created on a linguistic basis, each of them somewhat homogeneous and will facilitate the development of people and the languages of the respective people*" (*Kesari*: 17-9-1893).

In 1901, the secession of the North West Frontier Province from Punjab Province created a Pushto territory beyond Durand Line. The union of Agra and Oudh resulted in creation of United Province in 1902 and the union of Central Provinces and Berar 1903. These developments responded to local convenience without taking into account ethno-linguistic considerations (Berton, 1973: 150). In 1902, Lord Curzon recognised the necessity for re-distribution of provinces. Lord Curzon said: "*The question of territorial and administrative re-distribution is indeed in our judgement one of the most urgent and vital of any problems for which we are at present endeavouring to find a solution*" (*Op. Cit*. Rao, 1973: 114).

The linguistic principle figured for the first time in a letter dated December 3, 1903 from Herbert Risley, Home Secretary, Government of Bengal. Reference to it recurred in the dispatch of Lord Hardinge's Government to the Secretary of the State, dated August 15, 1911, promising annulment of the Partition of Bengal. The Bengal Province became the cockpit of the nationalist activities. 'In 1904, Curzon partitioned homogenous province of Bengal and amalgamated Marathi speaking areas of Berar with the Hindi speaking Central Province' (Pai Panandikar *&et al* 1999: 384). It helped the imperialist power to weaken the nationalist forces. But led to widespread protests all over the country. The Partition of Bengal was closely followed through Marathi and English press in Goa, particularly *Kesari* edited by Lokmanya B. G. Tilak' (Gaitonde 1987: 16). In 1937, Persian was abolished as the language of records and the courts and was replaced by English and other Indian Languages in higher and lower courts. The native languages were recognised and strengthened by the colonial rulers.

The Persian language was replaced as the official language by the vernaculars during the British Raj. The policy aimed making the people speaking these languages to think themselves as separate nationalities. It led to a phenomenal rise in development of native languages. 'The British were apparently more tolerant of the native languages but spread English out of policy' (Rahman, 1998: 24). They also maintained status quo over the traditional elitist tendencies of the ruling cultural and religious traditions in India and encouraged the higher education in English rather than the basic education in the vernaculars.

Nobel laureate Amartya Sen wrote: "*There is even some evidence that where Western imperialists conquered countries in Asia and Africa, they tended to expand rather than counteract the biases that had already existed in local cultures. The British in India took little interest in elementary education, but were quite keen on creating institutions of higher learning in the good, old Brahamanical mode, whereas the same British in Buddhist Burma gave much encouragement to the expansion of elementary teaching, even though they tended to do rather little for higher education*" (Dreze & Sen, 1996: 14-15).

The Indian National Congress (INC) championed the cause of united Bengal in 1905 and championed the linguistic principle for Bihar in 1908, Sindh and Andhra in 1917. On April 8, 1917, the All India Congress Committee (AICC) approved the constitution of eleven Telugu districts into separate Congress circles. Lokmanya B. G. Tilak supported the proposal to this effect, but Annie Besant vehemently opposed it. The Congress party lent its support to the linguistic reorganisation of states, but faced the question of evolving a common language through out India. 'Lokmanya B. G. Tilak at Kashi Nagari Prachyarani Sabha advocated Devanagari script for native languages in the country, which he felt would facilitate promotion of Hindi as a national language' (*Kesari*: 9-1-1906).

In 1917, Mahatma Gandhi, in his presidential address at the Second Gujarati Conference in Broach stated 'Hindi alone could become the national language. Moreover, Hindi and Urdu were the same, the difference being only in the style' (Munshi 1967: 215-16). Gandhi placed language issue at the core of the Independence movement. 'He supported the idea of having Devanagari script for vernaculars' (Rahman, 1998: 73). 'Pandit Jawaharlal Nehru preferred two scripts (Persian and Devanagari) in the north and one in the south. He stressed 'the efforts should be made to approximate Devanagari to the four scripts of the four southern languages—Tamil, Telugu, Kannada and Malayalam; if these were not favourable, a composite script for the southern languages should be devised' (Brecher, 1959: 235-236).

In 1918, Mahatma Gandhi remarked: "*It is my humble but firm opinion that unless we give national status to our provincial languages their due place in the life of the people, all talk of Swaraj is useless*" (Gandhi, 1960: 14).

In 1917, the demand for the unification of Maharashtra included the Marathi-speaking areas of Goa, too (Phadke, 1973: 67). The INC accepted the principle of linguistic reorganisation of the states at its Nagpur session in 1920. The Simon Commission (1927) did not accept language as the only test and referred to race, religion, economic interest, geographical contiguity, a due balance between coastline and interior, country and town, as other factors which determine the scheme of re-distribution of boundaries of the provinces.

In 1928, the All-Parties Conference at Allahabad concluded that, it became most desirable for the provinces to be reorganised on a linguistic basis. Language as a rule corresponds with a special variety of culture, tradition, and literature. In a linguistic area, all these factors would help in the general progress of the province. The sessions of the INC held between 1916 and 1931 accepted Marathi as the vernacular medium of Goa. At Seventh Session of the INC (1927), T. B. Cunha eminent Goan thinker and writer observed: "The use of Marathi language for primary education has been justified by the fact that it is a cultural language through which more than half of the population of this territory illustrates itself" (Angle, 1986-87: 7).

Mahatma Gandhi argued that linguistic redistribution would be conducive to the cultural advancement of the country. It would allow the provincial languages to grow at full height. And give impetus to education and trade. Hindustani should be the lingua franca— *Rashtra Bhasha* of India, but it could not take place of the provincial languages. Mahatma Gandhi did not subscribe to the Communists that linguistic communities constitute distinct nationalities in India. He subscribed for Hindustani to pacify the Muslim community. The sub-committee on fundamental rights adopted Hindustani in Devanagari or Persian script, at the option of citizens, should be the first official language of the Union. B. R. Ambedkar suggested that Hindustani should not only be the language of the Union, but also the States. The Partition of India shelved the Hindi-Hindustani controversy.

Mahatma Gandhi argued: "*I believe the linguistic basis is the correct basis for demarcating provinces. I should not mind two provinces speaking the same language, if they are not contiguous. If Kerala and Kashmir were speaking the same languages, I would treat them as two distinct provinces...Without linguistic re-distribution, it would be very difficult to enforce all teachings through provincial languages in our schools or colleges and it would not be easy to oust English from position unlawfully occupies today*" (Gandhi, 1960: 7)

Further, Mahatma Gandhi remarked: "*The re-distribution should not militate against the organic unity of India... if each province began to look upon itself as a separate sovereign unit then India's independence would lose its meaning and it would curb the freedom of the various units as well.... It would be fatal if it led to narrow provincialism, mutual bickering, and rivalries*" (Harijan: 1-2-1948).

From 1928 to 1947, the INC repeatedly declared in the favour of linguistic principle. The common tongue of India was the language of the conqueror, English. It was an important tool of British imperialism. It was used by elite enjoying power, culture and money in so many domains to limit the avenues of native languages to position of power and privilege.

Thus, strong emotional appeal for national language could not be denied. The British favoured multi-lingual provinces in order to dissipate the forces of nationalism, but Congress reorganised itself on a linguistic basis in the hope of making the party more acceptable to different regions. This helped, as Nehru claimed, to transform the Congress from a middle-class assembly into a mass organisation.

Linguistic Demands after 1947

The draft Constitution of India, 1948 suggested for formation of a Commission to make recommendation for the creation of the linguistic states. The Linguistic Province Commission (LPC) was appointed on June 17, 1948 with S. K. Dar as its chairperson. The Dar Report (13-12-1948) stated that 'the theory that linguistic boundary must coincide with political boundaries must not be accepted. Indian nationalism was still in its nascent stage and till it acquires sufficient strength— the creation of linguistic provinces would encourage disintegrating forces, thereby, weakening national unity. It involved merger of some states, which was not easy; after all, it was not a problem. It could wait until; more urgent problems such as defence, food, refugees, and others that the country faced were solved... It has given us no pleasure to come to a decision, which runs counter to the cherished desire of so many countrymen' (LPC, 1948: 33).

The task before free India was integration of 562 princely states. The alien powers had the bases on the Indian soil. The separatist forces in the Kashmir Valley threatened the unity and integrity of India. The Cabinet Missions Memorandum on State May 12, 1946 stated that all the rights surrendered by the princely states to paramount power would return to the States. On October 22, 1947, Pakistani forces invaded the Kashmir valley. On October 26, 1947, Maharaja Hari Singh, the ruler of princely state of Jammu and Kashmir, signed the Instrument of Accession, thereby, the accession of Jammu & Kashmir became full, complete and irrevocable. Indian Army was flown to Srinagar October 26, 1947 to vacate the Pakistan aggression. Ex-Prime Minister Pandit Jawaharlal Nehru lodged a formal complaint to the Union Nations Organisation on January 1, 1948 over Kashmir crisis. On August 5, 2019, Prime Minister Narendra Modi Government abrogated Article 370 which was temporary, transitional and provisional feature of Indian Constitution. The integration of the union territories of Jammu and Kashmir and Ladakh is complete. India has to vacate the aggression in Pak-occupied Kashmir and re-integrate the region of former Jammu and Kashmir state with the mainstream of the country.

The princely State of Hyderabad was integrated by a police action on September 13, 1948. The alien powers had bases on Indian soil. In this background, the Dar report went against popular sentiments. The INC came under fire within and outside party. It appointed a high-level committee comprising of Prime Minister Jawaharlal Nehru, Deputy Prime Minister Vallabhai Patel, and Dr. Pattabhi Sitaramayya (JVP Committee) to review the matter. The JVP committee report was released on 06-04-1949. The Report asked for a 'breathing time' and stated time was not ripe for taking up the linguistic reorganisation of the provinces.

Potti Sriramulu, a Gandhian, courted self-immolation and his death resulted in the emergence of the first linguistic State of Andhra Pradesh on October 1, 1953. 'The leadership of the Andhra movement had attached itself to resentment of the commonly accepted Brahmin monopoly on education, wealth, opportunity, and power in Tamil-dominated Madras Province. The Kammas and Reddies, their power diluted in Madras caste politics, became among the strongest advocates of an Andhra State whose creation would only strengthen their position of power' (Harrison, 1960: 110). 'The establishment of Andhra Province was *prima facie* a local and parochial demand incapable of attracting interest out side. The Andhraites demanded the reorganisation of all British provinces to make the demand broad-based and attractive to all' (Rao, 1973: 313).

Paul Brass wrote: "*In the course of the struggle for linguistic reorganisation one of the principle applied in relation to them in practice was that no reorganisation would be carried out on the basis of a demand which lacked demonstrably popular support even if language group spoken for was clearly a distinct and separate language from other multi-lingual provinces*" (Brass, 1991: 315).

Pandit Jawaharlal Nehru adopted evasive tactics and finally gave an impression that the Government of India yielded to coercive tactics. The Government of India appointed the States Reorganisation Commission (SRC) comprising of S. Fazal Ali, H. N. Kunzru, and Sardar K. M. Pannikar on December 29, 1953. The Commission felt that, the change in boundaries should suit the financial and administrative resources of the country. It recognised the fact that the language plucks at the deepest chords of one's sentiments. It did not want the parochialism to creep in, thereby, affecting nationalism and interplay of regional cultures. The SRC stated the constituent units should be economically viable to avoid strain on the regions. It relied on geographical contiguity and principle of common language, which promotes administrative convenience. It did not provide definite answer to the size of the constituent units and did not visualise weak states. The SRC stated 'every state must have adequate resources to fulfil the responsibility of a full-fledged constituent of the Union' (SRC 1956: 270).

The Commission released report on September 30, 1955 and placed it before the Lok Sabha on March 16, 1956. The 267-page document represented conclusions of three members after travelling 98,420 kms., interviewing about 9000 people from different occupations and examining nearly 1,52,000 documents. It recommended that the number of states be reduced from 27 to 16. The Parliament modified and enacted the Report, which showed 14 states and six union territories. It laid certain test, which a linguistic area must satisfy before it, could be formed into a province. These were: - geographical contiguity and absence of pockets and corridors; financial self-sufficiency; administrative convenience; capacity for future development; and a large measure of agreement within its borders and amongst people speaking the same language in regard to its formation, care being taken that the new province should not be forced by a majority upon a substantial minority of people speaking the same language (*Ibid*., 15-16).

The Samyukta Maharashtra movement gained momentum in the bi-lingual Bombay State. The Congress High Command conceded to the demands of Marathi-speaking and Gujarati-speaking population. The State of Maharashtra and State of Gujarat emerged on the map of India on May 1, 1960. The leaders of the Samyukta Maharashtra movement (1955-60), however, emphasised on the liberation of Goa rather than its inclusion in Maharashtra (Phadke, 1973: 77). The Congress adopted an ostrich-like posture on the issue of statehood for Vidarbha region. In case of bifurcation of the Bombay State, the threat of erosion of Congress base forced the ruling party at the Centre to bifurcate the Bombay State.

Prof. Y. D. Phadke aptly remarked: "*It was this potential threat to the Congress rule in Bombay that made the Congress High Command retract and finally concede the demands of the Marathi-speaking people. It is doubtful whether the CHC was convinced about the merits of the Maharashtra's case. Otherwise, it would have intervened on its behalf, when the Gujarat leaders extracted their 'pound of flesh'. The fact that Maharashtra's boundary dispute with Karnataka remains unsolved indicate that the CHC did not care to tackle such problems unless they threatened the very existence of the Congress rule in the State*" (*Ibid*: 324).

LINGUISTIC AFFAIRS OF INDIA

English-Hindi Controversy

The necessity for indigenous official language for the country is stressed on the premise that a self-respecting country must have its own native language at least for official purpose. The language of the government must be comprehensible to the governed. This would also standardise (give uniformity to language to be used in the domains of power), modernise (add new terms in the language to express realities of modern society, and enrich the language in use. Congress stalwart Purushottam Das Tandon a strong proponent of Hindi stated that 'India's real self must assert through its languages' (Austin, 1966:122).

Hindi was the most vocal and having potential for mass awakening during the freedom struggle. It was instrumental in the emotional integration of the country. The Constitution-makers took the historic decision to accord the status of the official language to Hindi. On September 14, 1949 Hindi became the official language by a single vote in the Constituent Assembly. Parliament enacted the Official Language Act, 1963 providing for continued use of English, in addition to Hindi, for official purposes of the Union and for transaction of business in Parliament even after January 26, 1965. The move to replace English by Hindi after 15 years of working of the Constitution met with failure. The regional forces adopted an anti-Hindi posture mainly in the South, West Bengal, and Assam to confront the Centre. It threatened to split the Congress party. Frank Anthony, Member of Parliament, argued in favour of inclusion of English in the Eighth Schedule to the Constitution. Pandit Nehru stressed the desirability of all India language growing from the people. Nehru stated in the Lok Sabha: "Our languages represent the continuity of our cultural tradition from Sanskrit. We have to develop our languages and we have to keep in touch with the masses of people. Therefore, we have progressively to function in our languages. At the same time, we have to remember that we live in the modern scientific age. We must have a foreign language to serve as a window to the modern age" (LSD, 1963: Vol. XXXII c.c. 1288-1305).

Rising demands of Reorganisation of States

It is argued that the linguistic reorganisation of states has provided the maximum opportunity to various linguistic and cultural regions to develop their ethos and economy within the national framework. Language was legitimised as a marker of sub-nation identity. 'Language no more poses a threat to national integration' (Kishore 1987:47). Development triggers the demands for the fresh reorganisation of states in the country.

Myron Weiner wrote: "*The integration entails the process of bringing culturally and socially discrete groups into a single territorial unit; the establishment of a national identity; the imposition of a central authority over subordinate political units; linking the government with the governed;*

and the promotion of common values through political socialisation so that the authorities can maintain order and carry out programmatic goal's" (*Op. Cit.* Rubinoff, 1998: 20). Donald Morrison and Hugh Stevenson wrote: "*The process of integration refers to the degree of cohesion that binds members of social systems together, and is generally thought of in terms of values, institutions and communication that facilitate escalating sequences of social contract, co-operation and consensus*" (*Ibid.* 20).

Arnold Toynbee argued, 'while linguistic nationalism is a disintegrating force, it is a fair price that India has to pay for the introduction of democracy...We really want to reach these millions through administration and education, we have to give fullest scope to these languages.' After bifurcation of bi-lingual Bombay State, the Punjab State was bifurcated into Punjabi-speaking State of Punjab and Hindi-speaking State of Haryana in 1966. Tribal affiliations were recognised as a basis of statehood after creation of a separate state of Nagaland in 1964. The Northeastern Area Reorganisation Act, 1971 reconstituted country into several states. Himachal Pradesh attained full-fledged statehood in 1971 whereas Meghalaya, Manipur and Tripura in 1972. The Sikkim joined as the associate State in Union of India on April 26, 1975. Goa attained statehood on May 30, 1987 along with Mizoram and Arunachal Pradesh.

The Parliament passed the Madhya Pradesh Reorganisation Bill 2000 followed by the Uttar Pradesh Reorganisation Bill 2000 and the Bihar Reorganisation Bill 2000 in August 2000 to create new states viz. Chhatisgarh, Uttaranchal and Jharkhand to encourage balanced economic development of the region. 'Punnu Lal Mohale, while participating in the debate over the Chhatisgarh Re-organisation Bill in the Lok Sabha urged the Union Government to provide Chhatisgarhi dialect the status of language under Article 347 of the Constitution' (LSD: 31-07-200). The three new States of Chhatisgarh (1-11-2000), Uttarakhand (9-11-2000) and Jharkhand (15-11-2000) emerged on the map of India. The BJP and Congress party favoured the bifurcation of Maharashtra to create a separate Vidarbha State whereas Shiv Sena opposed it. The Constitutional (Sixtyninth) Amendment Act, 1991 provides that the Union Territory of Delhi with separate status and re-named it as the National Capital of Union Territory of Delhi. The peculiar status of union territory of Delhi has ensued a tug-of-war between chief minister and lieutenant-governor of Delhi. The Aam Aadmi Party chief minister Arvind Kejriwal, since 2013 and Chief Minister Atishi Marlena in 2024 are demanding full statehood for Delhi. The 2025 NCT of Delhi Legislative Assembly elections ousted the AAP government with tally of 22 seats and the Bharatiya Janata Party staged a come-back with 48 seats in all 70-member state assembly. The number of states has gone up from 14 states and 6 union territories in 1956 to 28 states and eight union territories in 2025.

The Union of India has to meet the challenges of autonomy, statehood in the north-eastern states to contain violence in Manipur, Assam and other parts of India. The reorganisation of states should promote development and heritage. A good constitution has to provide good things of life to every citizen and protect its territory and culture. People are primary and law is secondary. There should be change in the living conditions of the citizens and not merely electing a government to power on the false promises to the electorate. It could turn the country into a banana republics. The linguistic reorganisation of the states has brought to the fore the problem of linguistic minorities in various states. Language is not a marker of identity. It is not a measure of political unity in the country and elsewhere. Prof. Granville Austin rightly opined that 'Indian problem has been and is, rather, one of sub-national sentiments and sub-national competition, which often take the form of linguistic rivalries' (Austin, 1966: 306). The linguistic reorganisation of the states has ended up into breaking up of the mega-states and creation of smaller states to cater to peripheral demands of political autonomy and integration as well.

Thinking on Regional Languages

The development of languages increase political consciousness of the masses. One can reach the people through their languages. Language became a powerful tool to mobilise masses politically in the multi-lingual set up in a country or region. The demands are raised for recognition of languages as national languages. The theory that a language remains neglected, if it lacks official patronage, gained currency. The official recognition given to a particular language, however, reflects the disdain or support of the people themselves, followed by will of the State. The Constitution of Ireland bestows the status of national language on the Irish language. It is the first official language of the country. English is the second official language. This legalism, however, is reverse of the Irish reality.

Robert King wrote: "*It is the most corrosive fallacy of them all among the language sensitive, the belief that a language would flourish if only the government cared more and did more... The plain fact is that almost nothing can be done in a free society to force unwilling people in multi-language countries to adopt, except on paper, one regional language as the national language even when that regional language has more native speakers and strong political power base than the others*" (King, 1997: 35-41).

Mahatma Gandhi wrote: "*A spirit that is so exclusive and narrow as to want every form of speech to be perpetuated and developed is anti and anti-universal. All underdeveloped and unwritten dialects should be sacrificed and merged in the great Hindustani stream. It would be a sacrifice...not a suicide*" (*Young India*: 27-8-1925). Rammanohar Lohia stated: "*The ruling classes (upper castes) have spread out and are now trying to use provincialism to retain power...Caste system is at the base of provincialism too... Language follows power*" (Lohia 1986: 2937).

The Constitution (Seventy-first) Amendment Act, 1992 paved the way for inclusion of Konkani, Manipuri and Nepali languages in the Eighth Schedule to the Constitution. 'In Kashmir, Urdu has been accorded official status of Raj Bhasha and not Dongri, which is the regional language. The need is stressed for evolving a standard format for all recognised languages and its uniform implementation all over the country' (*Times of India*: 2903-1999). The Urdu, Sindhi, and Sanskrit languages, which are stateless languages, have been incorporated in the Eighth Schedule.

The Constitution (Twenty-first) Amendment Act, 1967 paved way for inclusion of Sindhi in the Eighth Schedule. The Government of India stated that there had been persistent demands from the Sindhi-speaking people for the inclusion of the Sindhi language in the Eighth Schedule. Although Sindhi was not a regional language in a well-defined area, it used to be the language of a province of the undivided India and, but for partition, would have continued to be so. The Commissioner for Linguistic Minorities had also recommended the inclusion of Sindhi in the Eighth Schedule. 'The Sindhi literature flourished in the sixteenth century in the Arabic script. Now it has adopted the Devanagari script. Over forty lakhs population speaks Sindhi, but it is not regional language in any of the States of Union of India. The cultural question took a backseat as the average Sindhi struggled for economic survival' (*Indian Express*: 28-12-1999: 11).

Pandit Nehru said in 1952: "*The language problem is usually exceedingly important from the psychological point of view...It is clear to me that the Government must encourage the tribal languages. It is not simply allow them to prevail. They must be given all possible support and the conditions in which they can flourish must be safeguarded. We must go out of the way to achieve this*" (Nehru: 1952: 581).

The Maithili Maha Sabha in 1940 demanded for the formation of Maithili State (Brass: 1974: 53). The Maithili language is recognised by the Sahitya Akademi instituted by Government of India in 1965. The recognition by the Sahitya Akademi carries with it both literary and political significance. From literary point of view, recognition brings financial patronage from the Centre and funds for publications and prizes. From political point of view, it gives national recognition to language as an independent language. Maithili is spoken by three crore population in 18 districts of State of Bihar. Yet, it is not included in the Eighth Schedule. It is responsibility of the people to protect and nurture their respective languages spoken by a small or by a vast majority. The protection of languages should come from people themselves rather than literary organisation like Sahitya Akademi or inclusion in the Eight Schedules of the Constitution.

Official Languages and Indian Constitution

The part XVII of the Constitution of India deals with the question of official language. It provides for use of language(s) in the administration at the central and state level. The provision is made for use of language of all sections of the people provided its claim is genuine. The language provisions have been incorporated in the Article 29, 30, 120, 210, 343-351 and 394-A. The Eighth Schedule to the Constitution recognises the languages other than Hindi and the need for their development.

Article 29 deals with protection of interests of minorities: - (1) Any section of the citizens residing in the territory of India or any part thereof having a distinct language, script or culture of its own shall have the right to conserve the same. (2) No citizen shall be denied admission into any educational institution maintained by the State or receiving aid out of State funds on grounds only of religion, race, caste, language or any of them. 'Right to conserve the language of the citizen includes the right to agitate for the protection of the language' (Lok Sabha Debates: 30-3-1967, Col. 1918-19).

Article 30 provides right of minorities to establish and administer educational institutions: - (1) All minorities, whether based on religion or language, shall have the right to establish and administer educational institutions of their choice. In making any law providing for the compulsory acquisition of any property of any educational institution established and administered by a minority, referred to in clause (1), the State shall ensure that the amount fixed by or determined under such law for the acquisition of such property is such as would not restrict or abrogate the right guaranteed under that clause. (2) The State shall not, in granting aid to educational institutions, discriminate against any educational institution on the ground that it is under the management of a minority, whether based on religion or language.

Article 120 lays down that the business in Parliament shall be transacted in Hindi or English. The Presiding Officer of the House may, however, allow a member if he cannot adequately express himself in Hindi or English to address the House in his mother tongue. The corresponding language provision for the state legislature is Article 210.

In the Jagdev Singh V/s Pratap Singh, the Supreme Court stated: "*The question of speeches in regional language being made by members who would not adequately express themselves in English and Hindi was considered by the Speaker of the Lok Sabha on April 3, 1967 at a meeting with the leaders of various groups in the House. It was decided that member would speak in any of the Schedule languages without furnishing in advance any translation of their speeches in Hindi or English*" (AIR 1965: SC 183, para 6).

Article 343 to 344 deals with the languages of the Union: - Article 343 provides (1) The official language of the Union shall be Hindi in Devanagari script. The form of numerals to be used for the official purposes of the Union shall be the international form of Indian numerals. (2) Notwithstanding anything in clause (1), for a period of fifteen years from the commencement of this Constitution, the English language shall continue to be used for all the official purposes of the Union for which it was being used immediately before such commencement: provided that the President may, during the said period, by order 306 authorise the use of the Hindi language in addition to the English language and of the Devanagari form of numerals in addition to the international form of Indian numerals for any of the official purposes of the Union. (3) Notwithstanding anything in this article, Parliament may by law provide for the use, after the said period of fifteen years, of- (a) the English language, or (b) the Devanagari form of numerals, for such purposes as may be specified in the law.

Article 344 deals with the Commission and Committee of Parliament on official language: -(1) The President shall, at the expiration of five years from the commencement of this Constitution and thereafter at the expiration of ten years from such commencement, by order constitute a Commission which shall consist of a Chairman and such other members representing the different languages specified in the Eighth Schedule as the President may appoint, and the order shall define the procedure to be followed by the Commission.

Article 345 to 347 deals with the state languages. Article 345 provides— subject to the provisions of articles 346 and 347, the Legislature of a State may by law adopt any one or more of the languages in use in the State or Hindi as the language or languages to be used for all or any of the official purposes of that State: provided that, until the Legislature of the

State otherwise provides by law, the English language shall continue to be used for those official purposes within the State for which it was being used immediately before the commencement of this Constitution.

Article 346 deals with the official language for communication between one State and another or between a State and the Union: - The language for the time being authorised for use in the Union for official purposes shall be the official language for communication between one State and another State and between a State and the Union: Provided that if two or more States agree that the Hindi language should be the official language for communication between such States, that language may be used for such communication.

Article 347 deals with special provision relating to language spoken by a section of the population of a State: - On a demand being made in that behalf the President may, if he is satisfied that a substantial proportion of the population of a State desire the use of any language spoken by them to be recognised by that State, direct that such language shall also be officially recognised throughout that State or any part thereof for such purpose as he may specify.

Article 348 deals with language to be used in the Supreme Court and in the High Courts and for Acts, Bills, etc:- (1) Notwithstanding anything in the foregoing provisions of this Part, until Parliament by law otherwise provides- (a) all proceedings in the Supreme Court and in every High Court, (b) the authoritative texts- (i) of all Bills to be introduced or amendments thereto to be moved in either House of Parliament or in the House or either House of the Legislature of a State, (ii) of all Acts passed by Parliament or the Legislature of a State and of all Ordinances promulgated by the President or the Governor 304*** of a State, and (iii) of all orders, rules, regulations and bye-laws issued under this Constitution or under any law made by Parliament or the Legislature of a State, shall be in the English language. (2) Notwithstanding anything in sub-clause (a) of clause (1), the Governor 304*** of a State may, with the previous consent of the President, authorise the use of the Hindi language, or any other language used for any official purposes of the State, in proceedings in the High Court having its principal seat in that State: provided that nothing in this clause shall apply to any judgement, decree or order passed or made by such High Court. (3) Notwithstanding anything in sub-clause (b) of clause (1), where the Legislature of a State has prescribed any language other than the English language for use in Bills introduced in, or Acts passed by, the Legislature of the State or in Ordinances promulgated by the Governor 304*** of the State or in any order, rule, regulation or bye-law referred to in paragraph (iii) of that sub-clause, a translation of the same in the English language published under the authority of the Governor 304*** of the State in the Official Gazette of that State shall be deemed to be the authoritative text thereof in the English language under this article.

Article 349 deals with special procedure for enactment of certain laws relating to language: - During the period of fifteen years from the commencement of this Constitution, no Bill or amendment making provision for the language to be used for any of the purposes mentioned in clause (1) of article 348 shall be introduced or moved in either House of Parliament without the previous sanction of the President, and the President shall not give his sanction to the introduction of any such Bill or the moving of any such amendment except after he has taken into consideration the recommendations of the Commission constituted under clause (1) of article 344 and the report of the Committee constituted under clause (4) of that Article.

Article 350 deals with language to be used in representations for redress of grievances: - Every person shall be entitled to submit a representation for the redress of any grievance to any officer or authority of the Union or a State in any of the languages used in the Union or in the State, as the case may be.

Article 350A deals with facilities for instruction in mother-tongue at primary stage: - It shall be the endeavour of every State and of every local authority within the State to provide adequate facilities for instruction in the mother-tongue at the primary stage of education to children belonging to linguistic minority groups; and the President may issue such directions to any State as he considers necessary or proper for securing the provision of such facilities.

Article 350B deals with special Officer for linguistic minorities: - (1) There shall be a Special Officer for linguistic minorities to be appointed by the President. (2) It shall be the duty of the Special Officer to investigate all matters relating to the safeguards provided for linguistic minorities under this Constitution and report to the President upon those matters at such intervals as the President may direct, and the President shall cause all such reports to be laid before each House of Parliament, and sent to the Governments of the States concerned.

Article 351 deals with directive for development of the Hindi language: - It shall be the duty of the Union to promote the spread of the Hindi language, to develop it so that it may serve as a medium of ____ expression for all the elements of the composite culture of India and to secure its enrichment by assimilating without interfering with its genius, the forms, style and expressions used in Hindustani and in the other languages of

India specified in the Eighth Schedule, and by drawing, wherever necessary or desirable, for its vocabulary, primarily on Sanskrit and secondarily on other languages.

Article 394-A provides for an authoritative text of the Constitution in the Hindi language. In 1995, the Supreme Court in the Santosh V/s Ministry of Human Resource Development pointed out that 'the common culture and heritage of India, of which the foundation is the Sanskrit language, must play a leading part in promoting the unity of India.' (Basu, 2000: 30)

The Resolution adopted by both the Houses of Parliament on 18-01-1968 stated: "*It is the duty of the Union to promote the spread of the Hindi language and to develop it so that it serves as a medium of expression for all the elements of the composite culture...And as far as languages of Eighth Schedule are concerned, it is necessary in the interest of the educational and cultural advancement of the country that concerned measures should be taken for full development of the language*" (Mallikarjun, 1986: 39-40).

The languages incorporated in the Eighth Schedule to the Constitution are national languages. The languages included in the Eighth Schedule are - 1. Assamese; 2. Bengali; 3. Bodo. 4. Dogri. 5. Gujarati; 6. Hindi; 7. Kannada; 8. Kashmiri; 9. Konkani; 10. Malayalam; 11. Manipuri; 12. Marathi; 13. Maithili; 14. Nepali; 15. Oriya; 16. Punjabi; 17. Sanskrit; 18. Santhali; 19. Sindhi; 20. Tamil; 21. Telugu; and 22. Urdu. Hindi is the official language because largest number of people speaks and it is only first among the equals. Besides, 1. Tamil (2004), 2. Sankrit (2005), 3. Kannada (2008), 4. Telugu (2008), 5. Malayalam (2013), 6. Odiya (2014), 7. Marathi (2024), 8. Assamese (2024) 9. Pali (2024), 10. Prakrit (2024) and 11. Bengali (2024) enjoy classical languages status in the Eight Schedule of the Constitution of India.

The opposition to Hindi exists at political plane rather than socio-cultural front. In the non-Hindi heart-belt, the political masters often adopt anti-Hindi posture to confront the Centre. Also, the bureaucracy has given a lip service to cause of promotion of Hindi after 75 years of the Republic. It is argued that it was the conspiracy of the bureaucracy at the Centre not to allow growth of Hindi while making every effort to promote English has worked against the promotion of Hindi.

LINGUISTIC AFFAIRS OF GOA

Language became a thorn in the flesh of government that assumed power soon after the Liberation of Union territory of Goa, Daman, and Diu on December 19, 1961. A section of Goan people opposed the integration of territory with India. They were planning to have a dominion status for Goa having no link with India or Portugal. They lent support to the sub-nation theory. They argued that Goa had a separate identity *Goa Dourado* or *Golden Goa*. The 'Goa Dourado image saw Goa as an European enclave clinging to India' (Dantas, 1999 (a): 18). Goa has had no separate linguistic identity from the Konkani-speaking people in the *Konkan Kshetra*. 'The Portuguese, up to their last days, devising plans to induce Goans to learn Portuguese and they hoped that Goan Hindus might become Catholics, given sufficient motivation. The result of this policy, never backed up with sufficient educational facilities, was that while Brahmin elite among both Catholics and Hindus learned Portuguese, the common people learned Marathi or English, if they went to school at all' (*Ibid*: 23).

The masses learned Marathi at a very early age, before attending any Portuguese or English school. 'The Saraswat Brahmins for their ulterior political motives and hatred towards Maharashtra perpetuated misconceptions about Goa's old ties with the Marathi language' (Pai Angle: Interview: 11-6-98). Marathi remained as Goa's cultural language and written medium of expression. The Marathi language and literature witnessed renaissance in thirteenth century. Goans enriched it. It was not imposed from outside at no point of history. The Portuguese language enjoyed the official status and Marathi was also used in the administration during the colonial regime. The privileged class showed interest in learning Portuguese and masses used Marathi as the literary language. The masses speak Konkani. The Portuguese labelled it as *lingua da criads* or kitchen language. Marathi drew the masses closer to cultural mainstream and evoked nationalist consciousness. It acquired prestige and was sacred language of the majority of the population.

The Marathi language and literature had profound impact on the people for centuries. The Jesuit missionaries produced literature in Marathi and later on in Konkani in Roman script to alienate the converted class from the mainstream culture. The majority of the population favoured Marathi as a literary language. The Portuguese had no alternative, but to encourage Marathi as the medium of instruction at primary stage. The Census of 1961 recorded 6,689 speakers of the Portuguese language out of total population of 5,89,997 or barely 1.13 per cent. Thus, the Portuguese regime failed to impose the alien language on the native population in the span of 450 years.

Pundalik Gaitonde stated: "*The clear aim of the Portuguese Government in Goa was to change Goans in such a way that they should regard a foreign language like Portuguese as their own; forget their history, their culture, their sentiments and behave in every walk of life like*

Portuguese. They had forgotten that this had been tried in earlier times by their ancestors, using every method at their disposal, including force, but without much success. Undoubtedly, there had been a small percentage of Goans who, in past centuries, had been denationalised, but they were now trying to re-integrate themselves into the mainstream of Indian life" (Gaitonde, 1987: 38).

After India's Independence, the anti-integration groups— a section of Goans who opposed the integration of territory with India and adopted pro-feudal policy during the Portuguese rule and faced the problem of reintegration with mainstream of the country after Liberation. These groups attempted to carve out a separate linguistic identity. They proclaimed that Konkani is a distinct language. The United Goans Party (UGP) stood for recognition of Konkani and full-fledged statehood for the territory. The Maharashtrawadi Gomantak Party (MGP) cherished objective of merger of Goa with Marathi-speaking State of Maharashtra. The Bahujan Samaj or Hindu masses supported the MGP for its pro-masses and pro-Marathi stand. The demand for merger of Goa with Samyukta Maharashtra gained momentum until 1960. The Liberation of Goa raised question over future status of territory. The demand for merger of territory came from people of Goa rather than Maharashtra. The INC adopted a vacillating stand on the merger issue. The UGP opposed merger whereas the MGP swore by it.

The pro-Portuguese forces identified Marathi with the nationalist forces whereas Konkani evoked regional sentiments. The Marathi protagonists considered Konkani as a dialect rather than a separate language whereas the advocates of Konkani refuted their claim. The language controversy rocked the House for the first time in 1964 over the status of Konkani. The ruling M. G. party argued that Konkani was not a separate language but a boli. The language issue also brought to the fore caste and communal loyalties. The anti-integration groups espoused parochial loyalties for economic gain and political power. They reactivated and intensified lingual conflicts in the territory.

The Konkani language and literature flourished only after Vaman Varde Valaulikar's (1877-1946) effort to raise it to literary standard. A section of upper caste in Hindu community on the lines of Christian missionaries took active interest in the Konkani literary activities after 1961. Konkani had no script of its own. The Jesuit missionaries adopted the Roman script for Konkani to produce religious literature aiming at alienation of the neo-Christians from the mainstream culture. The Government of India gave recognition to Konkani as an independent modern literary language in 1975. The protagonists of Marathi and Konkani made unsuccessful attempts to accord the official status to the native languages. The language controversy in 1985-87 played a crucial role in shaping political destiny of the territory. The Official Language Act, 1987 was passed amidst chaos and democratic ideals were given a go by. The Government of India included Konkani in the Eighth Schedule to the Constitution in 1992. Moreover, Congress party implemented the agenda of the erstwhile U. G. Party to gain entry in the territory after 1980.

The advocates of Konkani claimed that 'Konkani is the cement, which binds all Goans across lines of religion, caste and class. Konkani is the common universal language among Goans and has a long history of use in church, popular literature and popular theatre' (Dantas, 1999 (a): 41). The anti-integration groups used Konkani to keep Goa separate in the intervening period of the Liberation of Goa (1961) and attainment of the Statehood of Goa (1987). The desire to promote separate identity of Goa with strong backing of the Roman Catholic Church affected the cause of Marathi. The Roman Catholic Church is favouring the Roman script for Konkani after 38 years of enactment of the Goa, Daman & Diu Official Language Act, 1987. The state government has continued grants to the Church-run English medium primary schools in Goa. Language has inherent limitation as a binding agent at political plane. It gives rise to linguistic conflict in a political community. The following discussion focuses on the genesis of linguistic controversy in the pre-Liberation era.

Chapter–III

LINGUISTIC AFFAIRS OF GOA: THE PRE-LIBERATION PHASE

The City of Goa was the flourishing place of maritime trade, strategically located on the coastline, one of the holiest of the cities in the country for pilgrimage and the seat of Vedic culture and Sanskrit language. Goa formed a part of Konkan Kshetra. The people followed Puranic pantheism based on the broad philosophy of Vedanta. 'The villages before Portuguese rule were far-advanced in Sanskrit pedantry' (Bhembre, 1979:1). It had neither a separate political set up nor distinct socio-cultural identity separate from the mainstream culture. It was fundamentally the same.

Tristao Braganza Cunha wrote: "There is great deal of uncertainty regarding the ancient history of Goa, although there is no doubt whatsoever that, from very remote times, it was integrated in Indian civilisation" (Cunha, 1961: 1).

The mythology traces the origin of the region to Parshuram, an incarnation of Lord Vishnu. It is believed that Parshuram had reclaimed Konkan Kshetra. The reference to a mountain known as Gomanchal is traced to Harsha Puran. 'Goa is known as Gova in Marathi and Goem in Konkani' (Gazetteer of Union Territory of Goa, Daman & Diu 1979: Part-I, 1). The name Goa is derived from Goparashtra— the land of cowherds. It is the ancient name of the southern Konkan and one of the seven divisions of the Parshuram Kshetra. Its origin is traced to epic Mahabharat. The other designations of the territory include— Gopakpattana, Goparashtra, Gove, Gomantak, and Govapuri.

The Konkan Kshetra is a long narrow strip extending from the Thane district in the North to Mangalore in the South. 'Until the beginning of the Christian era, it was called Aprant and only later Konkan' (Desai, 1965: 1). 'The Skanda Puran mentions the seven divisions of Konkan Kshetra– Barbar, Saurashtra, Konkan, Karhat, Karnat, Tulang, and Malayalam. The ancient Poet Kalidas makes use of word Aprant for Goa in Raghu Vansha {fifth century after Christ}' (Velingkar, 1998: 167). 'The mythological reference reveals that Lord Krishna once sought shelter in Goa when he was told to leave Mathura by Yadav Sabha' (Harsha Puran: 1910: Cantos 40-43). Goa Bhjoas lay on the southern border on the West Coast of Goa of the Ashoka's empire in the third century before Christ. Emperor Ashoka sent monk Dharmarakshita to propagate Buddhism in the Konkan Kshetra.

The various dynasties ruled over Konkan Kshetra of which Goa was a part, since ancient era. These rulers are: - From 3 B. C. to 1300 A.—D. Bhojas of Chandrapur; Satavahanas; Kshatrapas & Abhiras; Taraikutakas of Konkan; Kalachuris; Mauryas of Konkan; early Chalukyas of Badami; Shilahars; & Kadambas of Goa. From 1300 A. D. to 1500 A.D.— Kadamba Chalukyas & Delhi Sultans; Vijayanagar rulers & Badami Sultans; Adil Shah rulers of Bahamani; and Portuguese (Gazetteer of Union Territory of Goa, Daman & Diu, 1979: Part-I).

'Goa flourished during the reign of Hindu rulers. They built palaces, temples, forts, and other edifices. It became a great emporium of the Orient in the whole of country' (Government of India, Information Service of India 1960: 2). Goa remained as the capital of Konkan Kshetra. The original inhabitants governed the territory. The people worshipped Lord Saptakoteshwar— the deity of Sapta-Konkan or seven divisions of Konkan at Narve. Chandrapur or Chandor in Salcete was the capital of Kadambas for more than 1500 years until they shifted it to Gopakpattana in 1010 A. D. The Shilahars made Gove as the capital of the Konkan Kshetra. In 1469, the island territory of Gopakapattana fell into the hands of rulers of Bijapur who shifted their capital to Ela Goa in 1474.

'The geographical entity of Goa is traced to Tiswadi Mahal, popularly known as Kalyan, Kalyanpuri, or Kalapur' (Braganza, 1964:4). 'The Bahamani rulers also declared Goa their capital. The Portuguese attempted to shift it to Mormugao in 1684. Plans never materialised' (Tripathi, 1992: 431). Vasco da Gama (1469-1524) who was a sailor and pirate reached Calicut Port on May 20, 1498. He set on the sail on July 8, 1497 with four ships and 179 men in search of Christians and spices in India. There was a common belief in the West that Apostle Thomas who visited India in the first century after Christ had converted India.

Charles C. Nowell wrote: "This Vasco da Gama, whose fortune it was to initiate direct European contact with the East, was a man of iron physique and surly disposition. Unlettered, brutal and violent, he was nevertheless loyal and fearless. For some assignments, he would have been useless, but for this one, he was made to order the work lying ahead could not be accomplished by a gentler head" (Subrahmanyam, 1997: i).

Governor–General Afonso de Albuquerque occupied the City of Goa from Military-General Adi Khan of Bijapur Sultanate (1498-1510) on November 25, 1510 with support of petty chieftains Timoji Nayak and Bicaji Rau of Vijayanagar Empire. In commentaries of Afonso da Albuquerque, 'Timoji Nayak was referred as a man, Hindu by birth, very obedient to the interest of the King of Portugal, and being a man of low origin, but raised himself to the position of great honour' (Coutinho, 1987: 27). The Portuguese found to their utter dismay that there were no converts to Christianity in India. 'After realising that the native population was not Catholics, Afonso de Albuquerque strongly favoured the creation of a Christian-Portuguese Goa. He adopted the policy of inter-marriages between Portuguese soldiers and native women. A new race would be created which would have roots in soil of Goa but would be loyal to the Portuguese Crown and thus ensure continuity' (Hutt, 1988: 59). 'The Politica dos Casamentos (marriage policy) of Albuquerque aimed at making the community loyal to Portuguese Crown and happy to be in the region' (Garcia, 1997: 32).

'The original inhabitants of Goa are Kunbis, Gaudas, Velips, and Mahars amongst others. The Gaudas basically belonged to the central zone comprising of north and eastern Bombay, Rajasthan, Madhya Pradesh, Bihar, Orissa and Bengal and Kunbis in the southern zone of India' (De Souza, 1975: 36). 'The Kunbis— the semi-tribal agricultural community are the earliest settlers of territory and worshipped Betal, Tulsi and Naga deities of Hindu pantheon' (Saldanha, 1952: 12). The word Kunbi like Rajput denotes a status and not a caste. It is derived from word Kurmi. 'The Kunbis must have descended from Konk tribe, which gave the name Konkvan or Konkan. The people of Kukuna resided in Dhulia and Jalgao districts in the adjoining State of Maharashtra' (Gomes, 1996: 9). 'The Gauda was the chief Rayat or farmer in the village. He settled all the disputes in the village in the same manner as the hereditary chief of caste' (Satoskar, 1979: 36). The Chardes or Kshatriyas belonged to landed gentry and Rajput clan. The Kshatriyas were the masters of Konkan Kshetra, despite political power had passed on to Muslim rulers.

The original inhabitants of the territory were prosperous, cultured and well-knit community 'The Saraswat Brahmins dominated the Kunbis and Gaonkars. They are invisible in the literature of Goa. These communities are typically derided as backward and uncouth...' (Axelvord & Fuersch, 1990: 420-21). 'The early Portuguese realised fully well the dominance of Brahmins in Goan social life and they were wise enough to give due recognition to Brahmins in their local and political administration'

(Phal, 1982: 22). 'The population of island of Tiswadi between 1510-1543 was well over 40,000' (*Ibid:* 16).

The Portuguese occupied Goa in a phased manner. They merely staked claim over 5.76 per cent area of Tiswadi Mahal in 1510 A. D. of the present geographical area of Goa. They occupied Diu in 1535 A. D. and Daman in 1559 A. D., respectively. They occupied Bardez Mahal and Salcete Mahal of Velhas Conquistas in 1543 A. D. These areas constituted mere 23.76 per cent of the total area of Goa. The Nova Conquistas areas of Ponda, Sangue, Quepe, and Canacona on June 1, 1763; Bicholi and Sattari on August 25, 1781; and some areas of Pedne Mahal on April 2, 1783. The remaining area came under the Portuguese possession in 1788 A. D. (See Plate-IV). It took over 250 years for the Portuguese to occupy the Nova Conquistas areas. The Portuguese rule had different impact on these areas viz. Velhas Conquistas and Nova Conquistas.

The Portuguese labelled all these possessions as the Estado da India to draw international mileage. Portugal became a world power before British did. It opened the first route to colonialism in Asia. The colonial empire stretched from Lisbon to Brazil, Angola, Mozambique, East Timor and Macau. The Portuguese rulers encouraged the traditional elite bias in the ruling cultural and religious sphere.

LINGUISTIC PERSECUTION IN GOA

The Portuguese tried to uproot the native language, religion and culture in the span of 451 years of the rule in the territory. When Vasco da Gama and his co-sailors set foot on the native soil, they knelt down in prayer and sang: *salve raina, mai nossa, esparanca docura* in Portuguese. The army led by Afonso de Albuquerque after entering the fortress of Adil Shah of Bijapur sang Te Deum in Latin. The Portuguese adopted Latin for religious purposes.

Military-General Afonso de Albuquerque in his letter to King Dom Manual-I (1495-1521) wrote: "I have found here a box full of primers with which children can be taught (Portuguese) its reading and writing material. I see the interest with which you dispatched it. I have ordered a married man to teach youngsters writing and reading. They are very sharp and learn in a short time what is taught to them" (Shirodkar, 1988: 166).

Portuguese Policy towards Native Languages

It is baffling to note that up to the end of sixteenth century the most cultured Europeans did not even suspect the existence of a language called Sanskrit. 'In 1542, Rev. Fr. Francis Xavier (1506-1552) and his band of Jesuits arrived in Goa with the financial and moral backing of the

Portuguese Empire' (Borges, 1994: 15). 'In 1544, Rev. Fr. Francis Xavier in a letter to King of Portugal suspected the existence of Sanskrit' (Gaitonde, 1983: 28). 'He pleaded for establishment of the Office of Inquisition' (Priolkar, 1961 23). St Francis Xavier was author of Goa Inquisition and and foisted the Roman script on the converted class. The Portuguese, though living in the age of Renaissance, believed that the Church and the State were one, with their interests inter-linked. 'The papal empire in Portugal as well as India had three arms—Archbishops, Bishops with their secular clergy, friars or regular clergy and the Inquisition. All these three powers conspired to absorb within their jurisdiction the sovereignty of the King, at the same time competing among themselves for the supreme jurisdiction' (Priolkar, 1958: 211).

In another letter in April 1512 Afonso de Albuquerque requested King of Portugal to dispatch urgently trained teachers to teach efficiently the Portuguese language to the natives. The parish schools were set up first in Tiswadi Mahal, Salcete Mahal and Bardez Mahal during the reign of King Dom Joao-III to teach religious hymns in Portuguese and Latin. Interestingly, the Portuguese language remained far from developed. The writings of Joao de Barros and Luis de Camoes, which dealt with the Portuguese occupations of territories and virulent attack on the native culture and people contributed to literary development of the language. 'The higher education especially medicine was administered through French books. The Portuguese language possessed no scientific literature' (Cunha 1961: 25). The Asia's first medical institution Escola Medico Circugica de Goa (Medical and Surgical School of Goa) was set up in 1842. It became the vehicle of Portuguese way of life through medical practitioners scattered in the villages. Curiously, the viceroy, bishops and clergy favoured the native system rather than Western system of medicine.

The Portuguese language served as an effective means of forging the link between the ruling class and those over whom they ruled. At official level, Portuguese became the language for administrative, social and cultural intercourse. It was symbol of colonialism. 'The knowledge of Portuguese language was compulsory for those who aspired to join the civil service. The Portuguese language was taught as proposed in the decree but people being rude, poor, living by manual labour, unable to frequent schools and could not master the Portuguese language' (Priolkar, 1958: 191). A minuscule minority close to colonial power cultivated interest in learning the alien tongue. The Portuguese managed to consolidate their power through their propaganda of superiority of Portuguese language, religion and culture. 'The Portuguese language began to mix up with other native languages, thereby, giving birth to other linguistic forms, so called creoles and dialects' (Borges & Feldmann, 1997:231). Portuguese influenced the word order of the spoken language especially of the neo-Christians. Scholars like Phillip Neri Xavier (1801-1852) and others referred to the introduction of Portuguese word order in the native languages. Interestingly, 'the Portuguese ignored the native languages in other colonies' (Rahman, 1998: 23). In Goa, they adopted repressive measures to suppress the native languages in their so-called civilising mission in the territory.

'Konkani showed a total subservience to Portuguese word order in its sentence construction' (Katre, 1966: 187). 'The Portuguese policy, was to Christianise or to turn to Portuguese' according to Jesuit writer Fr. Pierre Dahme (Op. Cit. Priolkar, 1967: 62). The Portuguese regime adopted a systematic policy to eliminate all traces of pagan cult. The Padroado or the State-backed Church system realised that the effective religious instruction could only be imparted through Konkani— the spoken tongue of the masses rather than the Marathi— the literary language that nurtured strong religious, cultural and nationalist ethos. The Church believed that the road to be a true missionary was to know the language of the flock. The Christian missionaries feared that the use of Marathi would bring the neo-Christians close to Hindu pantheon. They banked upon the spoken language to propagate Christianity in the Latin script.

The Portuguese Government issued decrees in 1567, 1575, 1585, 1592 and 1606 for compulsory learning of the vernaculars. The change in policy led to systematic study of the native languages for effective evangelisation. The Christian missionaries could not make any progress in learning native languages from 1567 to 1575. The Order of Franciscans resisted learning the native languages. In the seventeenth century, there were dual currents in the Church one favouring vernacular and other Portuguese. The Fifth Provincial Council held in 1606 ordered that no secular or religious priest should be promoted to the post of parish priest unless he had the knowledge of his parishioners.

On September 6, 1556, the Jesuits first introduced the printing press in Goa. 'The establishment of printing press was intended to serve as an aid to effectual evangelisation. Printing actually continued to prosper so long as the importance of local languages for the purpose of conversions was fully appreciated' (Telkar, 1962: 23). The Christian missionaries published books of catechism and other religious texts in Portuguese, Marathi, Tamil, and Konkani in the Roman script until 1674. In 1851, William Carey translated holy Bible in Srirampur (Bengal) in Marathi prevalent in Nagpur but Modi script.

The Portuguese are described as the best record keepers of the world. Ironically, 'none of these books referred to atrocities perpetrated on the native population by the Inquisition' (Wakankar, 1986: 54). 'In 1585, the Third Goan Council recommended the use of vernaculars for preparation of textbooks of Christian doctrine' (Priolkar, 1967: 72). 'The vice-regal order of 1614 fixed a time limit of two years for village clerk of Cortalim in Salcete to begin writing office record in Portuguese language instead of using letre de tera' (Ghantkar, 1973:2).

Similarly, the order of the Viceroy, dated June 27, 1684 ordered the natives to abandon the use of their languages and began to speak the Portuguese language (Peasle, 1958:10). The Edict of April 14, 1736 imposed severe restrictions on the freedom of speech. It prohibited the 'neo-Christians to sing the songs called Ovio neither in public nor in private realm' (*Ibid.,* 21). The Archbishop Dom Frei Lourenco de Santa Maria in his pastoral order of 1745 'imposed restrictions to contract matrimony to any man or woman who was not used to speak or know the Portuguese' (Cunha 1961: 81). 'The missionaries pulled down 116 temples in Ilhas, 176 in Bardez and 264 in Salcete' (Hutt, 1988:61). The temples simultaneously functioned as places of worship, centres of learning and entertainment as well. 'The Carta Regia (08-03-1546) formally ordered that idolatry should be eradicated by dismantling temples, forbidding the festivals, exiling the Brahmins and severely punishing those who made idol of wood, stone or metal in Goa' (Pereira, 1978: 9).

The literature in the native languages was destroyed in the wake of the unholy Inquisition between 1560 A. D. and 1812 A. D. The Inquisition was suspended for a brief spell of four years between 1774-78. 'The Inquisitor Jose Antonio da Ribeiro Mota, in his report dated February 28, 1778, pleaded for the re-establishment of Inquisition. He stated that the natives did not speak Portuguese and, therefore, they did not acquire adequate conception of Christianity and rational love for Portuguese government and religion' (Priolkar, 1961: 182).

T. B. Cunha remarked: "The Jesuits and other religious orders are also greatly responsible for their attempt to exterminate Konkani language and to impose Portuguese... Even the Archbishop Dom Sebastiao de S Pedro accused them of neglecting the study of languages of the country" (Cunha, 1961: 396)… "The chief cause of cultural bankruptcy of Goans was the ferocious persecution of Konkani and Marathi and the forcible imposition of Portuguese. The official suppression of languages resulted in tremendous illiteracy and obscurantism to which Goans are condemned" (Cunha, 1961: 81-97).

GOA INQUISITION & NATIVE LITERATURE: 'The name Konkani applied to the language is of recent origin' (Cunha, J 1991: 1). 'The spoken mother tongue of the masses was no more different than the Marathi prevalent in the adjoining Marathi-speaking areas' (Priolkar, 1966: 11). Reference is made to word Konkani in the hymns composed by Saint Namdeo in Marathi. Some phrases in Dnyaneshwari, Leelacharita and other mainstream literature represented the regional dialect of Konkan. It was commonly believed that before the advent of the Portuguese there was flourishing Konkani literature in Goa, which was subsequently destroyed in the wake of Inquisition. The Christian missionaries were themselves studying the Marathi languages and literature. 'Rev. Fr. Thomas Stephen (15491619), an Englishman, wrote Christ Puran (1614) in Portuguese and rendered its Marathi version for parish' (Bhembre, 1979: 5-6). 'Bishop Fransisco Garcia who lived in Goa for about twenty years (1610-1630) collected thirty Marathi poems of religious nature and translated them in Portuguese' (Gaitonde, 1983: 30). The Inquisition directed not only at extirpation of religious beliefs but also of innocent usage and customs of the natives. To be precise there was no literature in Konkani at the time of Portuguese occupation of the tiny island or adjoining Konkan Kshetra. There is no historical or archaeological evidence to support the theory that the Portuguese destroyed literature in Konkani. If they had destroyed Konkani literature than it would have existed in the adjoining areas of the Nova Conquistas, which did not face the wrath of the Inquisition?

LANGUAGE & IDENTITY IN GOA

'The Portuguese rulers in the early period adopted the policy to suppress both Marathi and Konkani' (Gazetteer of Union Territory of Goa, Daman & Diu, 1979: 194-95). The impact of Portuguese legal-administration and their proselytising zeal drastically altered the linguistic identity of territory. The elite cultivated interest in learning the Portuguese language. Interestingly, the upper caste Hindus nurtured Marathi at home to retain their communal identity under the colonial set up. The neo-Christians were alienated from the Marathi under the influence of the Christian missionaries. In their so-called development of the native tongue, they sequestered Konkani from Marathi.

THE CASE FOR MARATHI: The Marathi language and literature flourished in Goa for centuries before Portuguese rule. The Marathi stone-inscription of 1348 A. D. is found at Vere in Goa after composition of the Dnyaneshwari, a commentary on Bhagavad Geeta, in the 1212 A. D. A copperplate of Nagdeva at Mhapsa in Bardez is written in Sanskrit and

Marathi. The date corresponds to 1402 A. D. (Angle, 1986-87: 5). The Varkari tradition had profound impact on the socio-cultural milieu in the territory and far-flung areas of Punjab in the North as well.

In 1943, Y. S. Desai, noted Marathi writer, speaking at Gomantak Marathi Sahitya Sammelan in Bombay stated: "The Marathi language made its imprint in the territory long before the word 'Marathi' was coined to denote the language and region beyond Sahyadri was labelled as Maharashtra. The people of Goa spoke original form of Marathi, which is called Konkani later. To be precise, Konkani is not a dialect of Marathi, not a separate language but original form of Marathi" (Op. Cit. Komarpant 1992: 33-34).

Sanskrit and not Pali was the court language during the Maurya Empire, which practically extended all over India. Pali lacked the legal precision of Sanskrit. From tenth century, onwards inscriptions are in popular speech forms; but at the same time, Sanskrit remained the cultural language. Similarly, Marathi pre-dominantly remained as the language of art, culture, communication of the masses in the territory. Konkani never became a serious medium of literature in the Konkan Kshetra. The Kadambas during their early period gave Prakrit the status of official language. Later, they preferred Sanskrit as the official language. The inscriptions of the Kadambas were written in the Sanskrit and Marathi—the literary languages of the region.

'It is very difficult to find a point of history where only one language was used as the language of the administration in a specific region. The languages of the people were used for all the necessary communicative purposes' (Mallikarjun, 1986: 15). 'In Goa, the Kadambas introduced Kannada script to write Marathi in many parts of Karnataka that continued until seventeenth century. The inscriptions of King Harihar II of Vijayanagar of 1391 are found on copper plates written in Kannada script, '(Sukhthankar, 1954: i). 'Adil Khan, the military-Governor of Bijapur accorded official status to the Marathi language whose court language was Persian' (Singh, 1993: 253).

Archaeologist V. R. Mitragotri wrote: "The attempts have been made to trace Konkani inscriptions from beginning of circa 1000 A. D. The Devanagari copper plates of Siroda and one line inscription on the solar disc of Haravale caves and Parel stone inscriptions of northern Silhara King Apardittya are considered to be Konkani inscriptions. The first two inscriptions are in Sanskrit but last two lines of inscriptions are in Marathi. Marathi and Konkani being Indo-Aryan languages are closely related. It is difficult to distinguish between old Marathi and Konkani. Hence it is extremely difficult to categorically state that Parel inscriptions is in Konkani" (Mitragotri, 1999: 226).

'The Goan place names have had a direct relevance to the words in Sanskrit, Marathi, Kanada, Malyalam and Tamil. These are: - Tiswadi (Janjire Goa), Bardez Prant, Sashti Prant, Phond Mahal (Antruj), Ashtagar Mahal, Balli Mahal, Kakode Mahal, Bhattagram, Sattari, Pedne amongst other' (Singh, 1993: 211). 'The Goa Government Gazette, which started publication in 1843, used to incorporate Marathi translations of important notices in order to ensure wider circulation a few years before Liberation. Temple notices published in the Gazette always carried a corresponding Marathi translation. In 1843, Government instituted a chair in Marathi and Marathi books compiled by Suriaji Rao were printed and published by Portuguese Government in 1847. By a Government order of October 22,1914, the Portuguese national anthem was translated into Marathi' (Angle, 1986-87: 6).

The Gramatica Marastta was published in Rome in 1778. Besides, the religious literature produced by the Christian missionaries was influenced by the variety of Marathi spoken by the natives in the Konkan Kshetra. 'The history of prominent Hindu temples in Goa is written in Marathi. The 'Kokankhyana', a Marathi chronicle of the Saraswat Brahmins narrates the escape of the deities from the area of Portuguese control' (Axelvord & Fuersch, 1996: 392). Sakharam Wagh wrote the first grammar of Marathi in Goa in 1819. Sir William Carey wrote grammar in Nagpuri dialect of Marathi and formal grammar came into existence in 1924. The earliest Marathi play dates back to 1818 in Goa and playwright was Raghunath Shet Sawant (Gomantak Times: 7-11-2001).

The dominant position enjoyed by the Marathi language led to issue decrees by the Portuguese government on December 26, 1883 to start two Marathi schools in Salcete and Quepe followed by Bardez and Sattari (1897) and other areas. On October 31,1892, Portuguese government issued a decree to authorise the local boards to start Marathi schools. 'After 1920, the Portuguese expedited their efforts in the field of education—promotion of primary and secondary education in vernacular language' (Pinto, 1996: 8-9). In 1937, the Portuguese Government made arrangement to provide translated copies of the Official Gazette and the Hindu Devasthan Act, the Hindu Customs and Traditions Act, the Civic Bodies acts the Forest Act, etc were translated in Marathi for publicity. Thus, the Marathi language and literature enjoyed dominant position in the territory.

THE CASE FOR KONKANI: The Christian missionaries designated the spoken mother tongue as lingoa bramana, lingoa de terra corrente, lingoa bramana vulgar, and lingoa Canarin before word Konkani was coined for the language. 'Konkani may be looked upon as an older off shoot of proto-Marathi, but it has some independent grammatical characters. It is split into number of dialects. In Goa, among the local Christians, the Roman Catholic missionaries have built up a literature, which is of Christian inspiration. This is written and printed in Roman characters in a Portuguese orthography' (Gazetteer of Union Territory of Goa, Daman & Diu 1979: Part-I, 221). The papal policy to produce religious literature in the native languages helped to create heathens for Christianity. Joquim Heliodoro da Cunha Rivara (1800-1879) the Portuguese secretary-general to the Government of Goa, in his essay Ensaio Historico da Lingua Konkani (1858), kicked off the controversy over the status of Konkani. Cunha Rivara asserted that Konkani was a separate language and called upon the native population to restore the mother tongue to its rightful place.

Cunha Rivara remarked: "The methodical culture of the mother tongue will bring you closer to Marathi language; it will facilitate the knowledge of the Asiatic and European languages, ancient and modern, and thereby useful knowledge will be opened to your intelligence; and the treasures of the world, till now hidden from you, due to the absence of this instrument of exploration, will be opened to you" (Priolkar, 1966: 111).

A. K. Priolkar wrote: "Cunha Rivara's ignorance of local languages led him to serious error. He wrongly assumed that some Marathi works written by Jesuits from which he profusely quotes are written in Konkani' (Priolkar, 1958: xiii).

'Nonetheless, Cunha Rivara fabricated tale that the native population was responsible for pitiable state— a kitchen language. Historians argue that Konkani had been an oral language until the advent of the Portuguese" (Larsen, 1998: 95). 'It was only under the inspiration of Latin West's scholarship that grammatical analysis of this defiant but ostracised tongue begun' (Pereira, 1971: 1). Rev. Fr. Andre Vaz wrote first grammar of Konkani in 1563 followed by Rev. Fr. Thomas Stephen (1540-1619), Gaspar de Sa Minguel, Diago Ribeiro (1560-1633), Joao de Pedro (1615-1672), Minguel de Almeida (1607-1687) and others. In 1630, the Archbishop circulated Cartilha de Dotrina Christa in Konkani for parishes. The majority of books of the Jesuits and Franciscans in prose are in Konkani and those in poetry are in Marathi. 'Arte de Lingua Canarin is the first printed grammar of Konkani whose name has not been recorded in the history' (Pereira, 1982: 15-57).

'The Flos Sanctorum or Lives of Saint by Padre Frey Amador de Soneta Ana completed in 1607 were written in Canadevi script and Konkani language' (Ghantkar, 1973: 2).' The famous Puranas of Padre Fransisco

Vaz de Guinaraes, a Portuguese missionary was first printed in Lisbon in 1659 followed by the editions in 1845 and 1876. The Grammatica da Lingoa Concani no Dialecto do Norte written by a Portuguese missionary in the sixteenth century was published in 1858' (Cunha J. 1991: 37-39). 'The Baron of Cumbharjuve was entrusted the task of writings books in Konkani to be used in schools, but idea bore no fruits' (Varde 1977: 23). Lucasinho Caridade Ribeiro staged the first Konkani drama Tiatro on 1704-1892 at New Alfred Theatre in Bombay (Gomantak Times: 7-11-2001)

T.B. Cunha wrote: "There is no single school, however, where Konkani is taught although it is the mother tongue of all Goans and is spoken by Hindus, Christians and Muslims. The persecution of Konkani is the chief cause of the illiterates prevailing among Goans. Konkani is spoken beyond area of Goa. Modern philologist call it Gomantaki, belonging as it does to Gomantak, the ancient name of Goa, in order that it might not be mistaken for a dialect of Marathi. By its grammar and vocabulary, it more closely resembles Sanskrit than Marathi and it is akin to the languages of northern India like Bengali. The Konkani of north, the Kudali, which is spoken as far as Malwan is influenced by Marathi and that of south, which extends as far as Mangalore is influenced by Kanarese.

The chief cause of the stagnation and decadence of Konkani is the systematic suppression and persecution to which the Portuguese have subjected it during their rule in Goa... Among the dozen or more newspapers published in Konkani in Goa, Karachi, Bombay and other places, majority were printed in Latin characters with various forms of spelling. One or two in Devanagari and other were in Kanarese alphabets. Konkani was opposed and suppressed by ruling powers, despised by educated class, by whom it is otherwise spoken. Its evolution either stopped or underwent abnormal conditions without any co-ordination, the process deforming and corrupting it" (Cunha, 1961: 23-26).

L. K. Khubchandani, a social scientist of international reputes argued: "The Konkan region can be cited as the best example of Kshetra or region in the traditional Indian framework. The members in the speech community live in the midst of powerful literary neighbours Marathi, Kannada, Malayalam with result that there are very few mono-lingual Konkani speakers. Konkani writings mostly inter-personal and journalistic are found in different scripts (Roman, Kannada, Devanagari and Malayalam) responding to the historical forces of conversions and migration" (Khubchandani, 1988: 8-9).

S. M. Katre revealed: "There was no literature worthy of its name in any of dialects of Konkani... The efforts of Rev. Fr. Thomas Stephen did not give any Konkani literature, his own Christ Puran being written in the form current during sixteenth and early part of seventeenth centuries. Konkani enjoyed no status of being a medium of serious literature or a court language...Konkani is pre-eminently fit to illustrate the case of non-literary language...It belongs to same group which include Marathi and shows close affinity with Gujarati also" (Katre, 1966: 1-176).

Pratima Kamat wrote: "The initial destruction of the Konkani literature and its subsequent development by the Jesuits in the Roman script not only sequestered Konkani from its parent and sister tongues, but also subjected the language to a communal divide that is difficult to eradicate today' (Kamat, 1999: 44).

Thus, Konkani purely had an oral tradition in the entire Konkan Kshetra. Goa had no separate linguistic identity from Konkan Kshetra. The Christian missionaries attempted to alienate Konkani from Marathi. The literature in Konkani was predominantly of Christian inspiration in the alien script. The elite enjoying power, culture and money identified themselves with the Portuguese rather than the native tongue. They did not make any efforts to raise the literary merit of Konkani for centuries. The Western scholars fabricated tale that the natives were responsible for the pitiable state of Konkani to severe the traditional interplay of oral and literary culture in the Konkan kshetra and make the natives to feel that they are the inheritors of the priceless heritage.

SCRIPT CONTROVERSY IN GOA

Marathi in its nascent stage adopted the different scripts before evolving into a literary language. 'In Goa, Marathi was written not only in usual Balbodh and Modi scripts but another kind of script called Canadevi or Canadi script. The land survey records in 1568 in Salcete were found to be in Canadevi script' (Ghantkar, 1973: p i). 'In mid-sixteenth century, the variant script of Kannada—Goykanadi was in vogue in the Konkan region. G. S. Ghantkar cited 149 documents written in the Goykanadi script. The language of these official documents is Marathi intermingled with words of dialect prevalent in the Konkan region and distorted words derived from the newly learnt Portuguese language' (*Ibid.* See Foreword). P. B. Desai stated 'the Konkani-speaking population had borrowed the Kannada script for writing. The western scholars were unable to clearly distinguish between Kannada and Konkani in early stage. The called both by name Canara' (Desai, 1965:2).

'The colonial missionaries wrote grammars of languages in India that interested them, the purpose being of course to win converts to the Christianity; but one cannot read far in the journals and reports of these men without soon appreciating that most of them were consumed by love of God not greater than the love of their languages' (King, 1997: 15). Else where, 'the Christian missionaries played a major role in purist literary movement started by Maraimalai Aitkal between 1875-1950 to rid Tamil writing of various non-Tamil especially Sanskrit words. They created an intellectual environment in which the non-Brahmin Hindus began to feel that they were inheritors of a great cultural heritage, which had been polluted by Brahmins. They perpetuated the idea that Tamil language can dispense with the greater part of the whole of Sanskrit and by dispensing with it rise to a purer and more refined style' (Palanthurai & Thandavan, 1193: 120-21)

Fr. Thomas Stephen was very eager to have Konkani writings in the local characters, but had to be satisfied with Roman characters, which he and other Jesuits adopted to suit the native tongue. The Roman script for native languages was adopted in 1674. It suited the colonial design to keep the neo-Christian insulated from the impact of the Marathi language and literature. In 1954, N. G. Gore stated 'the Catholics in Goa had been drifted away from the Marathi language under the impact of Portuguese rule. They adopted Konkani in Roman script. So they considered Marathi as an alien language' (*Op. Cit.* Komarpant, 1992: 261).

Bhiku Pai Angle remarked: "The Catholic priests produced literature in Roman script to alienate the converted class from religious literature prevalent in Marathi. Their efforts alienated the converted class from the mainstream literature" (Pai Angle: Interview: 11-6-98).

Ravindra Kelekar remarked: "The Devanagari is the natural script for Konkani language advocated first by a Portuguese scholar Monsenhor Sebastio Rudolf Dalgado in 1905 and later adopted in the first Konkani Sahitya Parishad in 1939" (Kelekar: Interview: 13-5-98).

Adv. Uday Bhembre pointed out: "Konkani has had a chequered life. In the sixteenth and the seventeenth centuries, Christian missionaries enriched it and gave it a literary tradition; but later they abandoned Konkani, as it was an obstacle for the colonialists in their attempts for denationalisation of Goans" (Bhembre: Interview: 14-5-98).

It is argued that 'Goan Christian Konkani has developed in its own way just as the Goan Christian people have developed a way of their own. They use Portuguese and English words in large proportion but only after they have been properly konkanized. There is certain amount of laxity in this, but good writers are already reacting against the tendency, and thus, a honourable mean will be struck which will no doubt produce the necessary balance required for formation of a standard type of Konkani literature'

(Saldanha, 1952:1). Vaman Varde Valaulikar stressed that 'Konkani had right to Sanskrit's script as any other Indian tongue' (Pereira, 1971: 69). The scholars argue against the use of the Roman script because it is not suited for the native languages. William Jones argued against use of the Roman script. He claimed the English alphabet and orthography are disgracefully and almost ridiculously imperfect. Sir William Kirkpatrick stated 'he employed Devanagari characters to help the student to pronounce more correctly than he or she could be taught either by Persian or English' (Wakankar, 1986: 8).

The advocates of Konkani argued that 'due to historical reasons Konkani speaking people born in Karnataka write Konkani in Kannada script. Kannada was and is the medium of education there and perforce had to use the same script for their mother tongue for lack of any alternative. Catholic Konkani speaking people use Roman script mainly due to Portuguese influence. Hindus in Goa were writing in Devanagari script not because it was an accepted script for Konkani but because they were studying in the Marathi medium and so had to learn Devanagari script... If language is written in one script than its development will be faster. Its literature follows wider readership. If this is not done, there is danger of these three streams going their separate ways and breaking out in three independent linguistic communities' (Rasmi, 1999: 77-79)

For colonial rulers, trade followed the flag and script followed the religion. The religious literature produced by the Christian missionaries in the Roman script gave the variant forms of Konkani. The Christian missionaries adopted the Roman script rather than native script for evangelical purpose. The missionaries created confusion in the minds of the people that they were inheritors of great cultural heritage and dispensing Konkani by Marathi words they could refine and raise its literary standard. In case of the Tamil language, they asked the non-Brahmins to get rid of non-Tamil words especially Sanskrit. The efforts to use the Roman script for native language aimed at creating a barrier between the neo-Christians and Hindus. It severed the neo-Christians from their Hindu past. Interestingly, these communities are united by common ancestry, which is still difficult to eradicate. The use of the Roman script for native languages gained momentum where Christianity was the major religious force. In the north-east, the anti-national forces under the influence of the Church opposed the use of native script for the languages. 'On August 19, 2000, Bineshwar Brahma, President of Bodo Sahitya Parishad, was killed by some anti-national elements owing allegiance to the National Democratic Front of Bodoland for staking claim for Deva Nagari script' (Indian Express: 20-08-2000). In Goa, the use of the Roman script has resulted into vital change in the spoken language. It distorted the intrinsic beauty of the native language. The lusitanisation—the civilising mission of Portuguese aimed at removal of all traces of pagan cult could not achieve the real expression of inner-self of the people. It resulted, instead, into intellectual and artistic degradation of the native population.

LANGUAGE ISSUE & GOA'S FREEDOM STRUGGLE: Goa enjoyed no civic rights under the Portuguese rule. The villagers from Assolna, Verna, Cuncoli, Veroda and Ambeli in Salcete laid the foundations for Goan freedom movement way back in 1582 A. D. The neo-Christians mainly Kshatriyas were in the forefront of the liberation movement to oust the alien power. The Portuguese adopted brutal measures to suppress revolts in the Salcete Mahal. The Maratha rulers had close historical, linguistic, and ancestral ties with the native population. Chhatrapati Shivaji Raje Bhosle attacked Portuguese from Bardez on November 19, 1667. The Portuguese signed peace treaty with him on December 5, 1667. Chhatrapati Shivaji recovered Phonda Mahal on May 16, 1675 and Antruj, Jambhavali Mahal, Sangue, Quepe, Canacona, Balli, Kakode, Hemadbarse became part of Maratha Empire. He also staked claim over Salcete and Bardez. Shivaji's demise in 1680 gave a breathing time for the Portuguese. 'The Portuguese had an eye over Konkan but plans never materialise' (Pissurlekar, 1979: 100).

There were as many as forty revolts recorded in the history against the colonial rule up to the beginning of the 20th century. The Pintos Revolt in Bardez coincided with the clarion call given by the French Revolution in 1787. The ruler of Sattari, Dipaji Rane captured fort of Nanuz in 1824. Dipaji revolted against Portuguese rule in 1852. Custoba Rane Revolt of 1869 continued up to his death in 1871. In 1820, the parliamentary form of government came up in Portugal. Goa elected six representatives by decree of 1821. The Portuguese Parliament was merely a decorative instrument. 'Jose Inacio Loyala launched a political party Patrido Indiano to fight for self-rule and a newspaper A India Portuguese in 1864' (Indian Express, 19-8-99: 9).

In 1910, Portugal became Republic. The Professor of Economics of University of Coimbra, Antonio de Oliveira Salazar took over government by a coup d' etat on May 28,1926 in Portugal. The territory witnessed extreme suppression and denial of basic rights under the fascist rule of Salazar. Goa became a Portuguese colony under the Colonial Act of 1930. The local civic bodies were disbanded. The Uniao Nacional the official Party of Salazar's regime grabbed the total number of votes and the opposition party left with nil. T. B. Cunha identified the Goan aspirations with the struggle for freedom in the country. The two organisations, which played major role in Goa's freedom struggle were Azad Gomantak Dal (AGD) and Goa Congress Committee (GCC). The Indian National Congress recognised the GCC formed by Cunha in its Calcutta session in 1928. The activities of GCC gained momentum in the territory. The INC, however, de-recognised the GCC for lack of provision in its constitution for overseas branches.

In 1930, Antonio de Oliveira Salazar expressed his mind: "It belongs to the organic essence of the Portuguese nation to fulfil the historic mission of possessing and colonising the native population which are compressed therein, by using also the moral influence granted to them by Patronage of the East" (George, 1959: 19).

Mahatma Gandhi wrote: "In free India, Goa cannot be allowed to exist as a separate entity in opposition to the laws of free state. Without a shot being fired, the people of Goa will be able to claim and receive rights of citizenship of the free state" (Harijan: 30-6-1946).

Rammanohar Lohia, who launched Satyagraha campaign for liberation of Goa on June 18, 1946 stated: "Konkani and Marathi are after all allied languages and growth of one cannot harm the other. Gomantak is not like its neighbours whose languages are fixed. Encourage growth of Konkani and Marathi and also spread Hindustani" (Lohia, 1947: 6).

Mahatma Gandhi in his letter dated 18-07-1946 to governor-general Jose Bossa wrote: "Though the politics of Lohia probably differ from mine, he has commanded my admiration for his having gone to Goa and put his finger on the black spot...No person or group can remain without civil liberty, without losing self-respect. He has lit a torch, which the inhabitants of Goa cannot, except at their peril, allowed to be extinguished. Both you and the inhabitants of Goa should feel thankful to the Doctor for lighting that torch... Therefore, your description of him as a stranger would exercise laughter, if it were not so tragic. Surely, the truth is that the Portuguese coming from Portugal are strangers exploiting the so-called weaker races of the earth" (Harijan: 2-8-1946).

Salazar stated 'Goa represented clearly a well defined type of culture and civilisation, a typical western manifestation' (Khera, 1961: 143-44). The Portuguese were inducing the people to learn Portuguese in the hope of making them Catholics at the fag end of their rule. They argued that Portugal was the motherland of Goans.

Mahatma Gandhi shot back: "It is ridiculous to Portugal as the motherland of Indians of Goa. Their mother country is as much India as mine is. Goa is outside British India but it is within geographical India as a whole. Moreover, there is very little, if anything, is common between the Portuguese and Indians of Goa" (Harijan: 8-9-1946).

'In Bombay Province, the Goa freedom struggle gained support from different political parties ranging from leftist to rightist parties. The British Government did not act against those freedom fighters who participated or escaped to Bombay' (Government of Maharashtra 1978: Vol. III, Part-I, ii). The Marathi-speaking population in the adjoining Bombay State and other parts of India actively participated in Goa's freedom struggle. 'The Kesari-Marathi institution played a prominent role in Goa's freedom struggle' (Gokhale 1981: 299). The leaders of Samyukta Maharashtra movement shelved the issue of unification of Goa with Maharashtra. In 1955, the Co-ordination Committee for Liberation of Goa was formed in Pune under the leadership of Keshavrao Jedhe, which included Jayantrao Tilak, N. G. Gore, and Vinayakrao Apte amongst prominent others.

On August 20, 1954, the Government of India severed diplomatic ties with Portugal. On 18-05-1955, Senapati Bapat marched along with a band of 54 Satyagrahis to liberate Goa. The volunteers of Praja Socialist Party (PSP), Hindu Mahasabha (HM), Bharatiya Jan Sangh (BJS), Communist Party of India (CPI) and the Indian National Congress took active part in the liberation movement. Jaganathrao Joshi of the BJS played a prominent role in Goa's freedom struggle. The Satyagrahis 'advocated violent line of action to dislodge Portuguese rule (Mascarenhas, 1989: 1). Interestingly, some prominent Goans including Bruto da Costa, Dr. Alvaro Loyola Furtado and Dr. Antonio Colaco did not form a part of Goan freedom struggle. These elements opted for Goa's autonomy within the Portuguese empire rather than Goa's independence and integration into the Union of India (The Navhind Times: 01-05-2001) Pandit Nehru assured the international community that his government would not resort to force to liberate Goa. The AICC in the meeting held on September 5, 1955, however, did not approve the strategy of direct action advocated by the Satyagrahis to liberate Goa.

On November 30, 1960, Salazar stated in the Portuguese National Assembly: "Goa is a small jewel, which because of its size holds no interests for Indian Union. It interests Portugal only by virtue of a mandate of history and is important to the West... It stands to reason that if it was unwise to create the question it would be even less wise to create a conflict, since, about it, we can neither negotiate nor compromise" (Government of Portugal, 1960: 21).

The President of Council of Ministers of Portugal declared: "If Goa is geographically India, from the social, religious and cultural point of view she is Europe. The Western, Indo-Portuguese, and Indians who live their politically speaking are Portuguese citizens" (*Op. Cit.* Shirodkar, 1992: 108).

The colonial rulers exaggerated the separate identity of Goa and went on to remark that 'Goans were Europeans of the East' (Gaitonde, 1987: xii). They alienated the neo-Christians from the Marathi language and literature. The idea of distinct identity of the territory did not gain support during Goa's freedom struggle because the roots of Konkani lay in Marathi. One is allied to other. The growth of one never harmed other. The Christian missionaries produced religious literature that aimed at sequestering Konkani from Marathi, which enjoyed the dominant position in the life of the people.

Chapter–IV

LINGUISTIC AFFAIRS OF GOA— THE OPINION POLL PHASE

The presence of European powers on Indian soil posed the threat to security and integrity of India after 1947. The diplomatic efforts failed to persuade the Portuguese regime to expedite the process of restoration of the civilian rule. The Government of India was forced to resort to military action after the failure of protracted diplomatic efforts to liberate territory. On December 18, 1961, the Indian Army moved in from Bardez in the North to flush out the Portuguese. Major-General K. P. Candeth led the Indian Army. It was the meticulously planned and executed 24 hours operation. 'The casualties during the 'Operation Vijay' recorded 22 killed, 54 wounded from Indian side, 30 killed, and 57 wounded from Portuguese side with 3,301 prisoners of war' (Khera, 1961: 238).

Major-General Candeth was appointed as Governor of the newly liberated territory from 20-12-1961 to 01-06-1962 to oversee the transfer of power to the civilians. On March 14, 1962, the Constitution (Twelfth) Amendment Act incorporated territory into Union of India. The President of India administered the territory in accordance with Article 239 of the Constitution of India. The military rule was taken over by civil administration between 08-06-1961 to 02-09-1963 after appointment of Tumkur Shivshankar as the first Lieutenant Governor of the territory. In August 1962, Dr. Antonio Colaco and Dr. Pundalik Gaitonde were nominated to the Lok Sabha.

Prime Minister Jawaharlal Nehru remarked in the Lok Sabha: "The Portuguese, however, decided to declare Goa as one of the overseas provinces of Portugal and maintained that Goa was Portugal, in fact, which was an extra-ordinary proposition" (LSD: Vol. LXI c.c. 37, 14-3-1962).

Portuguese governor-general Vassal e Silva in his report in 1963 observed: "Portuguese is the official language but has not developed much in spite of almost five centuries of our presence. All civil servants and educated people speak it but it is still far from creating desired ambience of Portuguese" (Gaitonde, 1987: 137).

Jaisingrao Rane Sardessai revealed: "The language conflict first raised its head in Goa during the military rule after Liberation. A circular was issued regarding the use of English, Portuguese and Konkani languages in the administration. The exclusion of Marathi led to widespread protests from cross-section of the society. Subsequently, the said circular was amended to allow use of Marathi along with Konkani, English, and Portuguese in the administration" (Rane Sardessai: Interview: 1-6-1998).

On October 24, 1962, for the first time people exercised their franchise in the panchayati elections. Out of total 1,95,000 electorate 1,21,000 or 62.05 % exercised their franchise for 56-member panchayati segments. The people showed a great deal of enthusiasm in the democratic exercise. The assembly elections mobilised political parties and groups at political plane. The MGP, UGP, PSP, INC and independents entered in the fray.

In the assembly elections held on December 9, 1963, the total electorate was 3,50,032. In the 30-member assembly, the Maharashtrawadi Gomantak Party-Praja Socialist Party (MGP-PSP) combine secured 16 seats with 40.13 per cent vote share. The MGP mobilised the masses on the issue of merger of territory with Maharashtra. The United Goans Party (UGP) opposed the merger and claimed that Konkani is a separate language independent of Marathi. The UGP secured 12 seats with vote share of 29.68 per cent. The INC bagged 16.72 per cent vote share and drew a nil whereas the independents bagged 11.63 per cent vote share and two seats (Assembly Election Ready Reference-1999).

Former Chief Minister Shashikala Kakodkar stated: "In 1963, the Indian National Congress fielded the majority of the candidates from the Saraswat Brahmin community whereas the M. G. Party drew the overwhelming support from the Bahujan Samaj" (Kakodkar: Interview: 13-10-1999).

The INC adopted a neutral stand on the merger issue. It drew a blank. It secured 16.72 per cent votes. The masses frowned upon the pro-feudal policy of the Congress party. The electorate gave a clean mandate to the MGP, which stood for cause of Marathi and majority of the population supported it. The Bharatiya Jana Sangh (BJS) and Hindu Mahasabha (HM) had limited influence amongst the masses. They supported the MGP. The BJS favoured merger of Goa with Maharashtra. The Frente Popular (FP) a party with leftist leanings participated in the first assembly elections. The FP had marginal influence. It secured 1.85 per cent votes. The Roman Catholic Church directed its ire against the FP on the ideological ground.

The Church scoffed at the forces wedded to the communist ideals and mobilised support in favour of the UGP.

Bertha Menezes observed: "On the issue of a separate state, alone United Goans Party (UGP) could not carry labouring masses with it. The UGP mobilised the Roman Catholic Church with its powerful hold on the masses steeped in religious superstition and bigotry and rendered fatalistic by their miserable conditions" (Menezes, 1992: 50).

On December 20, 1963, Dayanand Bandodkar a mine owner was sworn in as the chief minister of Goa. The Congress party attempted to woo both the regional parties— MGP and the UGP for carving out political base. 'Pandit Nehru had approached Chief Minister Dayanand Bandodkar to join the Congress party in 1964. Plan did not materialise, as both the parties did not pursue the matter seriously' (Kakodkar: Interview: 13-10-1999).

KONKANI— A LANGUAGE OF KONKAN: The penchant for separate identity gained momentum in the Iterritory. A section of upper castes within Hindu and Christian community identified themselves with Konkani to re-define their so-called roots. Gerson da Cunha believed that 'the Goud Saraswat Brahmins introduced Konkani into the Konkan from Trihut' (Cunha, J 1991: 35). 'Saraswat Brahmins migrated to Goa from the river Saraswati basin in the North', according to Swaraj S. Gupta, in his concluding speech at a seminar on Heritage Goa organised by Konkan Kashi, Goa, on 28-02-99 at (Panaji) Goa. Sir George Grierson (1851-1941) in his Linguistic Survey of India argued that Trihotra is not to be identified with Trihut (Bihar). Bhau Daji Lad Parsekar, a historian of repute, traces the settlement of Goud Saraswat Brahmins between seventh or eighth century. The second settlement of Goud Saraswat Brahmins came from Kanauj (north-west Province), according to Manguesh Mahatmya (*Op. Cit.* Singh, 1993: 249). Interestingly, there is no historical evidence how the Saraswat Brahmins adopted Konkani or introduced it in Goa. 'The Vedic river Saraswati disappeared about 3,500 years ago', according to Dr. S. Kalyanraman, Director of the Saraswati River Institute, Chennai, (Indian Express, 16-01-2000: 5).

S. M. Katre remarked: "The entry of Saraswat Brahmins into Goa is still a matter of historical investigation for they look upon Kashmir as their place of origin and depending upon mythological and semi-historical facts adopted in Konkani language…There was no evidence how Saraswat Brahmins adopted Konkani… The Caste as well as guild system in the social fabric of Goa and Canara before and during the advent of Portuguese helped the formation of several distinct dialects' (Katre, 1966: 176-77).

After Liberation, the anti-integration groups faced a task of re-integration with mainstream country. Konkani became a convenient tool to assert the so-called separate identity. Goa had no separate linguistic identity different from Konkan Kshetra. The anti-integration groups adopted Konkani primarily to counter the merger of Goa with Maharashtra. The merger issue brought to the fore communal divide. The majority of the population frowned upon the pro-feudal policy of the upper castes and whatever they stood for before and after Liberation.

DEBATE OVER STATUS OF KONKANI

Conventionally, whether speech of a given community is considered as an independent language or a variety of the wider community is decided on political or cultural grounds. The political boundaries and mutual intelligibility often do not coincide with each other. For example, Danish, Swedish and Norwegian are mutually intelligible, but are considered as separate languages on political or cultural ground. The origin of Konkani never failed to provide a subject for speculation and its inaccessibility adds to its fascination. The anti-integration groups attempted to construct a separate identity of Goa by de-linking Konkani from Marathi. The advocates of the Konkani language groups refuted the claim that Konkani had any affinity with Marathi.

ARGUMENT FOR KONKANI AS A SEPARATE LANGUAGE: At the end of seventeenth century, the word Konkani was used as Saraswat Brahmins were called Konkane, reference to which is found in the Konkankhyana— a Marathi chronicle of Saraswat Brahmins of 18th century. The advocates of Konkani argued that Konkani was chronologically older than modern Marathi as it represented the ancient form of Maharashtri Prakrit. Jose Pereira believed 'under the Kadambas (980-1350 A. D.) the Konkani language might have formed from an evolute of Maharashtri Prakrit' (Pereira 1995: 10).

Jose Pereira wrote: "Official and religious status was accorded to the vernaculars of the more powerful adjacent territories (of Konkan), Karnataka and Maharashtra. At the time the northern emigrants arrived in the Konkan, the prestige and power of Kannada extended over the land between Godavari and Kaveri; the great rock temple of the Deccan and Konkan has inscriptions on it. The latter region was for a long time afterwards under the sway of Kannada-speaking dynasties, and Konkani has felt the force of its Dravidian neighbour's domination.

To the north, in Maharashtra, the Yadavas speaking the nascent Marathi overthrew the rule of Kannada. The monarchs like Bahamanis and Bijapur Sultans, who used Persian as their official tongue, subdued them, in turn.

The Yadavas ruled over portions of Konkan for a time, and after them the Bahamanis did so too; both gave Marathi official standing. This continued under the Sultans of Bijapur whose enemies were the Vijayanagar emperors, who offered high post to Konkan Brahmins in the civil service. Their vacant places were taken by the less qualified Maratha Brahmin priests, who raised their own vernacular to the position of Konkani Hinduism's sacred speech" (Pereira 1992: 8-9).

V. P. Chavan argued: "Though it is difficult to prove by historical data, in the absence of Konkani writings, that Konkani must have preceded Marathi, the vocabulary and grammatical forms do induce one to think that Konkani had an independent origin and growth until it was subordinated by Marathi, which in the course became the court language and was cultivated by poets and philosophers who flourished in the seventeenth century and thereafter (*Op. Cit.* Velingkar, 1998: 169)… Both Konkani and Marathi have descended from common Prakrit and Konkani language is the example of the different stages of existence through which a merely spoken but not written language passes in its evolution" (Chavan, 1924: ii).

'The distinct identity of Konkani is put forth on following premises:- a) Marathi and Konkani descended from same Prakrit and that has literature in the standard tongue; b) Konkani branched-off from earlier Prakrit; c) Konkani has several forms peculiar to itself; d) The origin of Konkani or Saraswat bala bhasha community is traced to Trihotra by Puranas, which is not the corruption of Marathi. The Konkani language is allied very much in its phonetic structures to the Gaurian language of the North, especially Bengal. It represents most probably Sanskrit, which Orientalists regard as being extinct for those who introduced it into Konkan were emigrants from Trihotra' (Xavier, 1993: 20).

M. Madhav Pai wrote: "Konkani is a derivative of Magadh Prakrit and closer to Bengali, Oriya, Magadhi, Bihari and Maithili while Marathi is descended from Maharashtri Prakrit of Vidarbha. Konkani has followed independent course and developed as a language much earlier than Marathi. That would make Marathi younger sister of Konkani and not its mother" (Kamat, 1982: 7).

It is argued that 'Konkani is closer to Pali and Ardhamagdi, which were spoken by Saraswat Brahmins of Magadh Desh... It is not true that Konkani has derived from Maharashtri Prakrit' (Rasmi: 1999: 39-40). The scholars like Henriques Henriques (1520-1600), Rev. Fr. Thomas Stephen (1540-1617), Joao de Matias (1595-1624), Gaspar de Minguel (1595-1647), Simao Alvares (1695-1744), Prikryl Karel (1718-1785) pointed out that two languages were in use in Goa. They did not consider Konkani as a dialect of Marathi. Rev. Fr. Thomas Stephen argued 'that Konkani and Marathi were two distinct languages' (Saldanha, 1907: 93). 'In 1878, the German Rudolf Hoernle maintained that there were two principal dialects (of Marathi), Konkani and Dakhani. The former was spoken in the Konkan region and latter in Dakhan or central India' (Op. Cit. Pereira 1971: 16). 'In 1725, Bishop Inacio de Santa Teresa gave an account that the speakers of various provinces in the Konkan could not understand each other easily. Of the many dialects prevalent in that region, seven were to become literary media, in order of evolution: Sashtti, Kerali, Kodialli, Karwari, Bardexi, Mangaluri and Antruzi' (Pereira, 1992: 33).

J. Gerson da Cunha (1855-1922) argued: "To distinguish a language from a dialect there are two approaches, the practical and scientific. The former has two sorts of arguments; one based on the mutual intelligibility and other of the impossibility of a dialect having further dialects. Of the first, having applied this test to Konkani, it has been observed that, Marathi does not understand it as easily as he understands the dialects of Marathi, such as Nagpuri, Khandeshi. Of the second, again a dialect has not, as a rule, any sub-dialects. Konkani has Kudali, the southern, etc... The scientific language may lay emphasis on the basic vocabulary, phonetics and grammar. Konkani is closer to Sanskrit, but also Dravidian languages of southern India. Instead of calling Konkani another dialect of Marathi, it would perhaps be more to the purpose to designate it a language or one allied to Marathi' (Cunha, J 1881: 3-6).

Further, J. Gerson da Cunha remarked: "It is autonomous country that can preserve its language in a state of purity, and to its literature or rather to learned men of that country is confided the task of rendering its forms classic and unalterable. But, Goa has for centuries been swayed by foreign rulers, who have insisted on making their own language the official language, or the language of the court withdrawing at the same time all encouragement to the native language. Konkani has dwindled into a state of jargon or patois" (Cunha, J, 1881: 41)

'On cultural and political grounds the dominant cultural and official speech form of a community is counted as a language, whereas related speech forms in that are broadly similar in structure are classified as dialect or patois or regional speech forms. Based on speech forms existing within a given political community being either completely distinct from the official language' (Collinwood, 1996: 78-79). 'A standard language is understood as a matter of approximate uniformity of vocabulary, regularity of syntax, similarity of pronunciation and uniformity of meaning of term used. It is indisputable fact that no language has any intrinsic qualities or properties to become a standard language... A standard language evolves through a process determination by specific types of conditions prevailing in each country, although those different types usually combine in a particular way in each instance…' (Bapuji, 1993: 9-10).

Sir George Grierson in his Linguistic Survey of India stated: "Konkani is a Marathi dialect, having branched off from the common Prakrit at a relatively early period…The missionaries of Goa and Mangalore…. Contend that Konkani is not a dialect of Marathi. Their view, however, is based on too narrow conception of the idea connoted by the word dialect. They apparently think that a dialect is a deterioration of some other form of speech, and if such were the case Konkani would certainly be a separate language, as almost every dialect all over India" (Grierson, 1905: Vol. II, p.164).

S. M. Katre studied six out of nearly twenty dialects of Konkani, which were considered representative and rich in the form of grammars, dictionaries, glossaries and contemporary literature. 'These variant forms of Konkani are: - a) Konkani spoken by the Kanara or Chitrapur Saraswats; b) Konkani spoken by the Gauda Saraswat Brahmins; c) Konkani of Goa Hindus, representing particularly in the writings of Vaman Varde Valaulikar and in the quarterly journal 'Nave Goy' by Gomant Press in Bombay; Konkani of the Christians of Mangalore and South Kanara; Konkani of the Christians of North Kanara; & Konkani of the Christians of Goa' (Katre, 1966:1)

S. M. Katre argued: "Taking into account all the main features of Konkani we may definitely assign it to the south-western group (having Marathi and Gujarati as its nearest kin) with a tinge of central group (Hindi, especially in the dative postposition— ka). The difference noted formation of the direct sing masc norms in their extended form and the divergent postpositions, for the dative clearly mark off Konkani as a separate language (and not mere dialect) is thereby proved, but phonological considerations, show that both belong to common parent Prakrit… A new set of circumstances has been introduced into the already complicated history of Konkani and unless a great genius of the rank of Kalidas or Tagore gives a fresh lease of life to this language of homely communion and raise it to the level of a polished literary medium, the future for it is not too bright" (*Ibid.* 173-180).

R. C. Nigam, a noted linguist argued: "The declaration of Konkani as independent language in the Census of 1961 will only be a tentative re-classification and that the position may be considered open to further verification and research since a section of scholars is inclined still to agree with the old classifications in the Linguistic Survey' (*Op. Cit.* Mallya 1997: 12-13).

'A dialect in its widest sense is a form of language springing from common root. The term is popularly used to describe a localised form of language, which diverges from the standard dialect, that is, the dialect that has come to be accepted as the spoken or literary form. It is wrong to think such localised forms as corruption of the standard, which is also the dialect of the same language. When dialects of the same language become so different as to be mutually unintelligible, they become, in effect foreign languages. The dialect arises as a result of change and development, which takes place continually in all living languages. They develop as result of isolation of community, either geographically or socially' (Collinwood, 1996: 66-67).

'Normal language development takes place in a rather haphazard way, largely below the consciousness of the speaker whereas the standard languages are result of direct and deliberate intervention by the society. This intervention is called standardisation produce a standard language where before they were just dialects or non-standard varieties. The distinction between language and dialect can be made based on prestige, size and mutual intelligibility. Based on prestige, a language is a standard language. In principle, this distinction is absolute. Either a variety is a standard language or not.

The distinction based on the size becomes relative for example, in comparison with one variety a chosen variety may be large, yet compared with another it may be small. If speakers of given varieties can understand each other, then the varieties concerned are the instance of the same languages; otherwise they are not. The linguistic situations are influenced by three main factors, which are on the path to concisely delimit established and emerging languages from dialectal forms: - The existence of a superordinated standard or is in the grammatical, lexical or literary process; Its actual or potential, widespread use in mass-media; Its eventual legal status or wide consensus to reach it' (Berton, 1997: 17).

R. A. Hudson argued: "There is no real distinction to be drawn between language and dialect (except with reference to prestige, where it is better to use term standard 'language' rather than just 'language'... All we can assume that there are varieties of language, and that a given variety may be relatively similar to some other variety and relatively different from other. The search for language boundary is waste of time. When the boundary between two languages is clear to socio-linguists, it is clear to everybody else. Moreover, when it is unclear to ordinary people, it is equally unclear to socio-linguists" (Hudson, 1996: 36).

Interestingly, Jay Dubhashi, a noted columnist remarked: "It matters very little whether Konkani is a dialect of Marathi or Pushtu. It is good enough for me that it is Konkani a vehicle that takes me deep into my past, just as English takes you to Shakespeare and Sanskrit to Vedas" (Goa Times Jan. 1986 (a): 29).

ARGUMENT AGAINST KONKANI AS A SEPARATE LANGUAGE: A section of foreign missionaries in the beginning of the sixteenth century stated that 'the common idiom, which was current among the intelligent natives, was Marathi... the vernacular of the region' (Priolkar, 1958: 202). 'By the name, Konkani is meant a number of Marathi dialects, which were spoken along the West Coast of Maharashtra, Goa and parts of Mysore. The speech differed from one region to another and one social group to another' (Ghatge, 1963: iii). John Leyden (1775-1811) argued that Konkani was a dialect of Marathi. William Carey (1761-1834) did not refute Leyden's view. In 1858, Sir E. Perry (1806-1882) argued that, the Konkani appeared to him no other than Marathi with a large infusion of Tulu and Kanada words. 'The scholars like Sir Erskine Perry, Murphey, John Beames, Robert N. Cust, A. F. Rudolf Hoernle, Rev. Fr. Dennis L. Cottineau de Kloguen, Sir, R. G. Bhandarkar, Sir, Philippe Neri Peres, Joseph Saldanha considered Konkani not as a distinct member of Aryan group but as a dialect of Marathi' (Sukhthankar et la 1941: 23-24).

Further, J. Gerson da Cunha quotes Murphy: "The examination of the grammar of Konkani proves it to be decidedly that of the Marathi language. The distinguished scholars in Anglo-Indian linguistic agreed in considering Konkani not as a distinct member of Aryan group but as a dialect of Marathi" (Cunha, J. 1881: 4-5).

Sir R. G. Bhandarkar (1837-1926) stated: "There are five dialects differing in great many particulars from the main Marathi. Thus, the Goanese prevails in Goa; the Malvani my own native tongue in Sawantwadi, both of which, notwithstanding some minor differences, may be considered as one, are spoken in Malvan, Vengurla and Sawantwadi districts. The Chitpavani is used only by the caste of Chitpavan Brahmins in the district about Ratnagiri; the Salseti is spoken by the original inhabitants of the island and Bombay and the Khandeshi, which is the mixture of Marathi and Gujarati, and contains to an appreciable degree a barbarous element, probably from a Bhil source prevails in Khandesh" (Bhandarkar, 1914 (a): 20).

In 1884, Ramchandra Gunjikar (1843-1902) expressed moderate views in Saraswat Mandal that 'both Marathi and Konkani had sprung up from Saraswat bala bhasha. Konkani could develop only in association with Marathi' (Sharma, 1950: 77-78). Sir Richard Burton pointed out that 'the spoken language of Goans was the corrupt form of Marahatta called Concanee whereas Rev. Fr. A. F. Maffei considered 'Konkani. as an assemblage of dialects rather than a formed language' (*Op. Cit.* Priolkar 1966: 13). The Linguistic Survey Report (1921) stated that Konkani varies with the kind of speakers. The elite class speaks it with Portuguese and Kannada words whereas Muslims with Urdu and Arabic words and Chitpavan with Sanskrit words.

Sir George Grierson (1927) argued: "No less than thirty-nine names have been recorded in the Survey as those of dialects of Marathi. Few of these can be called genuine dialects, the majority being merely forms of the standard speech or one of the real dialects, pronounced in some peculiar way according to locality or to the caste of speakers.

For instance, the Marathi of the Konkan north of Ratnagiri is very nearly the same as the standard, but natives recognise two dialects, one spoken by Brahmins and another spoken by Muslims. The minute differences are all investigated in the pages of Survey...It will be sufficient to mention here the four main dialects (of Marathi) viz. Desi, Konkan standard, the Marathi of Berar and the Central Province and Konkani...' (*Op. Cit.* Priolkar, 1966: 19-20).

V. S. Khandekar noted Marathi writer, while delivering presidential address at the first Gomantak Marathi Sahitya Parishad on May 11, 1935 at (Margao) Goa stated: "The difference between spoken language and literary language is bound to prevail because variations occur in the spoken languages at twelve miles distance. The spoken languages should merge with the literary language" (*Ibid,* 13).

Acharya Kaksaheb Kalelkar argued: "Konkani and Marathi should be studied simultaneously and developed in the territory. Konkani language will wither or acquire a corrupt form without Marathi" (*Ibid.,* 99).

However, in 1952, Acharya Kalelkar remarked he would not involve himself in language-dialect controversy. (*Op. Cit.* Pereira 1971: 123). Laxamanshastri Joshi noted scholar stated 'Konkani was offshoot or subsidiary of Marathi language. It was not a separate language. The Konkani in Ratnagiri had merged with Marathi' (Op. Cit. Komarpant, 1993: 359-60). In 1983, B. L. Bhandare in his speech at Second Gomant Marathi Bhasha Parishad had quoted Acharya Kakasaheb Kalelkar who in 1936 had stated that it was suicidal to uproot Marathi from Goa. Konkani is a form of dialect rather than an independent language.

Sunit Kumar Chatterjee stated: "In the South, the Christians in Goa with Roman script have given a distinct form to one of the dialect Konkani that is intimately related to Marathi. Konkani is a subsidiary and not an independent language. However, Konkani cannot forge ahead without Marathi. One should not try to compete Konkani as a literary language as against Marathi" (*Op. Cit.* Bhandare, 1983: 22).

A. K. Priolkar stated "The people of Goa played a prominent role in the literary development of Marathi language and Konkani merely remained as a spoken dialect of the former" (Priolkar, 1966: 126-133;).

Noted writer and thinker B. D. Satoskar stated: "Konkani movement has political manifestations. Konkani protagonists have used language as a tool to perpetuate their influence in linguistic, religious and cultural sphere after Liberation. It will be suicidal for these people, if territory merges with Maharashtra" (*Op. Cit.* Komarpant, 1993:143).

G. V. Kamat noted Marathi writer revealed: "The Saraswat Brahmins alone do not enrich Konkani. The other castes that migrated to Goa along with Goud Saraswat Brahmins also contributed for evolution of Konkani like other dialects of Marathi language" (*Op. Cit.* Komarpant, 1993: 20910).

Sir Vithal Chandavarkar et al in Memorandum on Konkani as per the resolution passed by the All India Marathi Conference held at Solapur stated: "The Desh and Konkan are merely the two parts of the well-defined territory known as Maharashtra. Various dialects, communal and local, are spoken in both these parts. It is, however, a matter of common knowledge that different dialects are used merely for the purpose of speaking by the Hindus, while for the purpose of writing only one language— that is Marathi has been used over the whole region since the time of Dnyaneshwar…

The fact is that the literary Marathi and the various dialects noted above have a common parent, that is, they are immediately derived from the same transitional form of Apabhramasha of the Maharashtri Prakrit…It is the misfortune of our country that some people have thought it necessary to exaggerate even slight differences in our religious beliefs, communal characteristics and spoken tongues — and that too when the utmost possible unity in these matters is crying need of the day. As regard language, if each dialect were to be treated as a separate language it will result in babel of tongues to the great detriment of the best interests of our country" (Sukhthankar et al, 1941: 24).

M. N. Perason revealed: "The almost universally spoken Konkani language in Goa is far from standardised. Hindus and Christians spoke very different versions, as was revealed in 1950s by noted historian Pandurang Pissurlekar who tried to address the students of Rachol seminary in his Hindu Konkani. They could not follow him. Finally, both the sides spoke in Portuguese. Goan scholar D. D. Kosambi claimed that he could place any individual within five miles of locality of his origin by his speech" (Pearson, 1987: 150).

Jayantrao Tilak, former editor of Marathi daily Kesari, freedom fighter, ex-Speaker of Legislative Council of Maharashtra stated: "In fact, according to me, there should be no controversy about the Marathi language in Goa. Konkani is not a separate language. It is only a spoken dialect. A. K. Priolkar has long established this" (Tilak: Interview. 10-2-1999).

P. P. Shirodkar, the first Speaker of the Legislative Assembly of Goa, Daman & Diu remarked: "The infamous Inquisition altered the socio-cultural milieu in the Old Conquest areas of Tiswadi, Bardez and Salcete areas in Goa. Konkani remained as the dialect of Marathi representing entire Konkan region that also carried influences of Kanada, Tulu languages in the South. For that matter, Goa reflects no geographical or linguistic identity separate from the Konkan region

The entire Konkani movement in the territory lacked any historical or geographical base. A minuscule minority with their pro-Portuguese orientations perpetuated a myth amongst the masses that Konkani is a distinct language. The Saraswat Brahmins scattered within and outside territory whipped up the linguistic sentiments on utterly a false premise to further their own interests in the changing political milieu" (Shiriodkar: Interview: 10-3-1998).

Bhiku Pai Angle remarked: "The Konkani language movement had separatist and sectarian undertones. The Konkani protagonists attempted at denying rightful place enjoyed by Marathi in social, religious and cultural sphere. The Saraswat Brahmins for their ulterior motive and hatred towards Maharashtra perpetuated misconceptions about Goa's old ties with Marathi" (Interview: 11-06-1998).

Jaisingrao Rane Sardessai remarked "The Konkani language movement is spearheaded by the upper caste and Konkani is dialect of Marathi rather than an independent language" (Interview: 01-06-1998).

Shashikala Kakodkar, former Chief Minister of Goa, Daman & Diu stated: "Ironically, after Liberation, the Saraswat Brahmins who nursed Marathi at home and the Christians who identified themselves with the Portuguese or English adopted a pro-Konkani stand on the separate identity of the territory" (Interview: 13-10-1999).

All languages in India belong to parentage of Sanskrit and show affinities with each other. It is important to note that 'there are 70 per cent of unaltered Sanskrit (Tatsam) words in Bengali language; around 20 per cent words in Bengali are again derived from Sanskrit (Tadvaba)' (The Navhind Times: 29-10-2000). Precisely for this reason Konkani shows affinity with Bengali language. Konkani is a variant form of Maharashtri Prakrit or old Marathi. It has unique form. It is not proved whether Konkani had worthwhile literature or was destroyed in the fury of Inquisition. The native intelligentsia in the Konkan Kshetra made no efforts to raise the spoken language to a polished medium of literary ___expression. The spoken Konkani idiom of neo-Christian was rendered to the position of kitchen language. A language carries prestige and dialect lacks it. Hindus used various dialects at oral plane and Marathi at the literary plane. The evolution of Konkani as a separate language is fraught with many difficulties. Konkani had entirely an oral tradition not only in Goa but also in the entire Konkan Kshetra. The advocates of Konkani faced problem of separating Konkani from its sister or parent language namely, Marathi. Konkani is allied to Marathi. The growth of one depends on other. After 1961, the anti-integration groups brought to fore the theory of separate identity of territory. They claimed that Konkani as an independent language in its own right to further their vested political interests in the changing political milieu. The tentative re-classification in the Census records in 1961 was apparently under the pressure from the anti-integration groups and these groups had more material than linguistic interests did.

IMPACT OF NEIGHBOURING STATES ON INTEGRATION OF GOA

Goa remained an integral part of Konkan Kshetra before its occupation by the Portuguese. Culturally, Goa exhibited close affinity with the Marathi-speaking areas of its powerful neighbour— Maharashtra rather than the Kannada-speaking areas of the former State of Mysore. The Bombay Province bound Goa— an area stretching from Lahore in the North and Karwar in the South during the British rule (See Plate-V). The agriculture remained as the mainstay of Goan economy. In 1876, the principal items of export recorded were coconut, water melons, coir work, cinnamon, pepper, fire wood, jack-fruits fowls, fish and salt. Goan emigration began in 1779 when the British Government had anchored their naval fleet in the territory to protect their possessions against the French revolutionaries. 'The British never intended to industrialise India beyond the demand of their colonial needs, and the economic policies pursued by them clearly point towards this. Infrastructure was created more to exploit India's resources than to develop country, though unintentionally, it helped in binding the country, later' (Kanoria, 1999: xiv).

The Portuguese encouraged emigration to augment its resources. The migration could be considered as the most significant export of the Eatado da India. 'Goa had barely 7.67 per cent of trade with Portugal and other Portuguese territories' (Government of India, Information Service of India 1960: 13). 'The Government of India claimed that the remittances from India to Goa totalled sixty-eight million rupees, while those from Goa to India forty-six million rupees whereas remittances from Portugal to Goa 4.1 million rupees and from Goa to Portugal amounted to 11.5 million rupees' (Rubinoff, 1998: 38-39).

In 1839, British asked the Portuguese to relinquish Goa for five lakh pounds, which was refused. On 26-12-1878, Portugal and Britain entered into treaty to relax custom duties, monetary conventions, and construction of railway segment and port to facilitate trade. The Anglo-Portuguese treaty ended in 1891. 'The repercussions of the Treaty on the economic fabric of Goa were lethal and some time beyond repair' (Pinto, 1996: 24). Interestingly, the Portuguese put forth the argument that their possession of Estado da India was uneconomical drain on Lisbon. Nevertheless, it was patently false. Their presence became a thorn in India's loin. 'The Portuguese viceroy returned from Goa to Lisbon with three lakh pounds, each governor with one lakh pounds and petty officials with between 20,000 to 50,000 pounds' (The Navhind Times: 12-12-1997).

The Portuguese hardly tried to industrialise territory. Goans migrated to adjoining areas of Belgaum, Karwar, Pune and Bombay in the former Bombay Province and other British provinces in search of employment, business and educational facilities. In 1960, the Portuguese disbanded their airline and banking services, which rendered 3,500 persons unemployed (Techno-economic Survey of Goa, Daman & Diu 1964: 21). The Census of 1960 enumerated 16,704 persons or 6.5 per cent of the workforce employed in the industrial sector. Mr. Arun Sinha in his editorial wrote: '…The Portuguese never even once during their four and a half centuries of occupation of Goa encouraged agriculture. Their political design was to keep Goa as a starvation-diet economy, so that the people do not acquire consciousness and resources— which would, follow economic development— and begin to challenge the Portuguese rule…' (The Navhind Times: 15-06-01). Thus, the adjoining areas sustained Goa's economy during the Portuguese rule.

IMPACT OF MYSORE STATE: According to P. B. Desai, 'Konkana is purely Kannada __expression consisting of two parts, viz. Konku meaning the state of being bent and ana connoting a region. The name is thus physical formation of coastland. The antiquity of this name along with Karnata, Karahata and Tulva, which are basically Kannada, goes back to actually beginning of the Christian era' (Chavan, 1995: 6-7). It is argued that, 'Maharashtra was originally a Kannada-speaking region and that Marathi gradually displaced Kannada in this region' (*Op. Cit.* Israel 1983: 24). 'Goa was tagged to north Canara in the administrative divisions commenced in the end of seventh century and continued till the end of fourteenth century' (Shirodkar, 1989 (a): 22).

The place names like Panjikhalli or Panaji and Rai Bandar or King of Ports in the capital City are Kannada words. 'The poems of 'Yakshagana' resembling 'Jagar' are in Ovio form peculiar to Kannada but akin to Marathi and Konkani' (Desai, 1967: 94-97). Goa had established the trade links with the adjoining Kannada region. 'Goa depended for import of food, cloth supplies and precious stones on the Sultanate of Bijapur during the Portuguese rule' (De Souza, 1979: 34). Karnataka had close historical and linguistic ties with Konkan of which Goa is a part and the language of the Konkan in the fifth century A. D. must have been Kannada, according to P. B. Desai.

P. B. Desai remarked: "The influence of Karnataka culture and Kannada language on the social and cultural set up of the area underwent a change during the thirteenth and fourteenth centuries on account of various causes including migration of population, movement of communities and new settlements as a result of vicissitudes and other spheres in the country. The position that the Vijayanagar records (1336 A D) are all in Kannada goes to confirm once again the fact that it (Goa) was still integral part of Karnataka and the people and further to what their edicts were addressed were conversant with Kannada. Kannada was not merely the official language. It must have been the language of the people, too" (Desai, 1965: 2-3).

In Indian context, the language of the rulers and language of over whom they ruled were often different. It is very difficult to find that at any point of time only one language was used as the official language. 'For the first time, Konkani language spoken by Saraswat Brahmins was recognised in the court of Keladi rulers of Karnataka' (Desai, 1965: 11). The Kadambas during the early period gave Prakrit the status of the official language and later used Sanskrit for the official records. The inscriptions of the later period are in Sanskrit, Tamil, and Kannada languages. 'From the tenth century, onwards inscriptions are in the popular speech forms at the same time Sanskrit remained as the cultural language' (Mallikarjun, 1986: 11).

In 1883, the Konkani-speaking population was not separately enumerated from the Marathi-speaking population in the North Canara District of the Bombay Province. There were 2,44,895 (58.05) per cent Kannada speaking population out of the total 4, 21,840 in the District. The Marathi-speaking people constituted 1,52,774 (36.21) per cent followed by Hindustani 17,458 (4.13) per cent and others 6,484 (1.54) per cent, respectively (Bombay Gazetteer, Vol. XV, Part-I, 1883, Ch. III, p.114).

'In the South, Marathi was used as the official language in Travancore, Mysore, Tanjore and Kerala in the medieval period' (Gomantakachi Asmita November, 1999 (a): 5). 'In the Mysore plateau only half of the population of Mysore City spoke Kannada, a quarter of the population of Bangalore spoke Kannada, and the rest spoke Tamil, according to Census of 1961' (Berton 1997: 114). The various minority languages in Karnataka included Tulu, Coorgi, and Badaga related to Kannada, Telugu, Tamil and Malayalam, Marathi, Konkani, Urdu, Rajasthani or Banari-Lambadi dialects. The Mysore Government Gazetteer (Vol. I, p. 252) referred to Konkani as a dialect of Marathi rather than a separate language.

The Mysore Government in its submission to the M. C. Mahajan Commission Report, 1967 stated: "Konkani that is spoken in the northernmost region is moulded more or less by Marathi and south-west has been moulded by Kannada, Malayala, etc." (Telang, M K: 1966-67: 4).

'A. K. Priolkar and P. P. Pissurlekar submitted before the Commission (25-10-1966) that Konkani is a dialect of Marathi whereas the Konkani Bhasha Prachar Sabha (KBPS), Kerala, argued before the Commission that Konkani is an independent language' (Mallya, 1997: 116-17).

M. K. Telang remarked: "The Mysore Government laid claim not only over Goa by putting forth cultural and historical links with the mineral ore, scenic territory but also the Marathi-speaking areas of North and Kannada moulded Konkani-speaking areas South Kanara which had abundant forest wealth" (Telang, M K: 1966-67: 4-23).

IMPACT OF BOMBAY STATE: Goa had no separate linguistic identity from the neighbouring Marathi-speaking areas of the Bombay State. The areas of Karwar, Supa, Halyal, Bidar, Belgaum surrounded the tiny territory. Goans contributed to enrich the Marathi language and literature. The Bhakti movement— a Hindu devotional cult had profound influence on the native population.

'Father Sebastiao Goncalves in a letter dated November 25, 1565 revealed: "The Hindus, before their conversion to Christianity, used to walk on the streets of the City of Goa chanting the verses composed by

Saints like Saint Namdeo, Saint Eknath, Saint Tukaram in Marathi" (Gaitonde 1983: 29).

Teotonio De Souza wrote: "Goa shared the cultural life of the Maratha region around it. There is undeniable evidence to prove that the Varkari sect which gave shape to Marathi literature and brought about a cultural unification of Marathas had its devotees in Goa…In addition to the Maratha race and the Varkari sect, there was Marathi language, which had gained a firm foothold in Goa, or can be gathered from extant epigraphic and documentary evidence" (De Souza, 1979: 38).

'A critical examination of copper plates, inscriptions and other old material available and collected from different parts of that territory will completely bear out this view point. The Hindu saints, again, hailing from the remotest corners of Maharashtra have all written their poems and psalms in the same language; to give a few names, Dnyaneshwar, Eknath, Tukaram, Soiroba, Subanant of Ankola, Shiva Munishwar Kaikeni and Tukaram Baba of Goa— all those wrote in Marathi. Even foreign missionaries like Rev. Fr. Thomas Stephen, Rev. Fr. Crox, Rev. Fr. Gama and Rev. Fr. Minguel, who toiled in Goa in the 17th century wrote their Christ Puran in the same language, namely literary Marathi, for the benefit of converted Hindus who all spoke Konkani (Sukhthankar et al, 1930: 24).

The Kannada rulers did not interfere with the native language, culture or life-styles of the native population. The Kadamba dynasty ruled over Goa for three centuries. They could not make much impact on the native language and literature. The Marathi language and literature dominated the socio-cultural plane and administrative sphere before and after Portuguese rule. In this background, it is contended that 'Goa was an extension of Maharashtra— an extension of rest of India minus its poverty, illiteracy, and teeming population. The differences were only superficial. The core of Goa is Maharashtra— except for the Portuguese rule and its adverse consequences' (Borges & Feldmann 1997: 42). Thus, this contention holds well in case of Goa, which is a part of Konkan Kshetra.

MERGER ISSUE & PRESSURE GROUPS IN GOA

'In March 1963, the Maharashtrawadi Gomantak Party was temporarily formed to achieve the merger of Goa with Maharashtra' (The Navhind Times: 17-12-1963). 'Dayanand Bandodkar had consulted former Union Home Minister Yeshwantrao Chavan regarding the formation of the M. G. Party' (Narain 1976: 481). The anti-integration groups favoured the status quo over the future of the union territory. They perceived merger of Goa with Maharashtra as a threat to their communal identity and loss of power, position and patronage. 'The United Goans Party (UGP) was formed in September 1963 after coalition of political parties or groups like Goan National Union, Goencho Paksha, Patrido Indiano, United Front of Goans' (Coutinho, 1987: 167). Interestingly, these parties or groups had played no worthwhile role in Goa's freedom struggle. The primary objective of the UGP was to keep Goa separate. Peter Alvares, Member of Parliament, stated in the Lok Sabha that 'there was no demand from Maharashtra to take Goa. On the contrary there was demand from the Goan people to integrate territory with Maharashtra' (*Op. Cit.* Esteves 1989: 125).

'Economically and historically, Maharashtra is divided into four regions— Vidarbha, Marathwada, Western Maharashtra, and Konkan' (Misra, 1988: 41). Goa being a part of Konkan Kshetra had close linguistic and cultural ties with Maharashtra The Marathi-speaking people in the Vidarbha region put forth a demand for a separate state on economic, administrative and historical considerations. Prime Minister Jawaharlal Nehru favoured the status quo over the future of the union territory. He was not in favour of the Samyukta Maharashtra movement and vis-à-vis unification of Goa with Marathi-speaking areas with Maharashtra. Acharya Pralhad Keshav Atre noted Marathi writer and firebrand orator opined that, Pandit Nehru harboured anti-Samyukta Maharashtra sentiments.

Acharya P. K. Atre commented: "None other than Nehru was responsible for propagating idea that Konkani is the language of Goa. He propagated the myth in order to undermine the linguistic identity of territory and to oppose its inclusion in Samyukta Maharashtra" (Atre, 1977: 33-34).

Pandit Nehru said: "We have made it clear that we want Goa to maintain its separate identity, separate individuality, call it what you will, because in the space of 400 years Goa has had a separate identity and the course of history had imparted it some. In fact, some people have advised us to make another change in the Constitution and to recognise the Konkani language as one of the official languages of India" (*Op Cit.* Faleiro 1999: 44).

D. D. Karve remarked: "The pity is that even our top-most leaders are not clear in their minds about the fundamental principles. To take only one example, we went about declaring to the world that Goa was an integral part of India, that Goans were Indians by blood, sentiment, and culture. We justified our departure from oft-advertised policy of non-violence in order to drive out Portuguese. Soon after peace was established, no less than a person that Premier Jawaharlal Nehru went to Goa and made a declaration that Goa had a peculiar and special culture and that it would be carefully preserved" (Aiyer & Srinivasan, 1965: 422-23).

Interestingly, the Congress leaders in Maharashtra favoured merger and those from Mysore opposed it. Pandit Nehru exaggerated the separate identity of Goa to counter the Samyukta Maharashtra movement in the former bi-lingual Bombay State. He favoured status quo over the future of territory rather than its merger. In case of Goa, Nehru formulated political strategy based on his erroneous impression that Goa had carved out a distinct identity in the space of 451 years of Portuguese rule. The traces of lusitanian culture bore its imprint only in Velhas Conquistas areas, which came under the spell of Inquisition.

LANGUAGE ISSUE IN FIRST LEGISLATIVE ASSEMBLY OF GOA: The language controversy mired the proceedings of the first democratically constituted Legislative Assembly of Goa, Daman and Diu on January 7, 1964. V. S. Karmali, Minister for Education, drew the attention of the House over the language in which a member was allowed to express himself in the House.

The pro tem Speaker A. R. Tople stated: "The honourable member is allowed to speak in any language, but I would like to bring to their notice that, the speeches delivered in any language other than English or Hindi would not be recorded in verbatim, only substance will be recorded" (LAD 7-1-1964: Vol. I, 3-7).

On January 9, 1964, Chief Minister Dayanand Bandodkar delivered his speech in Marathi in the House. Jack Sequeira, the Leader of the Opposition, interrupted him. The Opposition threatened to boycott the sessions of the House, if the proceedings were conducted 'in a language unknown and unintelligible to the Opposition' (LAD 9-1-1964). Bandodkar switched over to Konkani and asserted that Konkani was a dialect of Marathi rather than a separate language. On January 14, 1964, Bandodkar preferred to speak in Konkani rather than Marathi and arranged for the translation of speech into Konkani. 'The demand for translation of Marathi speeches was politically motivated and therefore, not strictly justified. However, translation was certainly necessary to guarantee smooth transaction of business of the House (*Op. Cit.* Dias 1991: 39). 'Bandodkar doubted the sincerity of the Leader of the Opposition, because he came to know that the Leader of the Opposition was conversant with Marathi. The Leader of the Opposition himself apprised him that he opposes Marathi because it is a question of principle' (*Ibid:* 40-41).

The members consumed two full sessions of the House over the language controversy. The UGP opposed the use of Marathi for conduct of the business of the House. The move aimed at denying the rightful place to Marathi— the literary language of Goa. In fact, Konkani was not a language used in the domains of power— administration, judiciary, education, research and commerce. It was not the language in use but had entirely an oral tradition. The language in use was Marathi and Portuguese in the domains of power at the fag end of the Portuguese rule.

Kashinath Jalmi stated: "The real objective of the Portuguese regime was to turn the native population into black-Portuguese. The Portuguese followed a deliberate policy to isolate the converted class from the mainstream culture. Some were undoubtedly victims of the false propaganda of the superiority of Portuguese blood and culture. The identification with civilisation of foreign rulers gave material advantage and patronage. The black-Portuguese in the Old Conquest areas stood against the recognition of their cultural heritage— the Marathi language. The New Conquest areas were not much influenced by tyranny of conversions and the Inquisition instead continued to be culturally rich and prosperous. This historical fact is responsible for shaping different outlook and attitude of the people in the Old Conquest and New Conquest areas in Goa. Precisely for these reasons, Konkani although is spoken by all Goans cannot be called the language in use in Goa. (Jalmi: Interview 14-12-1999).

The Census of India recorded 5,89,997 population in the Goa District out of total population of 6,26,667 in the Union Territory of Goa, Daman & Diu in 1961. Konkani was spoken by majority of 5,56,297 94.29 per cent of the native population. The speakers of Marathi 11,630 (1.97) per cent; Portuguese 6,688 (1.13) per cent; Urdu 9,414 (1.59) per cent; Hindi 1,647 (0.28) per cent; Gujarati 1, 345 (0.23) per cent; and others 2,975 (0.5) per cent, respectively (Census of India, 1961).

In the census enumeration, a speaker, returns a particular language as his or her mother tongue not because of formal properties of the language but on the basis of group identity, socio-political pressure, and loyalty. Konkani remained as the spoken mother tongue of the people in the Konkan Kshetra. The majority of the population speaks it. The Hindus adopted Marathi as the literary language. The Roman Catholic Church adopted Latin script for Konkani to produce religious literature. The Christians were alienated from the Marathi language and literature for centuries. They nurtured Portuguese and later shifted to English.

DEBATE OVER MERGER ISSUE: P. P. Shirodkar, the first Speaker of the Legislative Assembly of Goa, Daman and Diu publicly stated that 'he was a mergerist since 1946 and he would be the happiest man if Goa is merged with Maharashtra' (The Navhind Times: 12-1-1965). On January 22, 1965, the House adopted the resolution for the merger of Goa with Maharashtra. On March 10, 1965, the Maharashtra Legislative Assembly passed the resolution in favour of merger. Jack Sequeira protested over the statement that 'Goa was predominantly populated by people with their mother tongue as Marathi or its dialect Konkani' in the merger resolution passed by the Maharashtra Legislative Assembly (Esteves, 1986: 122).

Prime Minister Jawaharlal Nehru in a letter to Chief Minister of Mysore S. Nijalingappa wrote: "I have made it clear that Goa is to remain separate and is not going to be joined as to either of two states" (Kelekar, 1965: 8).

'On March 12, 1965, The Mysore Legislative Assembly passed resolution for honouring the assurances given by late Pandit Nehru for no change in the status of the Union Territory and its future would be decided according to the wishes of the people' (Hindu: 14-3-1965).

The Goa, Daman & Diu Territorial Congress Election Manifesto (1963) declared: "The Government of India have made it clear that the future of Goa and whether it should merge into the adjoining territory of Maharashtra will be ultimately decided according to the wishes of the people of Goa. For the present, this question does not arise, as we have to stabilise and strengthen the economy and facilitate the changes that are taking place because of the integration of Goa in Indian Union".

On November 21, 1966, V. C. Shukla introduced the Bill in the Lok Sabha to ascertain the future status of the Union Territory of Goa, Daman & Diu. The Bill stated that the opinion poll should be taken for ascertaining: - a) The wishes of the electors of Goa as to whether Goa should merge in the State of Maharashtra or should continue to be Union Territory; b) The wishes of the electors of Daman and Diu to whether Daman & Diu should merge in the State of Gujarat or should continue to be the Union Territory.

Peter Alvares, Member of Parliament in the Lok Sabha stated that '72,000 children studied in Marathi while less than 2000 studied in Konkani'. K. Hanumanthaiya remarked that 'Bandodkar Ministry opened only Marathi schools to spread the cult of Shivaji, which had parallel in Hitler's Nazi Germany' (LSD 1-12-1966: c.c. 6658-70).

On February 2, 1966, Chief Minister Dayanand Bandodkar stated that 'Karwar, Goa and Belgaum sail in the same boat and their struggle for merger would end together and simultaneously…The people living in Goa only should exercise their voting rights during the Opinion Poll' (Radhakrishnan, 1994: 253-59). The notification for Goa, Daman & Diu Opinion Poll Act, (Act No. 38 of 1966) received assent of the President of India on December 11, 1966. 'Union Home Minister Y. B. Chavan declared in favour of merger and assured the pro-mergerists to have patience. Chief Minister Dayanand Bandodkar was in touch with Chavan over the merger issue' (Kirloskar, 1952: 2). 'The Chief Minister of Maharashtra V. P. Naik announced encouragement to Konkani and pledged that development of Konkani and Marathi shall go hand in hand' (Indian Express: 13-12-66).

'On November 17, 1966, the Anti-Merger Front was launched in Goa. The Konkani protagonists Laxmanrao Sardessai, Shankar Bhandari, Ravindra Kelekar, P. Mulgaonkar, M. Maximo Menezes, Enio Pimenta, and Marcelino Lima-Leitao' led the Front (Esteves 1986: 101). The vested political interests whipped up the linguistic, caste, communal and regional sentiments during the Opinion Poll campaign. The UGP asked the electorate to cast votes in favour of status quo so that Konkani may be encouraged and developed. Goa's cultural heritage retained. Its unique identity and personality preserved instead of allowing it to be lost in the vast ocean of Maharashtra.

On November 23, 1966, the Anti-Merger Front demanded that the electoral rolls should be revised to include all names of Goans of Indian nationality residing in and outside Goa and to exclude all non-Goans from it. The Front demanded for resignation of Chief Minister and his ministry and withdrawal of all civil servants on deputation from interested neighbouring States. They suggested that the alternatives in the Opinion Poll to be placed before the electorate should be merger and non-merger. The decision on the merger issue should be based on a substantial majority and not on simple majority. Also, the result of the Opinion Poll should be considered taking the entire territory as one unit. The pro-merger groups expressed their dissatisfaction over clubbing the twin-issue of merger of Daman and Diu in Gujarat and that of merger of Goa with Maharashtra. The mergerists argued that these two issues were fundamentally different. They did not approve the strategy of resolution of dispute over the future of the union territory through Opinion Poll, per se.

'Chief Minister Dayanand Bandodkar resigned on December 3, 1966 from the ministry to enable free and fair opinion poll' (Radhakrishnan, 1994: 253-59). A faction of the MGP leaders argued that the resignation of the chief minister on the eve of the Opinion Poll would encourage the anti-India forces to vitiate the process of free and fair polls rather than ensure its sanctity. V. N. Lawande, former Vice-President of the MGP stated that 'Chief Minister D. B. Bandodkar on his own gave consent to resolve the merger controversy through Opinion Poll. He either did not know the meaning of Opinion Poll or its implications or he was not sincere about the cause of merger" (*Op. Cit.* Esteves 1986: 107). The political parties were divided over the merger issue. The MGP, PSP, and Jana Sangh stood for merger whereas the UGP, INC and the leftist parties stood for status quo over the future of the union territory. The all-India parties like INC and the left parties encouraged the anti-integration stream in the territory.

Bertha Menezes, freedom fighter argued: "The United Goans Party is a grouping of most reactionary elements. Both its composition and processes used during the electoral campaigns speak for themselves. The top leadership of the United Goans Party is entirely made up of anti-national, feudal and wealthy reactionary elements wedded to the ideal of the Swatantra Party— the only Indian party, it must not be forgotten, which opposed operation Vijay and Liberation, to as to be in tune with its Western powers" (Menezes, 1992: 51).

Tariq Rahman remarked: "Language not only helps to imagine community, which was already imagined as a single kinship lineage but also to create living cultural artefacts: literature, a heroic tradition, history, new words, etc. In short, language creates devices for increasing solidarity and for creating pressure groups. In terms, the core of this political groups agitate for autonomy (or even secession), increased power in the peripheries, a larger share of goods and services, or at least for recognition as a separate cultural collectivity" (Rahman, 1998: 252).

The democratic institution in the territory was in the nascent stage. The party system was weak, unorganised and divided. The UGP was autocratic, reactionary and bourgeoisie party. The MGP banked upon the Hindu masses. The pressure groups assumed importance in the volatile political milieu. These groups became active and attempted to influence the public policy by mobilising masses steeped in semi-literacy, poverty and ignorance. The mine owners lobby had a finger in every pie. The Roman Catholic Church and advocates of Konkani vehemently opposed the merger. The pressure groups resorted to non-violent to violent tactics to stall the merger. The language became a powerful tool to mobilise the masses politically.

LANDHOLDERS & MERGER ISSUE: The institution of communidades or a village commune having its roots in the Vedic community is the unique feature of Goan socio-economic life. It provided lubrication to reduce friction between landowners and the land-less gentry. The Gaonkars or land controller nursed the communidades. The communidades were the collective farming societies endowed with land management and welfare activities in the villages. The Mahajans— the associations of religious nature and communidades existed in Konkan before year 1054 of the Christian era. In the pre-Portuguese era, the communidades were almost autonomous, self-sufficient, powerful and progressive bodies. They wielded judicial, fiscal and administrative powers, according to Rui Gomes Pereira. There were 224 communidades in 1961. 'Traditionally, the best lands came to be possessed by Brahmins after their migration to Goa, either in the form of communities or a farm in their capacities as landowners, the non-Brahmins too had their communities but of less important land' (Pereira, 1973: 15).

The land owned by different entities in Goa before Liberation is as under - The private land included 44.3 per cent followed by the communidades 34.8 per cent, government 17.7 per cent and temples 2.6 per cent of the total availability of land in 1958 (Portuguese Agriculture Mission in 1958). The bhatkars or landholders mainly were upper castes and mundkars or tenants were the masses. It is interesting to note that the bhatkar-mundkar (the landlord-tenant system) and the communidades (the collective land-ownership system) existed simultaneously in Goa. The Portuguese legal system favoured the elite class rather than the masses. The Bahujan Samaj had nursed a grudge against the elite class. The majority of the masses supported the MGP to retain their cultural identity and oppose a pro-feudal policy adopted by the elite enjoying power, culture and money.

INDUSTRIALISTS & MERGER ISSUE: In 1906, a Dutch traveller, John H. V. Linschoter predicted the possibility of iron ore in the red soil of Goa. The French, Italian and German firms staked their fortunes in the mining activity. The foreign and domestic industrialists began to explore frantically the vast areas of iron ore deposits leased to them by the Portuguese government and export it. In 1946, Goa exported 5,00,000 tonnes of iron ore. 'The mine owners substantial earnings of foreign exchange through the central office of Unio Banco Nacional in Lisbon, apart from raising their financial stature, it also reinforced the Goa exchequer' (Mascarenhas, 1999 (a): Vol-I, 26).

Before 1961, mine owners adopted a pro-establishment policy to further their corporate interests. T. B. Cunha in his last article Portuguese Occupation of Goa Supported by Indian Merchants in Free Goa (25-07-1958) revealed the nexus between the merchants and Portuguese. The Indian and foreign investors who contributed to the funds of the Shipbuilding Society and permanently co-operated with the Portuguese in strengthening foreign hold in Goa. The most important names are: Chowgule & Company Limited (India); Damodar Mangalji & Company (India) Limited; Gangadhal Agrawal; Khantilal & Company Limited; Shantilal Khushaldas & Brothers Subraya & Company; Timble Brothers Limited; V. S. Dempo Company Limited; V. M. Salgaonkar & Brothers Limited; Joao Hugo Sequeira; Madhav Sinai Talaulikar; Abdul Razak; Sesa Goa Limited (Germano-Italian); and WIP Railways (Bombay)' (Tombat, 1995: 217)

Jaisingrao Rane Sardessai stated: "To further their economic interests all mine owners were actively involved in the anti-merger activities.

The merger with Maharashtra would have threatened their position and business interests in Goa" (Rane Sardessai: Interview: 1-6-98).

Apparently, the mine owners were divided over the merger issue. The majority of them stood for the status quo over the future of union territory. They backed the anti-mergerists and supported Konkani literary activities. 'The Dempos and Salgaonkars supported the Konkani language movement. Industrialist Vasudevrao Salgaonkar became the financier during the Opinion Poll who believed Konkani to be a separate language and opted for a full-fledged statehood' (Keni, 1993: 11). Vishwasrao Chowgule, a mine owner, hailing from the neighbouring Maharashtra sided with the integration groups as well and 'supported the merger of Goa with Maharashtra' (*Op. Cit.* Chowgule 1975 (a): 115). The mine owners emerged as powerful pressure groups in Goa after Liberation. They controlled powerful print media. The merger with neighbouring states would have adversely affected their corporate interests. The Praja Socialist Party the alliance partner of the MGP had criticised Chief Minister Dayanand Bandodkar who had staked fortune in mining activity for adopting a go-slow policy over the merger issue.

PRINT MEDIA & MERGER ISSUE: On November 6, 1912, Govind Pundalik Hegde-Desai launched Bharat a Portuguese-Marathi bi-weekly on the lines of Kesari of Lokmanya B. G. Tilak and Sudharak of G. G. Agarkar in Goa. In its editorial (06-06-1946) Hegde-Desai warned that the advocates of Konkani who were in minority should not try to promote Konkani by suppressing Marathi, which is the language of the majority of population (Gomantak, 23-01-2000: 4). The Portuguese viewed Marathi print media as the foci of nationalist awakening in the territory. It had played a major role in shaping public opinion against the colonial regime. The Konkani print media backed anti-integration forces.

T. B. Cunha remarked: "Since the Konkani press is in immediate contact with the broad based Goan masses, who due to their semi-literacy resort this only source of knowledge and information, every effort should be made to see that it is not used by dubious elements for fostering anti-India propaganda in the Union of India... A large number of Goan institutions and newspapers many of them written in Konkani language and Roman script were run by or under the guidance of the foreign agents. The Jesuits controlled Goan Konkani press persuaded Catholics that their religion is safe under Portugal, which is a model Catholic State" (Cunha, 1961: 511).

The Goan writers based in Bombay gave vent to their legitimate aspirations in the Bombay press. In 1892, J. C. Francis started the first bi-lingual Portuguese-Konkani weekly entitled O Concan followed by O Luso Cocani of the same editorship and O Povo Goans a weekly published by Sebastiao Jesus Dias (Shirodkar 1995 (a): 95). In 1894, a bi-weekly, Udentachem Salok was launched by Eduardo Bruno da Souza whereas other papers which survived for less than a year include— O Intrasigente, A Luz, O Nationalista. In 1920, Antonio da Cruz started in Bombay a weekly Ave Maria. Dr. Vasco Da Gama and Felix Afonso brought out The Goa Mail, which was tri-lingual in Konkani, Portuguese and English later turned to be Konkani only. In 1930, R. A. Pereira founded the Goa Times. In 1939, Dr. Juio Menezes founded Gomantak Praja Mandal and weekly Gomantak in English-Konkani, which backed Goan freedom movement. In 1950s, Ravindra Kelekar edited Gomant Bharati a Konkani tabloid in Roman script. A Konkani paper Porjeacho Awaj was launched in 1953-54.

On January 26, 1956, Teb Mascarenhas started a weekly Resurge Goa and T.B. Cunha launched fortnightly Free Goa on October 10,1953. The other weeklies, periodicals included—Tar, Goan Affairs, Zuari by Bonafacio Dias; Goan Age by Gerald Pereira; Goenkar by E. Pereira; Konkani Life by Laura Rodrigues; Goan Life by Lucio Rodrigues. The other publications include— Free Goa, Amchea Goy, Amcha Goa by Nationalist Congress (Goa), the UG Reporter by the United Front of Goans, Navjivan and Jwala by the Azad Gomantak Dal, Deshsudhareanetshu, Dipagraha, Dudhasagar A Vida, Diaro de Noite, O Ultramarino, Goa Tribune by the Goa Liberation Council, amongst others. The newspapers viz., Bharat, Pradipa, Prakash, Utramar, Sadalcalo, and India Portugueza came under Portuguese censorship. Konkani tabloids adopted Konkani in the Roman script as the demand for Portuguese declined with popularity of English. Some of these tabloids indulged in pro-Portuguese activities even after 1946 when freedom movement gained momentum.

Late freedom fighter V. N. Lawande wrote: "The Christians who were sympathetic to the freedom struggle would have been more emotionally involved, if they could keep in touch with developments through newspapers and leaflets that were more easily available to Marathi reading Goan Hindus" (Goa Times: December 1986).

T. B. Cunha wrote: "Goan Konkani press provides the best example of a full-scale poisoning of people's mind against India. Whether it is in Bombay, Karachi or in Goa, this press always full of news of the alleged persecution of Catholics in India after Independence. The news is supplied to them by the agents of Propaganda Fide a Vatican congregation or by other missionary papers which tried to dissuade ignorant Goan Catholics from achieving integration of Goa into India' (Cunha, 1961 480-81). In a case filed by the Portuguese Consulate in Bombay against the publication of book Denationalisation of Goans by T. B. Cunha, Justice M. C. Chhagla remarked: "The whole aim of the author, it seems to us, is to trace historically the gradual denationalisation of Goans from the days of Albuquerque and point out what the consequences of this denationalisation are, finally emphasising the point that unless the Goans went back to their own culture and their own language, they would always remain servile and subservient, unfit for any progress and incapable of obtaining freedom... (Government of Maharashtra, 1978: 551).

The pro-merger press included Marathi dailies Gomantak launched on 24-03-1962, Gomantwani (1964), Pradeep, and Bharat Mitra. Gomantak maintained that Konkani was a dialect of Marathi and sided with the MGP. It did not subscribe to separate identity of Goa.

Adv. Uday Bhembre remarked: "In fact, this newspaper (Gomantak) ever since its inception, has been constantly anti-Goan, with one exception all its editors have been Maharashtrians who have always acted as external tentacles of the expansionist and colonial forces. This force opposed the preservation of Goa's distinct identity within the Indian Union and ferociously supported its merger with Maharashtra…' (Naik, 1987: See preface).

The Dempos launched the English daily The Navhind Times on February 18, 1963. The Navhind Times and Rashtramat— a Marathi daily adopted anti-merger and pro-Konkani leanings. 'The Rashtramat was launched on July 22, 1963 under the editorship of V. M. Phandse who was close associate of Acharya P.K.Atre. Phandse stood for cause of Konkani and opposed merger of Goa because the Vidarbha and Marathwada region had gained nothing after merger with Maharashtra in 1956' (Keni & Karwar, Chandrakant: 1994, 149). It is difficult to understand that how Phandse advocated cause of Konkani even though he associated with Acharya Atre in the Samyukta Maharashtra movement. The Rashtramat played an important role in mobilising the support merger in the Marathi camp. 'The Navhind Times though stood for status quo over the future of the territory was naturally sympathetic towards the Congress' (Hallappa, 1964: 58). The Konkani daily Sot was launched on August 15, 1962. Goa Today came up in 1966. O' Heraldo, a Portuguese daily launched in 1900 adopted anti-merger stand. The Vavrydeacho Ixtt a bi-lingual Konkani-Portuguese monthly vehemently opposed the merger. The local print media controlled by powerful mine owners lobby and the Konkani and Portuguese print media supported by the Vatican played a decisive role in moulding public opinion against the merger. The western powers conspired to send message to the international community that Goans were opposed the integration of territory with India.

The Marathi newspapers including Kesari and Maratha had wide readership in Goa. The English press in Bombay, the Times of India and Indian Express adopted pro-merger stand whereas Current and Goan Tribune favoured the status quo. The Kesari vociferously supported the merger whereas a Pune-based Marathi daily Sakal under the editorship of Dr. N. B. Parulekar adopted a neutral policy on the merger issue. The Sakal gave less coverage to merger issue compared to the Kesari. The merger news appeared in the columns of Sakal on 07-01-1967; 08-01-1967; 10-01-1967; 11-01-1967; 16-01-1967; 17-01-1967; 18-01-1967; 1901-1967; and 20-01-1967.

The Kesari provided regularly merger news in its columns. On January 7, 1967, a Marathi weekly Swaraj issued a special supplement on Opinion Poll in Goa. 'The Kesari-Maratha institution had played a prominent role liberation of Goa. Kesari maintained that Goa was culturally and geographically a part of Maharashtra...It claimed that Samyukta Maharashtra is incomplete without merger of Goa' (Gokhale, 1981: 299). The Samyukta Maharashtra movement, however, whipped up the sentiments of linguistic nationalism in the Marathi areas of the former Bombay Province. The Mysore State staked claim over Goa on historical and cultural affinity with territory. The Kannada press had no base and evoked no response amongst the masses. The advocates of Konkani mainly resorted to Marathi and English press to mobilise support in favour of the status quo over the future of the territory.

RELIGIOUS GROUPS & MERGER ISSUE: The Roman Catholic Church shared power with Portuguese regime. The Christian missionaries believed that Portugal was a model state. 'The Portuguese ruled under the sign of the Cross and the Sword. The State and the Church worked hand in hand.' (Cunha, 1961: 505). 'The order of Franciscans was the first to arrive in Goa after its conquest by Portuguese in 1510. The Franciscans and Dominican religious orders accompanied the first expedition of Portuguese in 1497. The Jesuits came in 1542 headed by Apostle Francis Xavier. In 1548, the Dominicans opened their monastery, followed by Augustinian (1572), Carmelite (1600) and Theanite (1640) who started to work under the patronage of Portugal in the East' (Costa, 1997: 3).

After Liberation, the Portuguese continued to maintain a fiction that Goa was part and parcel of Portugal and accordingly continued to appoint Governor and other officials for the Government of Goa in exile. The Vatican recognised it. The appointment of Auxiliary Bishop of Goa and

Apostolic Administrator of Goa was made under the Presentation clause of Concordat of 1928 till 1974. By virtue of Presentation, the Portuguese government had the right to nominate candidates for appointment of bishops only from the list of candidates submitted by it. As mentioned in the preamble of the Concordat this right was granted to Portugal to safeguard its interests. The amendment of 1940, although curtailed the powers of the Government of Portugal, retained those powers in full with regard to colonies in India. Thus, Church in Goa acted as external tentacles of the Portuguese regime even after Liberation of territory' (*Op. Cit.* Memorandum issued by Citizen's Forum to Members of Parliament, New Delhi, February, 2000).

The head of Roman Catholic Church Patriarch D Jose Nunes asserted: "The Catholics of Goa are westernised. They are as Portuguese as Portuguese of Portugal. They have nothing to do with the ancient civilisation of India and therefore they are opposed to Goa's incorporation into India" (Government of Maharashtra, 1978: 48).

In 1851, the Christians constituted 63.82 per cent followed by Hindus 35.41 per cent. In 1950, the Christians constituted 40.20 per cent and the Hindus 56.10 per cent. In 1961, the Christian constituted 38.07 per cent and the Hindus 59.92 per cent. In 1971, the Christians constituted 33.97 per cent and the Hindus 63.43 per cent, respectively. The Christian population steadily declined from 63.82 per cent in 1850 to 33.97 per cent in 1971 whereas the Hindu population shot up from 35.41 per cent in 1850 to 63.43 per cent in 1971 (Annuario Estatisco, Estadao da India, 1950 & Statistical Pocket Books, Government of Goa, 1961-91, Panaji, Goa).

Nirad C. Chaudhury to comment: "I do not think that any other group of Asiatic in naturalising to Christianity succeeded so thoroughly which was not of their own creation as did the Christianity of Goa in the Roman ethnic church" (Chaudhury, 1996: 321).

T. B. Cunha remarked: "In the whole of India, no people are so denationalised as Goans. A complete lack of national consciousness and most shameful subjection of foreign rulers, either Portuguese or British, render the Goans and particularly the Goan Christians strangers in their own land" (Cunha, 1961: 59).

In 1961, the overall population in Goa District the Hindus constituted 59.92 per cent followed by Christians 38.07 per cent and others 2.01 per cent respectively. The Christian population in the Old Conquest areas of Tiswadi taluka constituted 41.39 %; Salcete 75.27 %; Bardez 41.66 %; and Mormugao 53.57 %, respectively. The Church with its well-knit organisational structure and backing of the Vatican exercised considerable influence amongst its followers. In the New Conquest areas, the Hindus constituted 88.73 per cent in Ponda; Bicholi 92.12 %; Perne 87.13 %; Quepe 60.73 %; Sattari 73.70 %; Canacona 75.88 % and Sangue 92.62 %, respectively (See Appendix-9).

Prime Minister Jawaharlal Nehru expressed his mind in 1963: "In the first general elections were fought on communal lines the way, which the Congress party wanted to avoid. The Roman Catholics forming forty per cent of the population generally voted on the one side and the Hindus on the other. The Congress failed because it was trying to build bridge between the two" (Kelekar, 1965: 18).

Peter Alvares, Member of Parliament, on December 1, 1966 in the Lok Sabha stated: "The urge for keeping the territory as a separate entity, as a Union Territory, comes exactly from those four talukas, whereas the people in the remaining seven talukas representing the overall majority of the people of Goa have been and are and have always been rightly or wrongly for merger with Maharashtra" (Esteves 1986: 124).

Goan chronicler Mario Cabral e Sa wrote: "In Goa, unlike British and French missionaries, the Portuguese padres targeted the elites, the haves and not the have-nots like the others. They had to cushion the cultural shock. They allowed the neophytes to retain their Hindu caste. They also modified their liturgy and adapted the native hymnology and iconography' (The Navhind Times: 09-01-2000: 2).

The Roman Catholic Church considered the merger as a threat to the identity of the Christian community. 'Interestingly, a converted Saraswat Brahmin became Christian in the faith alone, retaining all caste prerogatives, untainted by any admixture of foreign or low caste blood, through generations to present aristocratic position' (Cunha, J 1881: 37).

LITERARY GROUPS & MERGER ISSUE: After 1961, the semi-conscious Konkani language groups began to transform into self-conscious force in the territory. The language strategists attempted to create new groups to have access to wealth and power. 'The cultural basis for Goa's independence or autonomy became clear only in the work of charismatic Vaman Varde Valaulikar alias Shenoy Goebab— a Hindu Brahmin, proud of his Brahmin lineage, but prouder still of his Konkani identity. The lineaments of which no one discerned so clearly before him' (Pereira 1995: 18). Dnyaneshwar Nadkarni argued that 'Vaman Varde Valaulikar directly influenced the renaissance of indigenous Goan culture' (Chowgule, 1975 (a): 15). Vaman Varde Valaulikar argued that 'Konkani is an independent language and directed his efforts to produce literature following the footsteps of the founding fathers of Konkani language movement (*Op. Cit.* Jaag: April 1999). 'He suffered from peculiar persecution mania. The only way by which he could give ___expression to his embittered feelings was to promote the cause of Konkani' (Telkar, 1962: 137). 'It was in Rachol Seminary— a prime institution in Asia devoted to spread of teachings of the Christ where Varde Valaulikar launched his magnificent efforts to revive Konkani and enrich its literature' (Faleiro, 1999: 60). Varde Valaulikar stated it was not necessary to adopt the defeatist plan of making Goa a part of Maratha community for acquiring freedom. Goa was never a part of Maratha country, it was not then, and it would not be in the future' (Goa Today, May 1995 (a): 13).

The Konkani writers mainly who actively associated with anti-merger movement included 'B. B. Borkar, Uday Bhembre, Laxmanrao Sardessai, Manoharrai Sardessai, Arvind Bhattikar, Anna Sarmalkar, Chandrakant Keni amongst others' (Simoes, 1990: 155-57). The literary organisations, which lit the torch of the Marathi literary activities at cultural plane, included Gomant Gayak Samaj, Gomantak Gayak Sabha, and Gomantak Marathi Samaj, amongst others. The mergerists derived support from the Marathi literary bodies and writers both in Goa and Maharashtra. Noted literature Acharya P. K. Atre, N. V. Gadgil, N. G. Gore, Sushil Kavalekar, Anant Kanekar and others attended the Marathi Literary Conference held in Goa in 1962. The cultural activities in support of Marathi always dominated the socio-cultural milieu in the territory.

Jaisingrao Rane Sardessai stated: "The upper castes spearheaded Konkani language movement and Konkani is a dialect of Marathi rather than an independent language...Konkani has traced or produced no literature of any worthwhile standard... The upper castes to promote their caste, linguistic and material interests after Liberation used Konkani as a weapon to mobilise the masses. They managed to perpetuate the myth that Konkani is a language in its own right" (Rane Sardessai: Interview: 1-698).

The Goa Vilinikaran Sahayak Samiti was formed on the eve of the Opinion Poll. P. G. Kher, President of Bombay Pradesh Congress Committee, headed the Samiti. M. S. Aney, a Vidarbha leader issued statement to vote against the merger in the territory (Amonkar, 1967: 9). The Western powers and Pakistan attempted to work against the integration of Goa with India. Chief Minister B. B. Bandodkar remarked that 'Konkani protagonists had joined hands with anti-national forces in the territory' (Sakal: 1-1-67). The Radio Lisbon showed a keen interest in the activities of the United Goans Party during the merger issue. Berth Menezes feared that 'it gave a clue to what part had been played by the Salazarist Gestapo agent left free by the Congress Government to operate in the liberated Goa and the links that existed between the United Goans and Lisbon' (Menezes, 1992: 50).

OPINION POLL VERDICT IN FAVOUR OF STATUS QUO: The merger was rejected by margin of 34,021 (10.71) per cent votes. There were 1,38,170 votes secured in favour of merger and 1,72,191 votes in favour of the status quo out of total 3,17,633 (81.78) per cent votes polled. The total electorate was 3,88,432 whereas 7,272 (1.87) per cent votes were rejected (Official Gazette, Goa, Daman & Diu, Series-II, No. 42, 21 01-1967).

The Old Conquest areas recorded 87.34 per cent voter turn out in Opinion Poll as against 81 per cent in 1963 assembly polls. In the New Conquest areas, voter turn out was 82.93 per cent as against 75 in 1963 assembly polls. The anti-integration groups had traditional hold amongst the masses in the Old Conquest areas. The integration groups derived support of the masses from sparsely populated New Conquest region. The Opinion Poll result exhibited strong communal, caste and linguistic pulls. A section of Maratha caste in Sattari, Quepe, Sangue and Canacona in the New Conquest tactically voted against the merger in the Hindu dominated areas.

The percentage of votes polled in favour of status quo includes is as follows: - Salcete 84.40 %; Tiswadi 57.63 %; Bardez 52.43 %; and Mormugao 51.50 % in the Old Conquest areas. Similarly, percentages of votes polled in the favour merger include— Tiswadi 42.37 per cent; Bardez 47.57 per cent; Salcete 15.60 per cent and Mormugao 48.50 per cent votes, respectively. The percentage of votes in the Hindu dominated areas in the New Conquest include— Perne 70 per cent; Bicholi 70.50 per cent; Sattari 52.48 per cent; Ponda 71.67 per cent; Sangue 41.50 per cent; Quepe 45 per cent; Canacona 56 per cent, respectively. Similarly, percentages of votes polled in favour of status quo include— Perne 30 per cent; Bicholi 29.50; Sattari 47.52 per cent; Ponda 28.33 per cent; Sangue 58-50 per cent; Quepe 55; and Canacona 46 per cent, respectively (See Appendix-10).

Union Railway Minister S. K. Patil stated that Congress always stood for status quo over the future of Goa. Mohan Dharia, General Secretary of Maharashtra Pradesh Congress Committee, stated 'some elements in the anti-merger group were close to Lisbon than to New Delhi. He criticised the Goa Congress for being involved in contrary to Congress President's stand...that it should have been neutral in the matter' (Esteves, 1986: 133).

The Jana Sangh leader, R. K. Mhalgi, expressed party's displeasure over the outcome of the Opinion Poll. Mhalgi argued that the Opinion Poll was not the appropriate strategy to decide the future status of the territory.

In Pune, Congress leader Vishvasrao Dhere charged that Acharya P. K. Atre, S. M. Joshi, N. G. Gore did not turn up in Goa for the Opinion Poll campaign whereas the non-Congress parties targeted Union Home Minister Yeshwantrao Chavan for not properly putting up Goa's case at the Centre. Pune-based Sakal commented 'the defeat of the MGP on the merger issue was due to its poor performance in three years of rule… A separate state of Goa should be carved out by amalgamating the adjoining coastal areas, irrespective of linguistic considerations" (Sakal: 20-1-67 & 21-012-1967).

Former Chief Minister of Goa Shashikala Kakodkar argued: "The Maharashtrawadi Gomantak Party played a crucial role in emotional integration of the people after the Liberation in 1961. The merger of Goa with neighbouring State of Maharashtra was a means rather than end in itself. The M. G. Party's emergence on political map of Goa was a reaction to the anti-national forces that were pitted against the integration of the territory with India and to usher in welfare of the Bahujan Samaj who were subjected to social, cultural and economic discrimination under the erstwhile Portuguese rule.

Ironically, the Saraswat Brahmins who nursed Marathi at home and the Catholics who identified themselves with the Portuguese or English adopted a pro-Konkani stand on the ground of separate identity of the territory. These pro-Portuguese forces, however, attempted to de-link themselves from the Western culture after Liberation" (Kakodkar: Interview: 13-10-1999).

Jaisingrao Rane Sardessai stated: "The Congress party heavy weights at the Centre maintained anti-merger posture. The political leadership in Maharashtra on the eve of Opinion Poll left the merger workers to fend for them. In addition, large number of pro-merger voters residing in Maharashtra did not turn up for voting as compared to anti-mergerists.

The Government of Maharashtra showed lack of interest in motivating the pro-merger voters residing in Maharashtra during the Opinion Poll for Goa' s merger with Maharashtra. Chief Minister D. B. Bandodkar should have not agreed to resolve the dispute through the Opinion Poll as his party had majority in terms of seats and votes secured in 1963 assembly elections. This weakness altered the outcome of the Opinion Poll in favour of the status quo over the future of the union territory" (Rane Sardessai: Interview: 1-6-1998).

Adv. Uday Bhembre stated: "The movement for Konkani right from its inception was a cultural movement as its objective was to give Konkani its rightful place and opportunities for its development. Political parties supported it at some stage; but it was not a political movement. The issue of Goa's merger with Maharashtra was a political movement and similarly anti-merger was a political activity. As language was a crucial point for both the sides, the movement for Konkani gathered momentum in the anti-merger activity and it served as a strong basis for anti-merger movement. The merger movement was bound to fail as Konkani was never a dialect of Marathi nor Goa was part of Maharashtra at any point of time" (Bhembre: Interview: 14-5-1998).

Ravindra Kelekar remarked: "The entire Konkani movement is political rather than literary in its form and content. The literary merit plays a secondary role in asserting the linguistic identity of the state...The Konkani movement was dominated by Saraswat Brahmins in the beginning because they were only educated and enlightened section of the society. In addition, Konkani was the mother tongue of majority of the people. The Saraswat Brahmins were actively involved in the Marathi literary activity within and outside the territory.

In fact, they (Saraswat Brahmins) were the main leaders of the Marathi political movement. The caste conscious Chitapavan Brahmins in Maharashtra were responsible for fuelling inferiority complex amongst the Saraswat Brahmins. The Konkani movement in the beginning was the reaction to that inferiority complex which culminated into demand for a separate Konkani state…" (Kelekar: Interview: 14-5-1998).

Tanaji Halarnkar stated: "The Konkani movement was not political but linguistic in its nature. The Konkani movement, however, resorted to encash upon prevailing political groups, ideas identical to its interest. The linguistic identity of Goa co-existed with the adjoining Konkan region. Konkani movement had upper caste orientations.

The masses had a grudge against Saraswat Brahmins who were landowners and adopted a pro-establishment feudal policy during the colonial rule and thereafter. The masses frowned upon their motives and whatever they stood for resultantly mainly non-Saraswat Brahmin Hindu community identified themselves with Marathi and the merger with the State of Maharashtra as security against a traditional fear of the upper caste (Saraswat Brahmins). However, further course of movement was shaped by all sections of the Konkani community" (Halarnkar Interview: 5-5-1998).

Bhiku Pai Angle pointed out: "For centuries, the Marathi language played a prominent role in the cultural life of the people in Goa. The

Saraswat Brahmins are responsible for distorting this historical fact. They attempted to elevate the spoken Konkani, which had hardly any literary merit. It is the egoistic venture of late Vaman Varde Valaulikar, which has become the basis of Konkani language movement in Goa. Before Liberation, the Portuguese tried to transplant alien culture, language, and religion on the natives. The Konkani language movement had has separatist and sectarian undertones. The Konkani protagonists attempted at denying the rightful place enjoyed by Marathi in the social, cultural and religious spheres (Pai Angle: Interview: 11-6-98).

Thus, the Opinion Poll verdict went in favour of status quo over the future of the Union Territory of Goa, Daman & Diu. Konkani had merit from the psychological and sentimental point of view. The anti-integration groups adopted Konkani as a tool to keep Goa separate. The Congress party had stressed on the separate identity of territory to counter the claim neighbouring States over territory. It resorted to appease the anti-integration groups that faced the problem of re-integration with the mainstream of the country after Liberation. The 'Aqui Portugal' or 'This is Portugal' depicting lusitanian culture had no takers in the post-Liberation era. The anti-integration groups banked upon separate linguistic identity to perpetuate their dominance in socio-cultural, economic and political plane in the changing political set up in the territory. The people of Goa rejected the idea of linguistic nationalism and chose cultural nationalism to usher in peace, harmony and progress in Goa.

Chapter–V

LINGUISTIC AFFAIRS OF GOA— THE STATEHOOD PHASE

The anti-integration groups mobilised support for the separate identity during the merger issue. In fact, Goa has had no socio-linguistic identity apart from the Konkan Kshetra. Konkani originates in Konkan Kshetra. The MGP soft peddled on the merger issue. The outcome of the Opinion Poll went against the MGP. Ironically, the electorate gave mandate to the M. G. Party in the assembly elections held after the Opinion Poll in 1967. The Praja Socialist Party (PSP) severed ties with the MGP. The regional parties assumed importance in the post-merger era. The UGP criticised the ruling party for neglecting the development work in the territory. The MGP refuted the charges. In fact, the MGP had attempted to implement the welfare measures after assuming power.

The total electorate constituted 4,18,404 in the assembly elections held on March 28,1967. The MGP secured 16 seats with 40.37 per cent vote share followed by the UGP (Sequeira) 12 seats with 37.98 per cent vote share. The UGP (Furtado) and Praja Socialist Party drew nil with 2.88 and 0.10 per cent vote share. The independents got two seats with 17.68 per cent vote share, respectively (Assembly Elections Ready Reference-1999).

The UGP was divided into Furtado and Sequeira groups. The INC was out of the electoral race. The MGP shelved the language issue for political convenience in the post-merger era. The ruling party had a marginal base in the Christian pockets in the South Goa. The MGP leadership tried to woo the Christian voters to the party fold. A faction of the ruling party criticised the party leadership for diluting its stand over the language issue. The MGP made hardly any efforts to accord the official status to regional languages— Marathi and Konkani and allowed English to dominate the domains of power. Section 34 (1) of the Union Territories Act, 1963 provides: 'The Legislative Assembly of a Union Territory may by law adopt any one or more of the languages in use in the Union Territory or Hindi as the official language or languages to be used for all or any of the official purposes of the Union Territory'.

Adv. Ramakant Khalap, former Union Mister for Law & Justice stated: "In case of Marathi, the M. G. Party did not adopt a consistent policy. The ruling M. G. Party did not introduce a bill to accord official status to Marathi. Jack Sequeira, the Leader of the Opposition had argued in the House that the ministry headed by D. B. Bandodkar is competent to introduce the bill to adopt any one or more of the languages in use in the Union Territory as official language." (Khalap: Interview: 03-10-199).

The total electorate constituted 4,51,484 in the assembly elections held on March 11, 1972. The MGP secured 18 seats, the UGP 10, INC (Sanjivayya) and independent one seat each, respectively (Assembly Elections Ready Reference-1999). The Nav-Maharashtrawadi Gomantak Party (NMGP), the breakaway faction of the MGP drew a blank. The new parties in the fray were the Socialist Party (SP), Bharatiya Jana Sangh (BJS), Communists Party of India (CPI), and Communist Party of India Marxist (CPI-M), respectively.

Biblial Dias argued that 'the language controversy was at its height during the first and second sessions of the first Legislative Assembly in the House. Speaker P. P. Shirodkar (10-01-1964 to 11-04-1967) partially solved the problem of the House by arranging for translation (of Marathi speeches in Konkani). However, these arrangements were short-lived and ended with ending of Shirodkar's Speaker-ship. His successors did not make any serious attempt to provide for translation. Speaker G. A. Kamat (12-04-1967 to 23-03-1972) thought that demand for translation was unjustified and firmly discouraged it. Speakers that followed Kamat were not compelled to take a stand on translation because the members from both sides did not press for translation in the House (Dias 1991: 46).

The total electorate constituted 4,85,811 in the assembly elections held on June 1, 1977. The MGP bagged 15 seats under the leadership of Shashikala Kakodkar. The INC got 10 seats, the Janata Party secured three seats and Independents two seats, respectively (Assembly Elections Ready Reference-1999). The UGP asserted the demands for separate statehood and official recognition to Konkani. The failure of the MGP to accord the official status to Marathi strengthened the forces that stood for recognition to Konkani and statehood. Interestingly, the MGP attempted to shed its pro-Marathi image. The hard-liners within the party expressed their resentment over the lack of commitment of the party leadership over the language issue or ideology. The charismatic leadership of D. B. Bandodkar discouraged erosion of party base or intra-party feuds.

The total electorate constituted 5,22,652 in the assembly elections held on January 3, 1980. The MGP got a set back and had to content with seven seats. The Congress (Urs) got 19 seats and independents and others bagged four seats (Statistical Pocket Book-1980, Department of Statistics, Planning & Evaluation, Government of Goa).

The political opportunism became rampant after 1980 when the candidates elected on the Indian National Congress (Urs) joined en-bloc to the Indian National Congress (Indira) after the failure of the Janata party experiment at the Centre. The INC (I) managed to lure the legislators owing allegiance to the regional parties. The INC adopted pro-Konkani stance to win over the traditional voters of the United Goans Party. The MGP's relevance faded after 1980 assembly polls in the territory. No political party genuinely stood for recognition of Marathi. Instead, they in a bid to capture power wooed the advocates of the Konkani language groups.

Former Chief Minister Luizinho Faleiro remarked: "Indeed, MGP was a born loser although it was in power for eighteen long and disastrous years. If one were to write an epitaph for that regime, it would read some thing like this 'There lies the champions of lost causes', because whatever they tried ended up in smoke, luckily in a big way for Goa. They tried to merge Goa with Maharashtra and failed, they tried to impose Marathi as the official language and failed. However, they also tried to portray themselves as the protectors of poor and disadvantaged and only ended in creating social chaos and disaster" (Faleiro, 1999: 37).

The total electorate constituted 5,86,709 in the assembly elections held on December 27, 1984 in the territory. The sympathy wave after assassination of former Prime Minister Indira Gandhi gave a swing in favour of Congress (I) party. The INC got 18 seats followed by the MGP 8 seats. The Goa Congress— a regional outfit won one seat whereas three seats went to the independents (Assembly Elections Ready Reference-1999).

The Communist Party of India (CPI), Communist Party of India-Marxist (CPI-M), Bharatiya Janata Party (BJP) of the erstwhile Bharatiya Jan Sangh, Janata Party (JP), Bhausaheb Bandodkar Gomantak Party (BBGP)— the breakaway faction of the MGP, and Gomant Lok Paksha (GLP)— a regional outfit entered the electoral fray. After 1984, the INC tried to derive political mileage on the twin-issue of the recognition to Konkani and statehood. It helped the INC to consolidate its power base. Interestingly, the anti-integration groups believed that the statehood would permanently bury the ghost of merger.

ELEVATION OF STATUS OF LANGUAGES

Konkani became a tool to keep Goa separate in the post-Liberation era. The anti-integration groups mobilised the masses for cause of Konkani. Pandit Nehru 'called upon people not to fritter their energies on the linguistic controversies' (The Navhind Times: 23-03-1963). On May 23,1963, Pandit Nehru stated that 'a popular spoken language had a particular merit from the psychological and sentimental point of view. Whether it could develop or not into something more than that, it was difficult to say' (*Op. Cit.* Kelekar 1965: 8). On 14-03-1962, Nehru revealed 'some people had advised him to make another change in the Constitution and to recognise Konkani as one of the official languages of India' (Nehru, 1963). The AICC resolution (5/6-11-1968) appealed that 'the Government of India should include Konkani in the Eighth Schedule to the Constitution and urged the Government of Maharashtra, Mysore and Kerala and particularly to the Government of Goa to give further encouragement and active support to Konkani' (De Souza, 1986: 49).

Kashinath Jalmi, M. G. Party leader stated: "In the past, the word Konkan had different references and different regions were included in the so named territory not limited by the present political boundaries of the State of Goa. The language of Konkan cannot be Konkani merely because the territorial boundaries of Goa fall within the ancestral Konkan region. The regional boundaries extended beyond the Western Ghats and included territories presently on the plateau of Indian peninsula.

Interestingly, a different phenomenon has evolved as regards the language of inhabitants of then Konkan, now included in the State of Karnataka. A few people believe that it to be Kannada and inhabitants of Karwar district and migrant population of Mangalore claim that language of people is Konkani. In these areas, majority of the people are speaking and using Tulu language. Most of the people residing in the disputed border areas between Maharashtra and Karnataka believe that their language is Marathi. The people residing in the Malvan taluka of Sinddhudurga district claim that their language is Malvani although it is a dialect of Marathi with some efforts are made to get it recognised as separate language. The inhabitants of that part of Konkan now included in Kerala believe that their language is not Konkani but Malayalam. In addition, those people included in Gujarat of then Konkan region claim that their language is Gujarati and so on. Thus, Goa being part of the ancestral Konkan, its language of use and usage cannot be called as Konkani.

The Marathi was the language studied, read and written by Goans during the colonial rule and after Liberation. It was the language of art, culture, literature, communication and freedom struggle of Goa. On this line, MGP sought to impart primary education in Marathi as medium of instruction in Goa. The Konkani protagonists argued that Konkani and not the Marathi is the language of Goa. They wanted to keep the masses perpetually cut-off from the cultural heritage. They advocated that primary education should be imparted in the mother tongue of the child, irrespective of merit of the language. However, speaking a language makes us humans and writing makes us civilised" (Jalmi: Interview: 14-12-1999).

In the post-Liberation era, the advocates of Konkani opted for English rather than the native language in the domains of power. They faced the problem of separating Konkani from the literary Marathi, as both were allied languages. The so-called development of Konkani under Jesuits had sequestered Konkani from Marathi. The bureaucracy favoured English rather than the regional languages. Arthur Rubinoff revealed that 'the use of English in the domains of power was a technique to avoid choosing between Konkani and Marathi. The advocates of statehood believed that inclusion of Konkani in the Eighth Schedule to Constitution would encourage development of Konkani' (Rubinoff, 1998: 116-17).

ATTEMPTS TO ACCORD OFFICIAL STATUS TO MARATHI: A section of legislators owing allegiance to the M. G. Party attempted to accord the official status to Marathi. The Legislative Assembly of Goa Daman, and Diu passed the non-official resolution tabled by Jaisingrao Rane Sardessai on March 23, 1968 'for use of Marathi and / or Gujarati for the purpose of replies by the Government whenever the correspondence was received in that language; for publications of the Government Gazette, bulletins, circulars, etc. issued by Government and Government sponsored institutions; a compulsory subject in Government and aided schools; and also a language of the subordinate Courts' (LAD 23-3-1968: Vol. V, No. 5, Col. 713-14).

On September 24, 1971, D. K. Chopdekar, K. B. Naik, N. B. N. Gaonkar and J. B. Gonsalves introduced the non-official Goa Daman & Diu Official Language Bill, 1971 seeking official recognition to Marathi and Gujarati languages. The UGP opposed the said Bill tooth and nail. The Bill was supported by a faction of the MGP who resented the evasive tactics of the party leadership to accord the official status to Marathi. The Bill No 21 of 1971 lapsed on the dissolution of the House.

KONKANI—A MODERN LITERARY LANGUAGEI: The advocates of Konkani geared up to accord the official status to Konkani after the MGP's inability to introduce official bill to bestow the official status to regional language(s). The advocates of Konkani scattered in the State of Kerala and Karnataka took active interest in putting forth the cause of

Konkani. 'The Konkani Bhasha Prachar Sabha (KBPS) formed on May 14, 1966 in Kochi (Kerala) had pleaded for recognition of Konkani as an independent literary language'. (Mallya, 1997: 42). The KBPS believed that the official apathy during the pre-Liberation period led to stunted growth of the Konkani language. The official recognition could only expedite the development of Konkani, the KBPS claimed.

On October 30, 1969, the KBPS in its memorandum put forth before former Prime Minister Indira Gandhi the case of recognition of Konkani by the Sahitya Akademi. The KBPS maintained that Konkani satisfies the criteria laid down by the Sahitya Akademi for granting the recognition to language for its literary development. The resolution (30-6-1974) of the KBPS dated to that effect was placed before the meeting of the Executive Board of the Sahitya Akademi on 3-12-1974. The Executive Board resolved that the question of Konkani being recognised as an independent language be referred to the General Council for its consideration and approval. Eight members out of 20 voted in favour of the resolution and four against. Interestingly, eight members abstained at the crucial time of voting on the resolution in the General Council. Late P. L. Deshpande, renowned Marathi literary figure, supported the cause of the Konkani language.

The General Council passed the resolution in its meeting held on 26-2-1975. The resolution stated: "As Konkani fulfils the criteria formulated by the Sahitya Akademi for recognition of a language. It is recognised as an independent modern literary language of India. About programmes in Konkani like the annual expenditure, Sahitya Akademi should request the Government of India to provide necessary extra funds. Such programmes and other activities should be undertaken only when extra funds are available" (Mallya, 1997: 18-19).

The MGP provided the safe passage for recognition of Konkani by the Sahitya Akademi as an independent modern literary language to encourage its literary development. Manoharrao Sardessai stated 'the MGP, in fact, had facilitated the recognition accorded to Konkani by the Sahitya Akademi' (Sardessai, 1994: 336). The MGP indicated that the ruling party was not opposed to recognition being given to Konkani by the Sahitya Akademi. Naguesh Karmali stated 'some leaders and literary figures from Maharashtra and protagonists of Marathi in Goa had attempted to block the recognition accorded to Konkani by the Sahitya Akademi' (Karmali: Interview: 28-04-99).

The Gomantak Marathi Bhasha Parishad (GMBP) raised doubts over the literary merit of Konkani. The GMBP challenged the claim of the advocates of Konkani that it constitutes a separate language. The Sahitya Akademi, however, ruled out the objections raised by the GMPB, since the Government of Goa had not given its opinion over the criterion laid down by the Sahitya Akademi for recognition of the languages. The MGP contended that Konkani was a dialect of Marathi in 1963. After a decade, the ruling party diluted its stand over the literary status of Konkani. The advocates of Marathi could not mobilise the support on the vital issue. They lacked political and financial backing. The MGP leadership allowed the advocates of Marathi to fend for them.

Shashikala Kakodkar, former Chief Minister stated: "The Sahitya Akademi's decision in 1975 to declare Konkani, as a separate language need not necessarily reflect the literary merit of the language. The M. G. Party allowed the Sahitya Akademi to adopt its own course to decide the status of the Konkani language in the territory" (Kakodkar: Interview: 13-10-1999).

Adv. Ramakant Khalap, former Union Minister for Law & Justice stated: "The M G Party sent wrong signals by airing the views that the Party is not opposed to development of Konkani, per se. It was a fundamental mistake or 'Sahyadryan' blunder on the part of the M. G. Party. It was responsible for recognition given to Konkani as a separate language by the Sahitya Akademi. The ruling party did not respond to the information asked by the Sahitya Akademi to determine whether Konkani constitutes a separate language or not (Khalap: Interview: 13-10-199).

The Government of India accorded the recognition to Konkani to appease the anti-integration groups in the territory. The advocates of Marathi did not raise a false alarm over the recognition given by the Sahitya Akademi to Konkani, which even had not adopted its own script. The Christian community favoured the Roman script for Konkani. They considered the Devanagari script for Konkani as another version of Marathi only. The attempts were made to recognise the Roman script for Konkani by the Sahitya Akademi. 'The Sahitya Akademi maintained that it had recognised Konkani in Devanagari. No other script had been recognised for Konkani (Mallya 1997: 119). The Sahitya Akademi's recognition gave the status of an independent modern literary language to Konkani for its literary development in the mainstream literature.

KONKANI LITERARY ACTIVITIES: There is no evidence in the history of literature to support the theory that Konkani had rich literary tradition. The Konkani literature is primarily of the Christian inspiration in the Roman script. The intellectuals, saints, poets in the Konkan Kshetra hardly made any efforts to raise the spoken language to a polished literary medium of ___expression. The opinion among scholars differed over the status of Konkani as a separate language. The Konkani literature began to flourish only after 1961.

The literary figures who contributed for literary development of Konkani in the first decade between 1961-1970 include— 'B. B. Borkar, Laxamanrao Sardessai, Devrai Baidoor, R. V. Pandit, Sadanand Jambaulikar, Vishvambar Usgaonkar, Ravindra Kelekar, Pandurang Bhangui, Manoharrai Sardessai, Shankar Ramani, Vijaybab Sarmalkar, Shankar Bhandari, Dattaram Sukhthanka, Vaman Sardessai, and Kamladevi Rao Deshpande amongst prominent others.

The second decade (1971-1980) writers include— C. D. Costa, Felicio Cardozo, Atchyut Totekar, Govind Mudras, Chandrakant Keni, Gajanan Raikar, A. N. Mhambre, Datta Nayak, Laxminarayan Paraj, Uday Bhembre, Shantaram Valulikar, Suresh Kakodkar, Olivinho Gomes, Damodar Maujo, Mina Kakodkar, Narayan Borkar, Sheela Nayak, Mahabaleshwar Sail, Prakash Thali, Jaymala Danayat, Prakash Acharya, Prakash Padgaonkar, and N. Shivdas amongst prominent others.

Lastly, those writers belonged to the third decade (1981-90) include— Shyam Verenkar, Pundalik Narayn Naik, Gajanan Jog, Hema Pundalik Naik, Ramesh Veluskar, Shashank Sitaram, Gokuldas Prabhu, Madhav Borkar, Dilip Borkar, Vasant Savant, Durgadas Gaude, Jayanti Naik, and Sudesh Lotlikar amongst others' (Keni 1993).

Prof. Partha Sarthi Gupta argued: "The efforts for improvement of a dialect into a written language with enlargement of its vocabulary and preparation of standard rules of grammar and lexicology come from the privileged class. Their success of dissemination alternative pure vocabulary would depend on the control on the educational institutions and support from the ruling dynasty or ruling coterie if latter could protect its vested interests by this process. If the pure language fails to replace the written prose of the people (the prose of commercial transaction and litigation) it will show the resilience of the language of the masses, however, hybrid or rustic it may sound to the upper strata of the society. A situation can arise when there are two parallel languages existing in one territory, corresponding to the social division, but both capable of expressing basic human emotions' (Mainstream: 11-9-99).

Vaman Varde Valaulikar, following the footsteps of the Christian missionaries, launched magnificent efforts to produce literature in Konkani. The Konkani literary activities created a base for asserting the separate linguistic identity. The initiative for so-called development of Konkani came primarily from a section of upper caste Hindus in the post-liberation era. A few writers from the Bahujan Samaj were encouraged to enrich the Konkani literature and lead the Konkani movement in the post-merger era. The move helped to broad base the Konkani language movement. The recognition accorded by the Sahitya Akademi in 1975 opened the avenues for funds for the budding writers, publishers and literary bodies. The advocates of Konkani argued that the official patronage could only expedite the process of development of the language.

POLITICS OF OFFICIAL STATUS TO REGIONAL LANGUAGES: The recognition given by the Sahitya Akademi to Konkani encouraged the advocates of Konkani to accord the official status to it in the territory. The attempts were made to introduce the bill in the Legislative Assembly to adopt Konkani as the sole official language. Herculano Dorado, MLA, tabled the non-official the Goa, Daman & Diu Official Language Bill, 1982 seeking official recognition to Konkani. The Bill No. 6 of 1982 was withdrawn on January 14, 1983 (See Appendix-11).

On March 31, 1982, Luizinho Faleiro introduced the resolution in the House. The resolution stated: "...This House strongly recommends Government to establish an Independent Centre for all round development of the Konkani language by: i) promoting research in the Konkani language, its literature, culture, history, and Lokved; ii) publishing research work carried out; iii) translating and publishing in Konkani the selective literature from other languages; iv) publishing the standard grammar for Konkani, vocabulary, and books on linguistic science in Konkani; and v) taking necessary efforts to develop Konkani in all respect in order to adopt it as an official language of the Government of Goa, Daman & Diu and in Vidhan Sabha" (LAD 1987: Vol. XXIV, No. 10).

The Sahitya Akademi although declared Konkani as an independent modern literary language, it was not developed as an effective medium of literary __expression for its subsequent adoption by the government as the official language. The advocates of Konkani demanded the sole recognition to Konkani despite its inherent limitations. In 1985, Luizinho Faleiro, lone MLA of the Goa Congress, tried to introduce the Bill seeking the sole official recognition to Konkani. The move aimed at embarrassing the Congress-I Ministry headed by Pratapsing Rane. The ruling party opposed the non-official Bill on technical ground. The said Bill was not accompanied by the Rule 131 of the Rules of Procedure of Conduct of Business of the House. When Bill was put to vote, it was not admitted. The MGP legislators abstained, three MLAs including Luizinho Faleiro, Adv. Uday Bhembre and Monte Cruz in the 33-member House supported the Bill.

Subsequently, the non-official Goa, Daman and Diu Official Language Bill, 1985 was introduced by Ramakant Khalap, F. Monte Cruz and Luizinho Faleiro. The Bill, however, lapsed. Again Babuso Gaonkar introduced the non-official Goa, Daman and Diu Official Language Bill, 1986. The Speaker of the House refused leave to introduce the Bill.

The anti-integration groups directed their ire against the Chief Minister Pratapsing Rane for his so-called pro-Marathi leanings. In a face-saving device, the Cabinet made the knowledge of Konkani desirable for registration with employment exchange to protect the interest of the sons-of-the-soil. The move aimed at pacifying the advocates of Konkani and diffusing the impending language crisis. The advocates of Konkani floated idea of linking language as a pre or post-condition for employment for making their demand broad-based and attractive to youth at political plane. The language became a measure for economic gain. Its link with regulation of recruitment and service conditions in the public services reflected vested political interests. The employment opportunities in the government sector are abysmally low. The Konkani literary activities are held not only in Goa, but also in the south-western coast till Cochin. It is difficult to presume that how the sole official status to Konkani would have been safeguarded the employment opportunities of the sons-of-soil?

The official status to Konkani would have only widened the economic opportunities of the writers, printers, publishers, et al by creating avenues of income on the one hand and asserting the separate linguistic identity on the other. Prabhakar Angle remarked that 'the people need not consider the question whether Konkani is a full-fledged language. The issue would be decided most probably based on political expediency and linguists may have hardly any say in the matter' (Angle, 1986-87: 2-3).

PRO-KONKANI AGITATION: Pundalik Naik who led the Konkani Porjeacho Awaz (Voice of Konkani People) during language controversy in 1985-87 stated: "The Konkani Porjeacho Awaz (KPA) spearheaded the movement for the sole recognition to the Konkani language, statehood and inclusion of the Konkani language in the Eighth Schedule to the Constitution of India. The KPA drew support from Konkani writers, poets, artistes, journalists and activists. The KPA had stated in a memorandum (10/09/1985) to the Government of Goa that it is a non-political association having no link with any political party formed to defend the interest of Konkani and Goa and to preserve Konkani 'asmitaya' or identity. The political parties like Congress, Goa Congress, Janata Party and Gomant Lok Pox supported the movement. The KPA had managed to shelve the controversy over the adoption of common script for Konkani language and unite the people cross-cutting communal and caste loyalties" (Naik: Interview: 10-10-1999).

The anti-integration groups argued that the liberation of Goa is incomplete without the sole official status to Konkani and statehood. These groups who wanted to keep Goa separate during the Opinion Poll reenacted the scene to accord the sole official status to Konkani by denying the legitimate interests of Marathi. Marathi became a hurdle in their move to accord the sole official status to Konkani. In the past, the anti-integration groups always had attacked Marathi as a symbol of nationalist movement and link with mainstream culture. Interestingly, they argued that the advocates of Marathi are nursing extra-territorial loyalties.

PRO-MARATHI AGITATION: The Marathi Rajya Bhasha Prasthapan Samiti (MRBPS) was formed in a bid to counteract the move of the anti-integration groups to deny the official recognition to Marathi. P. P. Shirodkar, ex-Speaker of the Legislative Assembly of Goa, Daman and Diu headed the MRBPS. On October 2, 1985, the MRBPS held mammoth rally in support of the official status to Marathi along with Konkani. It criticised the decision of the ruling Congress party (10-09-1985) to accord the sole official status to Konkani. The advocates of Marathi termed the resolution of the Congress Legislative Party (CLP) and Goa Pradesh Congress Committee (GPCC) as unilateral, insensitive and unjust (MRBPS 1985: 1).

The advocates of Marathi did not oppose the move to accord the official status to Konkani, but vehemently opposed the anti-Marathi posture adopted by the ruling party. Prof. Datta Bhikaji Naik of Akhil Bharatiya Vidyarthi Parishad stated 'the KPA though headed by Pundalik Naik was guided by Dr. Wilfred De Souza, President of Goa Congress, a party formed by communal elements, who had deserted the Congress-I party to form a regional political party on the lines of Kerala Congress. They had appealed to boycott Liberation Day celebration. They never had attended such days of national importance. So, it failed' (Organizer: 1-2-1987, 7).

The Konkani language movement exhibited regional sentiments. The use of the Roman script for Konkani had communal overtones. The Census of 1981, recorded 15.84 lakhs speakers of Konkani whereas Bhili 44.50 lakhs, Santhali 44.08 lakhs and Gondi 19.54 lakhs, Nepali 12.54 lakhs and Manipuri 9.06 lakhs, respectively. The speakers of Konkani were scattered in the adjoining states of Maharashtra, Karnataka, and Kerala. In the South, the Konkani-speakers opted for the local scripts rather than the Devanagari script. In fact, they had played a crucial role in putting forth the case of recognition of Konkani by the Sahitya Akademi in 1975.

In Goa, there were 6,00,004 or 37.88 per cent Konkani speakers out of the total 15,84,063 persons; 6,40,738 or 40.45 per cent in Karnataka; 2,12,214 or 13.39 per cent in Maharashtra, according to Census of 1981 (Adapted from Mallya, P. Purushothama, Selected Seminar Papers / Writings On Konkani Language & Culture (1954-97), Konkani Bhasha Prachar Sabha, Kochi, Kerala, 1997).

The Konkani-speaking population in Konkan Kshetra considered Konkani as a dialect of Marathi rather than a separate language. The Konkani-speaking population mainly the Christian community in Maharashtra claimed otherwise. The Konkani-speaking population until 1950s used Marathi as the literary language in the neighbouring states of Karnataka and Kerala. The linguistic reorganisation of the states in 1956 encouraged the Konkani language groups to assert their identities in the South.

CONGRESS PARTY'S STAND OVER LANGUAGE ISSUE: In 1984, the INC Manifesto stated: "The Congress-I Party believes that Konkani is the majority language of this territory and is spoken in almost every Goan home. The policy of the Congress-I Party will be to work for the growth of Konkani on scientific lines and its inclusion in the Eighth Schedule to the Constitution... Side by side, the Government will also take care to further the growth of the other two important languages of this Territory viz. Marathi and Gujarati".

A few Congress leaders at the Centre raised the fears that the official recognition to Konkani would trigger similar demands elsewhere in the country. Former Chief Minister Luizinho Faleiro argued that 'the thinking of the Congress at the national level was a continuation of the Morarji Desai doctrine, though the men were no longer in the party. They believed that if Konkaniwadis were appeased, then campaigners of Maithili and Bhojpuri and such other languages and dialects would have claimed inclusion in the Eighth Schedule to the Constitution' (Faleiro, 1999: 62).

In 1985, the Congress party at the local level was divided over the issue of the sole recognition to Konkani. A section of Congress legislators were forced to side with the cause of Marathi overwhelmingly due to constituency pressure in the Marathi dominated areas. Luizinho Faleiro (who later joined Congress and became chief minister) stated 'many of the leaders had transited to the (Congress) party from the MGP and they were true to their first love, in so far as Goa's language and constitutional status were concerned. Those in Congress who were truly Konkani lovers abounded only in sentiments, but lacked the guts. They feared if they come out in open would transgress the party line' (*Ibid.* 62-63).

M. G. PARTY'S STAND OVER LANGUAGE ISSUE: The Maharashtrawadi Gomantak Party stood for official recognition to Marathi along with Konkani to counter the move of KPA-Congress-I combine to accord the sole official status to Konkani. Apparently, the MGP was not opposed to the official recognition being given to Konkani. The MGP leaders like Shashikala Kakodkar, Babuso Gaonkar, Kashinath Jalmi and others adopted hard-line over the issue of official status to Marathi. M. S. Prabhu, the MGP leader (who later became a staunch supporter of Konkani) stated 'Marathi gave them enthusiasm during Goa's freedom struggle. It preserved culture. Therefore, Marathi was their religion and culture' (Gomantak: 22-2-1985).

The Goa, Daman & Diu Official Language Bill, 1986 was introduced in the Legislative Assembly on July 17, 1986 by Chief Minister Pratapsing Rane (See Appendix-3). 'The contents of the Bill were leaked to the press before it was tabled on the floor of the House' (LAD: Vol. XXIII, No. 10, 1986). It raised furore in the House. The Bill stated over 95 per cent of the people speaks Konkani. It conveniently overlooked the fact that the language in use by the majority of the population was Marathi, which is used in the influential section of media, education and also has long history of use in the administration. It nursed the cultural identity of Goa during the 451 years of Portuguese rule. The Bill stated that a substantial section of population had studied through the medium of Marathi. So, it gave liberty to those who would like to communicate with the Government in Marathi. It was mandatory on the part of the Government to correspond with such people in that language. It assured use of Marathi in social, educational and cultural fields. The advocates of Marathi claimed that the provisions in the Bill were as superficial, insensitive and aimed at uprooting the traditional hold of the Marathi language and literature in the territory.

The cultural and literary movement in support of Konkani always remained at low key compared to Marathi in the territory. 'The staunch Konkani protagonists aired their views in Marathi and English. The English press speaks for it. (LAD: Vol. XXIII, No. 10, 1986). There is no conflict at socio-cultural plane over the language issue. The Christian masses favoured use of English or Konkani in the Roman script. Arthur Rubinoff argued 'as was the case at the Opinion Poll, a coalition of Christians and Saraswat Brahmins was formed to advance a political demand for promotion of Konkani in 1985-87' (Rubinoff, 1998: 199). The leaders who belonged to the Bahujan Samaj were in the forefront of the Konkani language movement as against the Opinion Poll in 1967. Narayan Athavale, the editor of an influential Marathi daily Gomantak stated 'the people, the masses, appreciated the fact that individuals like Pundalik Naik, N. Shivdas and Tanaji Halarnkar were leading the Konkani movement. Otherwise, the monopoly of Konkani had remained in the hands of Saraswat Brahmins' (Gomantak: 22-2-1986).

On 18-12-1986, the KPA passed a resolution in its meeting that all the jobs in the government, semi-government and private establishment should be reserved for Konkani-speaking people (The Navhind Times: 19-12-

1986). The INC under the pressure from its pro-Marathi legislators decided to pass the Bill with amendments to accommodate the legitimate interests of Marathi. The advocates of Konkani stood for passage of the Bill without any amendments. They lacked the support from the majority of the Congress legislators to back their demand in toto. The advocates of Konkani supported the Congress party in the hope of according the sole official status to Konkani. The ruling party, in turn, relied on these groups to derive political mileage.

In a memorandum submitted to the state government, 101 or 68.24 % out of 148 village panchayats at the grass root level supported Marathi as the official language (Mallikarjun, 1986). The masses opted for Marathi as the literary language and Konkani as the spoken language in the affairs of Panchayati Raj Institution. The administrative machinery favoured English as the language of correspondence at the panchayat level. The Goa Congress, Gomant Lok Paksha, and trade unions and the student wings owing allegiance to the left parties supported the Bill. On November 19, 1986, the KPA gave ultimatum to Rane Ministry for passage of the Bill without any amendment. The Roman Catholic Church backed the Bill. Interestingly, the agitation in favour of Konkani as the sole official language lacked support of the majority of the population. The KPA resorted to pressure tactics to accord the sole official status to Konkani.

Jay Dubhashi, the BJP think-tank, stated 'Congressmen like Chief Minister Pratapsing Rane had given communal twist to the whole thing—something Congressmen were experts at. The language controversy was turned into a contest between Catholics (who are painted as Konkani activists) and Hindus (who are described as Marathi chauvinists)... Konkani is as much a Goan, an Indian language, Marathi, and even those who swear by Marathi used Konkani at home and nearly everywhere else..." (Organizer: 04-01-1987). M. V. Kamath a noted columnist stated 'Konkani should be the main language of the State. In fact, his mother tongue is Konkani' (Goa Today: January 1986, 38). Interestingly, the top sympathisers of the BJP, who cherished party's nationalist ideals, like Jay Dubhashi and M. V. Kamath, advocated line thinking similar to the anti-integration stream in the territory.

B. D. Satoskar, noted Marathi writer, stated that "Konkani was neither a dialect nor a language. It was a former form of Marathi. It was a tongue of people no doubt about it. The Sahitya Akademi gave Konkani a status of a literary language. It had not developed as language of culture and administration. Both Konkani and Marathi should be state languages. If one state becomes bi-lingual then a time will come when the difference between Marathi and Konkani would not exist... However, these two languages should come together. Moreover, perhaps a new language would come into a being" (Goa Today: September 1987, 17).

Luizinho Faleiro stated 'in that, strange setting was born one of Goa's most powerful public movements— Konkani Porjeacho Avaz. They had, wittingly or unwittingly, unleashed a tidal wave. Soon, all hell broke loose. There was no way those in the movement could retract. There was no way either, for the fence sitters in the Legislative Assembly and in the Government to ignore the movement' (Faleiro, 1999: 65). The language agitation turned violent after death of Florenco Vaz, a labourer in police firing at Margao in South Goa. The KPA claimed Vaz as the first martyr in the cause of Konkani. In the scattered violence, the property dispute claimed another six lives coinciding with the language agitation. The KPA claimed that 'all seven young men had sacrificed their lives in the cause of Konkani and one was killed in police firing while others were killed in an attack by the opponents of Konkani'. (The Navhind Times: 14-05-2000).

Prof. Datta Bhikaji Naik stated 'the main targets of the advocates of Konkani during the language agitation were members belonging to the majority community… In Margao, one Churchill Alemao (who became Chief Minister later on) tried to pull down the national flag on the Liberation Day... It was wrong to suppose that Marathi was imposed on Goans. Most of the Goan Hindus regarded Konkani as the dialect of Marathi and the Roman Catholic Church had always attacked it as it was a symbol of nationalist movement and cultural tie with the rest of India' (Organizer: 1-2-1987: 7). In the background of violent agitation, the Legislative Assembly deferred the consideration of the Bill with the administrator proroguing the Assembly. The Congress leaders at the Centre argued that the official status to the regional languages, Konkani and Marathi would trigger similar demands in the Belgaum district of the State of Karnataka. The MRBPS stated that the sole status to Konkani aimed at appeasement of the minority community. The MGP leadership charged that 'the Congress was hatching a conspiracy to uproot the Marathi language in the territory' (Sardessai, 1994: 369).

ENACTMENT OF OFFICIAL LANGUAGE BILL, 1986: On February 4, 1987, Chief Minister Pratapsing Rane sought the leave to move the Goa, Daman & Diu Official Language Bill, 1986 in the House. Kashinath Jalmi, M. G. Party legislators stated 'it was unfortunate that the Bill aimed at according official status to a language that people did not learn, read and teach to their children…' (LAD: Vol. XXIV, No. 1, 1987). Babuso Gaonkar, M. G. Party legislator stated 'the House did not decide the official language of the territory. It was unfortunate that the Congress-I party legislators had no say. It was strange that observers who came from

Delhi decided the matter for them' *(Ibid)*. Luizinho Faleiro demanded that the Konkani language should be used both in Devanagari and Roman script for twenty-five years after enactment of the Bill. *Ramakant Khalap* demanded for official status to both the regional languages.

The ruling party suggested that for the first proviso of the Clause-3 following should be substituted namely: - "(i) provided that the Administrator may, by a like notification, direct that in case of Goa District, the Marathi language, and in the case of Daman & Diu Districts, the Gujarati language, shall also be used for all or any of the official purposes and different dates may be appointed for different official purposes; (ii) in third proviso for the words Provided also the words provided further shall be substituted;(iii) the fourth proviso shall be omitted".

The House passed the Bill after amendment proposed by the ruling party. It had 21 votes in favour and eight votes against. Luizinho Faleiro termed the Bill in the amended form as 'the black mail of the people who wanted to merge Goa with Maharashtra and the Government had succumbed to the black mail. They had murdered Konkani…' (LAD: Vol-XXIV, No. 1, 1987) Adv. Uday Bhembre stated 'the Government had betrayed the people after amending the Bill. It would not facilitate the use of official language in the territory…' (Ibid). Uday Bhembre, Fransico Branco and Luisinho Faleiro staged a walk out for adopting the Bill after modifications to accommodate the legitimate interests of Marathi.

The enactment of the Bill in modified form did not satisfy the advocates of Konkani. It was a celebration neither for Marathi nor for Konkani protagonists. The 555-day agitation spearheaded by the KPA ended with the enactment of the Bill after amendments. The advocates of Konkani failed to push through the Bill without any amendments. They expressed dissatisfaction over the fact that the amendments provided for entry of Marathi from the back door. The notifications were issued for use of Konkani and Marathi for the official purposes on the same date and for the same official purposes. The notification (19-12-1987) provides: 'Konkani language shall be the official language for the purpose of replies by the Government whenever communications are received in Konkani language'. The notification issued on the same date also provides: 'Marathi shall be used for the purpose of replies by the Government whenever communications are received in Marathi language' (See Appendix-6).

Language flourishes at the socio-cultural plane and not alone due to state patronage. The anti-integration groups used Konkani for political power and economic gain. A language cannot be imposed on the masses through legislative measures. 'R L Bhatia, AICC General Secretary revealed that all the representations were received in English and none in

Konkani or Marathi in 1985-87' (The Navhind Times: 040-2-1987). Pundalik Naik stated the KPA movement took a violent turn because the local and the central government took no initiative in diffusing the language crisis. The KPA had no blue print of the bill seeking official recognition to the Konkani language. The Official Language Act, 1987 declares Konkani as the official language provided that the Marathi language shall also be used for all or any of the official purposes in the territory...' (Naik: Interview. 10-10-1999).

Arthur Rubinoff stated 'no political party got what they wanted as the MGP had championed Marathi. In reality, the issue was moot, as English was entrenched as the language of both education and administration' (Rubinoff 1998: 1990). Narayan Athavale, former editor of Goa based Marathi daily Gomantak, stated: 'Marathi lost the battle but Konkani did not win either. It was the (Congress-I party) observers from Karnataka who won…' (Op. Cit. Dantas 1999: 45). Shashikala Kakodkar charged that 'Athavale who had supported the M. G. Party over the language issue, subsequently diluted his stand when the anti-integration groups resorted to violence" (Kakodkar: Interview 13-10-1999).

Ramakant Khalap, former Union Minister for Law & Justice stated: "The Congress Ministry headed by Pratapsing Rane resorted to accord the sole official status to the Konkani language not out of love for the language but for his own survival in the party. The nine MLAs including. J. B. Gonsalves of the ruling party did not favour the Goa, Daman & Diu Official Language Bill, 1986 in toto. They stood for according the official status to the Konkani language along with Marathi language. Chief Minister Pratapsing Rane, Eduardo Faleiro, MP, Shantaram Naik, MP, Purushottam Kakodkar, MP, and GPCC chairperson Sulochana Katkar in consultation with former Prime Minister Rajiv Gandhi approved the final draft of the Bill. There is no ambiguity in the Goa, Daman, & Diu Official Language Act, 1987 about the status of the Marathi language. The Act explicitly states that 'Konkani language shall be the official language for all or any of the official purposes, and different dates may be appointed for different official purposes.

Provided that the Administrator, may by like notification, direct that that in case of the Goa District, the Marathi language and in the case of Daman and Diu Districts, the Gujarati language, shall also be used for all or any of the official purposes and different dates may be appointed for different official purposes...'

The official status given to the Konkani language is based on the explicit proviso that in case of the Goa District, the Marathi language and in the case of Daman and Diu Districts, the Gujarati language, shall also be used for all or any of the official purposes. Under Article 345, a state legislature may adopt any one or more of the languages in use in the State or Hindi for all or any of the official purposes. Thus, above proviso reveals that both the Konkani and Marathi languages are the official languages of the Union Territory. However, the official recognition is given to the Konkani language only to satisfy the political aspiration of group of people owing allegiance to it. It seldom reflects the literary merit in case of the Konkani language" (Khalap Interview: 28-10-1999).

Kashinath Jalmi, the MGP leader, stated: "The Konkani protagonists disowned Marathi, which is the carrier of our cultural heritage. This is due to 'denationalisation' of Goa and severing of ties with Indian culture during the colonial rule and post-Liberation era. So far as Konkani written in Devanagari script is concerned, large population of Catholics considers it as Marathi...

The sole Konkani daily 'Sunaprant' published in Devanagari Konkani is not picking up circulation figures among Konkani lovers. It proves that the Christian community did not want Konkani in Devanagari script. In fact, there is feeling amongst the Catholics that the Hindu protagonists of Konkani took them for a ride…

Konkani has many scripts like Devanagari, Roman, Kannada, and Malayalam. Writing is merely a convention. We can change the convention merely by agreeing to do so. This was an important issue during the language agitation. Practically speaking Konkani, literary conventions are convened at different places outside Goa, too. The Konkani speakers on the dais and off the dais happen to be Konkani writers in different scripts. As far as Goa is concerned, the majority of Christian population writes Konkani in the Roman script. Even after a consensus was arrived at and 'Konkani' means Konkani in Devanagari script. The amendment to the Goa, Daman & Diu Official Language Bill was moved in the House by a member of legislative assembly from the opposition for continuation of the Roman script for a period of twenty-five years. It is pity that the Goan Catholics have not bothered to learn Devanagari script even after twenty-five years of Goa becoming part of Union of India" (Jalmi: Interview: 14-12-1999).

Pratpsing Rane, Speaker, Goa Legislative Assembly and former Chief Minister of State of Goa stated: "A language cannot be imposed on the people merely through legislative measures. In 451 years, the colonial policy to impose Portuguese language on the native population met with utter failure. The people who raised the language controversy in 1985-87 in Goa should take steps to develop the language. The advocates of Konkani have produced no literature of serious literary merit so far" (Rane: Interview: 28-10-1999).

The political leaders who were at the helm of the affairs during the language agitation (1985-87) revealed that the advocates of Konkani were not serious about the language. They had political purpose behind it. The advocates of Konkani failed to secure passage of the Official Language Bill, 1986 without amendment. They had no support of the majority of the legislators in the House. The anti-integration groups whipped up linguistic, caste and religious sentiments to mobilise masses politically. The entire Konkani language movement aimed at alienating the Christian community from the Marathi language and literature. The anti-integration groups used the masses politically. Thus, language dispute exists in the political community rather than at socio-cultural plane.

LANGUAGE & STATEHOOD OF GOA

Language is not merely a creative device. It has implications for cultural identity of the region. 'At socio-cultural level, the cultural entrepreneurs build up the ideological forms to sub-national communities whereas language strategists are those literary figures who innovate prudently to promote linguistic identities' (Palanthurai & Thandavan, 1993; 180). The Official Language Act, 1987 did not satisfy the advocates of Konkani. The Congress party favoured the Devanagari script for Konkani rather than the Roman script. The advocates of Konkani had to resort to coercive tactics to accord the official status to Konkani. They lacked popular support although Konkani was recognised by the Sahitya Akademi in 1975 as an independent modern literary language. The political considerations weighed in favour of official recognition to the Konkani language 'In a free atmosphere the more virile, potential or actual, would take dominant role, which is cultural rather than political' (D' Mello, 1963:11).

Tariq Rahman wrote: "The groups react to situation for goal-oriented, rational reasons (jobs, power, etc) as well as extra-rational ones. The latter aspect is vague desire to promote something intangible which can be described as identity, way of life, or culture. Often impersonality and homogeneity imposed by modernity create loss of identity" (Rahman, 1998: 20).

Konkani exhibits strong regional moorings. The anti-integration groups adopted Konkani as a tool to assert the regional identity. They faced the problem of re-integrating with mainstream culture after 1961. The

Liberation of Goa had brought mixed results for them. They had toyed with an idea of dominion status for Goa or put forth sub-nation theory. The differences within the divergent groups wedded to separatism and integration rather than Gandhian or militant line of action followed by the freedom fighters delayed Goa's liberation for 14 years after India's Independence.

Ravindra Kelekar stated: "The entire Konkani movement is political rather than literary in its form and content. The literary merit plays a secondary role in asserting the linguistic identity of the state. The first Konkani Sahitya Parishad asserted in 1939, the creation of a Konkani speaking State comprising of areas from Vasai in Bombay Province to Malabar in Madras Province.

The concept of United Goa or Samyukta Goy propounded by the father of modern Konkani literature Vaman Varde Valaulikar. Goa had no distinct identity separate from Konkan region... The Konkani movement in the beginning was the reaction to that inferiority complex which culminated into demand for a separate Konkani State" (Kelekar: Interview: 13-5-1998).

The idea of Vishal Gomantak by including Marathi-speaking areas of adjoining states gained momentum in 1950s. Kakasaheb Kalelkar subscribed to the idea of Coastal State or Sagari Prant. In 1980, Pandit Mahadeoshastri Joshi stated 'some politicians in Goa were toying with idea of statehood. He was not against statehood, per se. Statehood should not confine to borders of Goa but it should include Vishal Gomantak or Greater Goa... Goa Government had not adopted a clear-cut language policy. It had not followed a consistent policy in case of Marathi in the territory…' (*Op. Cit.* Komarpant 1992: 502-07).

M. V. Kamath, noted columnist remarked: "When I proposed the idea of Vishal Gomantak forty years ago and suggested the name 'Aprant' I had support no less a patriot than Kakasaheb Kalelkar...If Goans are really serious Konkani being their state language, they must fight for Vishal Gomantak and the breaking of mega-states. If they do not do that, they are liable to the charge that they are selfish and small-minded and do not care for Konkani-speaking people elsewhere" (Goa Today: January 1986, 29).

The Government of India was reluctant to apply the linguistic principle to Goa for reorganisation of the state. The Konkani speaking population was scattered in the Konkan belt of the adjoining states of Maharashtra, Karnataka and Kerala. It would have encouraged demands from other regions, too. The anti–integration groups cherished the dream of keeping Goa separate rather than allow it to merge with the neighbouring Konkan Kshetra or amalgamated with those areas to carve out a separate Konkan

State. The demand for a Konkan State had no popular support in the territory although the region would have ushered in economic and democratic development, administrative convenience and raised its own resources for viable state. 'But, the people of Karwar, Supa and Haliyal areas of Karnataka harped upon inclusion of these areas after statehood of Goa. Mr. C. V. Pavaskar, President of Karwar, Supa and Hailyal Samyukta Gomantak Front, in a letter urged the Prime Minister Atal Behari Vajpayee for inclusion of these Konkani-speaking areas in Goa and focused on the Kadamba stone inscription of 1160 A. D. when Karwar, Gokarna and Chitakul formed part of Gomantak' (Tarun Bharat: 08-07-2001).

The United Goans Party had demanded for statehood way back in 1963. The UGP did not subscribe to concept of Konkan State by incorporating the Konkani-speaking areas of adjoining states. The sole aim of the UGP was primarily to keep Goa separate. The Maharashtrawadi Gomantak Party after 1967 was not averse to the full-fledged statehood for Goa. 'In 1971, Chief Minister Dayanand Bandodkar stated that the statehood to be his ultimate aim' (Rubinoff, 1998: 114). The MGP, however, made no serious efforts towards this end. The statehood meant raising one's own resources. The Congress party favoured the statehood but stressed on emotional integration after Liberation. In 1977, the Janata Government promised the people of Goa that it would confer the statehood on the territory.

Pratap Singh Gill (16-11-1977 to 30-03—1981), former Governor of Goa, Daman & Diu, argued that reorganisation of Goa could help improving administration, and benefit economic and political development 'Gill recommended to Prime Minister Morarji Desai handing over Daman and Diu to Gujarat and Dadra Nagar Haveli to Maharashtra. In turn, Maharashtra should hand over adjacent equivalent area with rich forests to Goa. Perhaps Daman could also be given to Maharashtra in exchange of equivalent area to Goa. Goa then could be declared as full-fledged state. It was wrong to continue Goa as a union territory indefinitely' (Gill, 1984: 15). In 1980, the candidates elected on the Congress (Urs) had shifted their loyalty to the Congress-I. The Congress party had committed itself to implement the agenda of the erstwhile U.G. Party viz. recognition to Konkani and full-fledged statehood to territory in the hope of making party acceptable to Goan people.

Chandrakant Keni wrote: "The Indian National Congress right from the day it stepped in Goa and even earlier like the United Goans Party has been categorical in its stand on Konkani. In fact, that facilitated the merger of UGP with the Congress. The historic victory of Congress (Urs) Party at the 1980 polls was possible only because it had asserted on unequivocal terms its commitment to make Konkani the sole official language of Goa" (The Navhind Times: 28-7-1986).

On March 15, 1984, Eduardo Faleiro, Union Minister of State for External Affairs stated in the Lok Sabha that 'the people of Goa should be given statehood immediately. It was the birthright of people of Goa' (Faleiro, 1996: 80). The advocates of Konkani argued that the language agitation was a movement to define their roots and the statehood to bring about the changes in the institution of the polity. Moreover, the Konkani language movement exhibited sub-national sentiments and sub-national competition. The anti-integration groups diluted their stand over dominion status to territory after Liberation. They espoused separate identity to keep Goa separate.

After passage of the Official Language Bill on February 4, 1987, a pro-Konkani English daily Herald wrote: "Konkani is the soul of the red soil of Goa. Statehood will be body, which will provide a home for the soul. For, only statehood will give a permanent burial to the ghost of merger with Maharashtra' (Herald: 20-3-1987). On July 2, 1986, former Prime Minister Rajiv remarked that 'he was opposed to the very idea of linguistic states. He urged people to harness the trend and halt the approach of some people trying to have tiny unit for themselves' (Press Trust of India: 2-7-1986).

Arthur Rubinoff argued 'Goa's small size and its financial dependency on the Centre worked against the demand for a full-fledged statehood. Both former Premier Indira Gandhi and her successor Morarji Desai opposed the creation of small states' (Rubinoff, 1998: 116). Some central leaders stressed that Goa would need the resources from the Centre for another 100 years. Geographically, Goa is of size of a district of the neighbouring state. It had representation of only two members in the Lok Sabha. The geographically contiguous areas of Daman and Diu were to be merged with Gujarat. It relied on the Centre for the cent per cent assistance. The mining and tourism industry catered to its economic power. The major part of the foreign exchange from tourism and mining goes to the Centre. The mining industry is on decline. Goa could not attract industries due to its limited resources— land, power and water especially to cater to the needs of large-scale industrial units. The statehood meant raising the resources by resource-staved territory.

On August 5, 1987, the Legislative Assembly unanimously passed the resolution to grant statehood to Goa. Pratapsing Rane, former Chief Minister of Goa and Speaker, Goa Legislative Assembly, stated 'late Prime Minister Rajiv Gandhi conceded to the demand for full-fledged statehood to Goa in 1987. Language was not a criterion to accord statehood in case of Goa. Language should not be a measure for economic gain" (Rane: Interview: 28-10-1999). The Constitution (Fifty-sixth) Amendment Act, 1987 introduced by Home Minister Buta Singh on May 6, 1987 read as follows: -

"The Constitution (Fifty-sixth Amendment) Act, 1987

Statement of Objects and Reasons appended to the Constitution (Fifty-seventh Amendment) Bill, 1987 which was enacted as THE CONSTITUTION (Fifty-sixth Amendment) Act, 1987

Statement of Objects and Reasons

The Government of India have proposed to constitute the territories comprised in the Goa District of the Union territory of Goa, Daman and Diu as the State of Goa and the territories comprised in the Daman and Diu districts of that Union territory as a new Union territory of Daman and Diu. In this context, it is proposed that the Legislative Assembly of the new State of Goa shall consist of forty members. The existing Legislative Assembly of the Union territory of Goa, Daman and Diu has thirty elected members and three nominated members. It is intended to make this Assembly with the exclusion of two members representing Daman and Diu Districts, the provisional Legislative Assembly for the new State of Goa until elections are held on the expiry of the five-year term of the existing Assembly. It is, therefore, proposed to provide that the Legislative Assembly of the new State of Goa shall consist of not less than 30 members.

2. In order to give effect to the above proposal, it is necessary to make a special provision in the Constitution. This Bill accordingly seeks to amend the Constitution. A separate Bill for the re-organisation of the existing Union territory of Goa, Daman and Diu so as to form the new State of Goa is also being introduced".

Thus, Goa became a full-fledged State on May 30, 1987 with the strength of the legislative raised from thirty to forty (See Plate-VI). Former Chief Minister Luizinho Faleiro remarked: "Even almost thirty years after the historic Opinion Poll, the great event of the time. In fact, the most important landmark of the post-Portuguese history of Goa, the citizenry had tended to forget it. The focus changed to Goa's struggle for the recognition of Konkani as the official language and the granting of statehood, as full-fledged member of the Union of India. Those were and remain, liberated Goa's most important events..." (Faleiro 1999: 44).

'The Hindu commented that serious consideration for granting statehood to Goa coincided with the drubbing the Congress received in Kerala, a result that left Goa as the only party's government in the South' (Rubinoff 1998: 119). Arthur Rubinoff stated the manner in which Goa had achieved statehood suggested that Indian politicians were not avers to reviving communal issues such as language, in order to achieve selfish objectives' (*Ibid,* 21). The Konkani-speaking population in the states of Kerala and Karnataka supported the cause of Konkani. The Centre ruled out inclusion of these Konkani-speaking areas to carve out a separate Konkan State. The advocates of Konkani were divided over the issue of Samyukta Goy or Unified Goa by amalgamating the Konkani speaking areas of the neighbouring states with Goa. The States Reorganisation Commission (1956) did not provide definite answer to size of the constituent state. It suggested that the every state must raise its own resources to meet their financial needs.

The demand for statehood camouflaged the parochial interests, per se. It at keeping Goa separate rather than reorganise the territory by amalgamating Konkani-speaking or Marathi-speaking areas of the adjoining areas to carve out a economically viable unit. The advocates of Konkani believed that the attainment of statehood alone would promote the cause of Konkani. They managed to secure the support of the Congress party for statehood and inclusion of Konkani in the Eighth Schedule. Pundalik Naik, noted Konkani writer and activist revealed 'the official recognition accorded to Konkani language and statehood facilitated inclusion of Konkani language in the Eighth Schedule to the Constitution. However, the KPA's stalwarts had committed a mistake by joining the Congress-I party in the State' (Naik: Interview. 10-10-1999).

The anti-integration groups have succeeded because Goa is a full-fledged State. The advocates of Konkani are yet to raise the standard of the Konkani language. They have realised that it is difficult to separate Konkani from Marathi, which is deeply rooted in the socio-cultural milieu or to implement the official language act without accommodating the legitimate interests of Marathi in the State. The Official Language Bill, 1986 could not be passed without modifications in the provisions of the Bill to accommodate the legitimate interests of Marathi. The Congress party's amendment to the Bill defeated the original intention to accord the sole official status to Konkani. Thus, the passage of the Bill neither satisfied the protagonists of Konkani nor Marathi

MEDIUM OF INSTRUCTION CONTROVERSY: The total electorate constituted 7,34,317 in the assembly elections held on 22-11-1989. The INC and MGP bagged 18 seats each and four seats by the independents and others in the forty-member assembly (Assembly Elections Ready Reference-1999)

The 1989 assembly verdict and fall of Congress party at the Centre led to political instability in the State. The defections became rampant and gave rise to alliances of extreme elements to capture power. Goa had three chief ministers from 1963 to 1989. The MGP rule was marked with stability and attempts were made to implement the welfare measures in the territory. The corruption stood at low mark. The Progressive Democratic Front (PDF) government came into existence with strange coalition of extreme regional parties— the MGP, GC and UGDP in 1990.

The PDF Government discontinued the policy followed by the Congress government to give state grants to the Church-affiliated English medium primary schools in the State. It raised the doubts over the survival of the PDF government. The Church-affiliated schools sought refuge in the court of law under the Article 29 and 30 of the Constitution. They argued that their fundamental rights are violated by the decision of the state government to discontinue the state grants to them. The minorities would have been eligible for the state grants, if English was the mother tongue of the substantial section of the population. Ironically, the Roman Catholic Church, which had backed the agitation seeking the sole official status to Konkani, demanded state grants to the English medium schools at primary stage. The Action Committee for Medium of Instruction (ACMI) spearheaded the agitation to reverse the decision of the PDF government. The state government adopted a policy to encourage the instruction at primary stage in the regional languages rather than English.

Former Education Minister in PDF government, Shashikala Kakodkar, stated 'she had adopted a firm stand that the primary and pre-primary schools imparting instructions in Marathi and Konkani languages or mother tongue should only be eligible for the state grants in 1990. However, Mauvin Godinho, Fransisco Sardinha and L. P. Barbosa of the previous Congress-I regime had encouraged the Church-affiliated schools to impart instruction at primary stage in English. The Congress-I had backed the medium of instruction issue when it was out of power. The Roman Catholic Church had resorted to pressure tactics to reverse the policy decision of the government. But, she had offered to resign rather than succumb to pressure" (Kakodkar: Interview: 13-10-1999).

'Initially, it (Church) showed resistance and a determination to challenge the policy, and seek grants for its many English medium primary schools… Later, the Church changed its stance and readied to implement a policy of switching over its primary schools to the regional language i. e. Konkani'. (Dantas, 1999 (a): 51). Kashinath Jalmi, M. G. Party leader argued 'the Church managed primary schools in Goa had opposed the decision of the PDF Government in 1990, that seriously aimed at implementing the Official Language Act, 1987. The PDF Government experiment was short-lived. So the aided primary schools got grants where English and Konkani were taught as one of the subject only' (Jalmi: 14 12-1999). The advocates of Konkani opted for English rather than regional language(s). The Congress party resorted to double-speak on the issue of the official language. It had introduced the official language bill stating that it was high time that people's language must replace the English language as the official language. Neither the ruling party nor the Konkani literary institutions were serious about implementing the Official Language Act, 1987 in the State.

INCLUSION OF KONKANI IN EIGHTH SCHEDULE OF THE CONSTITUTION OF INDIA: The advocates of Konkani attempted for inclusion of the language in the Eighth Schedule to the Constitution. They believed that 'such an action would enable exams at the state level to be taken in Konkani enhance the language's development, and expedite statehood (Rubinoff, 1998: 116). They argued that inclusion of Konkani in the Eighth Schedule would permanently settle the controversy over the status of Konkani and pave the way for its entry in the mainstream literature. The Congress party backed the advocates of Konkani for recognition of the language.

The language mainly spoken in the household in Goa accounted 2,65,803 (30.70) per cent Marathi and 6,00004 (69.30) per cent Konkani The urban areas included 53,178 (20) per cent Marathi speakers and 1,80,224 (30.04) per cent Konkani speakers whereas the rural areas were 2,12,625 (79.99) per cent Marathi speakers and 4,19780 (69.96) per cent Konkani speakers, respectively (Census of 1981).

The household population by languages outside the Eighth Schedule to the Constitution constituted 4.4 per cent of India's population in 1981. There were 44.5 lakh speakers of Bhili languages, 44.08 lakh speakers of Santhali, whereas Gondi speakers of population constituted 19.54 lakh, Konkani 15.84 lakh, Dongri 15.20 lakh, Tulu 13.76 lakh, Kurukh 12.64 lakh Nepali 12.54 lakh, Khandeshi 11.86 lakh and Manipuri— 09.06 lakhs, respectively (Ministry of Information & Broadcasting, Government of India, 1999). According to Census of 1971-1991, the number of Konkani speakers from 15,08,432 in 1971 shot up to 17,60,607 in 1991. Interestingly, the Bhili and Santhali lacked languages lacked the political backing for inclusion in the Eighth Schedule.

The strength of Hindi speakers constitutes 39.85 per cent followed by Bengali 8.22 per cent, Telugu 7.80 per cent, Marathi 7.38 per cent, Tamil

6.26 per cent, and Urdu 5.13 per cent amongst other languages included in the Eighth Schedule. Hindi, which is the official and link language of the country enjoys dominant position. The Schedule languages which constitutes less than one percent of total number of speakers include Sindhi 0.25 per cent, Nepali 0.25 per cent; Konkani 0.21 per cent, Manipuri 0.15 per cent, Kashmiri 0.46 per cent, Sanskrit 0.01 per cent respectively (India 1999, (New Delhi: Publications Division, Ministry of Information & Broadcasting, Government of India, 1990).

The Statement of Objects and Reasons appended to the Constitution (Seventy-eighth Amendment) Bill, 1992 introduced by Union Home Minister S. B. Chavan on August 20, 1992, which was enacted as the Constitution (Seventy-first Amendment) Act, 1992 stated that there had been demands for inclusion of certain languages in the Eighth Schedule. It is proposed to include Konkani, Manipuri and Nepali languages in the Eighth Schedule. The Bill sought to give effect to that decision. The Nepali language is also known in some areas as Gorkha Bhasa. In the census operations, other nomenclatures such as Gorkhali, Gorkdhi, Gurkhiya, Khaskura or Naipali have also been used. The Konkani language has been included in the Eighth Schedule along with Nepali and Manipuri under the Constitution (Seventy-first) Amendment Act, 1992. 'On August 20, 1992 the last day of the monsoon session, both the Houses of Parliament without any discussion passed the Bill' (Mallya 1997: 112).

The struggle for inclusion of language in the Eighth Schedule of the Constitution is political rather than based on the literary merit of the language. The Government of India has not evolved any standard for inclusion of the language in the Eighth Schedule. It has encouraged various linguistic groups to agitate for recognition of their languages at political plane. Noted constitutional expert Durga Das Basu argued that 'Government of India failed to amend the Constitution to lay down any definite standard for inclusion in the Eighth Schedule itself, instead, they have been obliged to amend the Eighth Schedule itself to include three new languages, viz. Konkani, Manipuri and Nepali, because of the time being, their demand became irresistible. But even then the case for elevation of other languages continues unabated '(Basu, 2000: 404). There is long standing demand for inclusion of Tulu language in the Eighth Schedule and other small languages in the country. The inclusion of Konkani in the Eighth Schedule was under the pressure from the vested interests. In other words, the official recognition given to Konkani is not based on its literary merit.

OFFICIAL LANGUAGE POLICY IN GOA

'The official language is a language used in the business of the government, legislative, executive and judicial where as the national language is the language of a political, social and cultural entity' (Mallikarjun, 1986: 6-7). 'A language used in administration occupies a central place in the context with language use in the society. It shows following characteristics: - a) easy to comprehend, simple to use, economic to express and amenable to process of standardisation, modernisation and innovation; b) able to make finest distinction of meaning to legislate and interpret; c) reflect the political system it represents; d) in active use among the people governed by it; e) history of its use in the administration; f) have competence to express the aspirations of the government and those who are governed; g) in a position to gain the respect from the people who are going to be governed by it; h) find acceptance from all those governed by it; and i) a part of educational system' (Mallikarjun, 1986: 69-70).

A language has to fulfil all these conditions of the literate culture for its effective use at the official level. The official recognition given to a particular language often exhibits political undertones. The state patronage alone cannot elevate the literary merit of a language. A language grows in a given socio-cultural milieu. The voluntary efforts encourage and expedite the process of use of a language at the practical plane. 'The notion of developing a language means...adding to its range of social functions' (Hallyday, 1968: 78). The widespread impression that multi-lingualism is uncommon is promoted by government policies less than quarter of world's nation give official recognition to two and only six recognise them more. In the countries that have a single official language used by the majority of the population, sizeable groups use other languages.

In the USA, at the time of nation's founding, there were as many as twenty languages including foreign and native languages spoken in daily life of the people. The languages other than English have always been a part of American history and culture. The debate over establishing a national language dates back to the country's beginnings. In 1780, the proposal to Continental Congress to create an official academy to purify, develop, and dictate usage of English was rejected as undemocratic and a threat to individual liberty. The restrictive language laws— 'Only English' have violated the rights of the immigrants and the indigenous people. The American Civil Liberties Union stated: 'The best insurance against social isolation of those who immigrate to our nation is acceptance and celebration of the differences that exist within our ethnically diverse citizenry. The bond that unites our nation is not linguistic or ethnic homogeneity but a shared commitment to democracy, liberty, and equality' (ACLU, New York, 1996).

The discord arises when the official recognition is given to a single language in a bi-lingual or multi-lingual set up. It gives rise to psychological fear that development of the official language will work against the other languages. The fear is that the official language will slowly dominate over other languages. It will replace the other languages in the educational system. It will encourage migration of the speech community from other areas. And there will be low prestige of the other languages in the region.

Shivendra Verma wrote: "What experts have called an undeveloped language is a language that has been deprived of its right to perform certain functions in its own society. It is fallacy to argue that, language should first become developed, then put to use in new domain...In fact, an undeveloped language is one that has not been used in all the functions that a language serves in the society. English in the medieval England was not a developed language, since many of the social functions of the language in the community could be performed only in Latin or the French' (University News: 1996).

The linguists argue that all the languages show vitality, elasticity, and creativity when used in the new sphere. It is not a monolithic system with one standard form. One of the remarkable features of the language is the creativity— the power to generate new linguistic expressions. This creative language use is universally present in all languages. In short, all people in all languages can transform, re-create, and generate alternative forms of expression. No language, however, is inherently incapable of conveying ideas be they sublime or mundane, metaphysical or technological. Small languages have grown up into the big languages and some small languages have vanished under the impact of prestige languages and technological development.

Pandit Nehru stated: "One should not try to suppress a language, one has to be as liberal as possible. One should not coerce anybody into a language as far as possible. Whenever an attempt is made to suppress a language or coerce the people into some other language, there has been trouble" (Mallikarjun, 1986: 1).

The prestige language often overtakes the function of mother tongue, which is the language of the formal occasions. The language maintenance and shift depends upon the factors such as— socio-economic status of linguistic groups, status of language, demographic profile, mass media, and institutional support base. Sometimes the mother tongue plays a ceremonial role under socio-political pressure. Singapore recognises Tamil,

Malay, Mandarin and English. However, English plays a dominant role in the national linguistic framework. The official status to people's language need not necessarily replace the prestige or elite language. The language that does not travel, it decays. No linguistic group could hope to enrich the language without accommodating words from other languages. Besides, no language could survive as a closed system. A standard language passes through process of selection (use for political and commercial activity), codification (preparation of dictionaries, encyclopaedia), elaboration of function (use as medium of instruction, media, government) and acceptance by people. It serves as a strong unifying force for the State as a symbol of independence of the states and as a marker of difference from other states. So, the state tries to somewhat develop it.

S. M. Katre stated "Unless we build up the linguistic resources of the Konkani speakers and publish enough soul-satisfying texts, there is no future for the language" (Katre, 1957: 11).

Bhiku Pai Angle stated: "There is lack of literary merit in Konkani and its scarce use at practical plane. The Konkani movement exhibits a parochial phenomenon...Even after Konkani was made the official language along with Marathi, the application and correspondence received by the government offices at Sachivalaya (Secretariat) were in Marathi and that in Konkani was negligible, say less than ten per cent. This was disclosed in the state assembly. Thus, the official recognition given to Konkani in no way reflects its literary merit" (Pai Angle: Interview: 11-6-98).

Raju Nayak, while speaking at the Fourteenth All-India Konkani Literary Conference held (23-01-1998) in Margao, Goa, stated: "In the eye of an outsider, Konkani is state language. Marathi is also the state language of Goa and English is widely spoken. Hindi, of course, is our national language. Such impression of the State was not conducive to linguistic identity of Goa" (Konkani Bhasha Mandal 1998: 16).

IMPLICATIONS OF OFFICIAL LANGUAGE POLICY: The word mother tongue is defined as the language of one's mother, the language naturally acquired during infancy and childhood, one's first language. The mother tongue is a language with which one is emotionally identified. To some, it is divine, something sacred, part of cultural heritage, shadow inseparable from the personality. The word mother tongue was not in vogue in the ancient Indian literature. In the past, different languages existed in the same territorial unit. The ruling elite adopted more than one language as the official languages. Pandit Nehru argued that the state education and all public activities should be carried out in the dominant language of each linguistic area, with suitable provision for minority groups. (*Op. Cit.* Brecher 1959: 235-36).

Tariq Rahman argued: "The domains of power are networks of the administration, judiciary, education, media etc, through which distribution of goods and services and other gratification are controlled. Other domains of power, not necessarily under direct control but influenced by it, are domains of culture, research, commerce and ideology" (Rahman, 1998: 9).

The dominant languages were used at practical plane. The oral culture and literary culture both flourished simultaneously in the country. In the modern period, the choice of a language as an official language affects different spheres of life— linguistic, academic, socio-cultural, economic and political. The official recognition given to a particular language promotes it in the new territories. It encourages growth of the language and its increased use in the domains of power. The official language becomes part of the educational system. It becomes the medium of instruction at various levels. Its knowledge becomes pre or post-condition for public employment. It acquires prestige and develops distinct identity. It becomes a bond that unites people irrespective of caste, language or religion and other such variables. It opens up avenues for economic benefits of the speech community. At political plane, the official status leads to polarisation of political parties. The use or non-use of state language at official level invites pressure on the political parties. It becomes a tool mobilise people, politically.

USE OF OFFICIAL LANGUAGE IN MEDIA: The newspaper and periodicals published in a particular region sufficiently indicate the principal language of the land. There are three local English dailies published from Goa which, include The Navhind Times, O Herald O, and Gomantak Times. The Marathi dailies include Gomantak, Navprabha, Tarun Bharat, Rashtramat, Sakal, Sanatan Prabhat, Pudhari, and Goa Times. Besides, the Marathi dailies published from Mumbai, Maharashtra Times, and Loksatta are popular in the State. The Marathi periodicals published in Goa and Maharashtra have wide readership. The sole Konkani daily Sunaprant launched in 1985 in the territory struggles for its bare survival. It has low readership and not an influential paper in the State. Its circulation went up to 2700, according to Raju Nayak, the former editor of the paper.

The average circulation of newspapers as per audit bureau of circulations report are as follows:- Marathi dailies— Tarun Bharat 28047 (ABC: July/December 2000); Gomantak 20117 (ABC: July/December 1999); Navprabha 10507; Rashtramat 7000; Sanatan Prabhat 6000; whereas English dailies— The Navhind Times 31,605 (ABC: July/

December 2000); O Herald O 30,905 (ABC: July/December 2000; Gomantak Times 4,890 (ABC: January/June 1999).

In 2001, the circulation of national or regional dailies are— Times of India 10000; Express Indian 2000; Financial Express 450; and Economic Times 2000 and Marathi dailies are—Lok Satta 1500; and Maharashtra Times 800. Besides, the other newspapers popular in the State are— Pudhari, Goa Times, Samana, Nav Shakti (Marathi); Nav Bharat Times (Hindi); The Inquilab (Urdu); Asian Age, Mid-Day, Hindu (English), Kannada Prabha (Kannada) amongst others. The circulation of English and Marathi newspapers dominates in the State.

The English periodicals published from Goa include— Goa Today, Gulab, Goa Post, Goa Revolution, Vanaguarda, Marg, and Goan Review. There are seven Marathi periodicals published from Goa include— Gomant Shakti, Gomantakachi Asmita, Gomant Kalika, Lokbhumi, Sangam, Hindavi, and Shabdha Yatra. The reported periodicals published in Konkani include— Jaag, Kulagar, Urba, Konkan Times, Zaitt, Hemangui, Rajhaunsa, Bhimba in Devanagari script, Vavryadeacho Ishtt, Konkan Mail, Goencho Awaj in Devanagari and Latin script (Government of Goa, Department of Information & Publicity, 1998).

The electronic media is in the nascent stage in the State. It does not influence the social or commercial advertising. The origin of All India Radio (AIR) dates back to May 28, 1949, which was popularly known as Emissora da Goa (Catulo 1951: 147). The Konkani news bulletin was aired from Bombay station of All India Radio before 1961. In 1982, The Door Darshan of India started its programme generating facilities in the state. 'It is an intellectual bankruptcy that no credible Konkani programmes are being produced and quality Marathi programmes are being stopped from telecast apparently by Konkani supporting organisations', according to President, Gomant Marathi Akademy, Goparao Mayenkar (The Navhind Times: 29-04-2001). However, attempts are being made to air Konkani news bulletin from New Delhi for Goans residing abroad after inclusion of Konkani in the Eighth Schedule to Constitution.

USE OF OFFICIAL LANGUAGE IN EDUCATION: The process of thinking and power of thought are inseparably linked with each other. The formation of ideas and the exchange of ideas are inseparable without a language. Man needs two kinds of languages— a language of emotions, unexpressed associations and a language of fact, knowledge, exact argument, scientific truth. The small language fulfils the first function but it proves insufficient for the latter. Language meant the issue of mother tongue instruction at primary to university level. The medium of instruction at university level in Goa is in English. The extra-mural studies and extension services under Section 5 sub section (5) of the Goa University Act, 1984, carried out by the Director of Students' Welfare and Culture provides for use of English, Konkani or Marathi for lectures and discussions by academics and post-graduate students (Statute (SA-25 V), Goa University: 1998)

'The factors which have bearing for determining the medium of instruction for community include: - size of community; compact or diffuse nature of the community in a region; isolated or interspersed communities; relations with dominant regional language; extent of bi-lingualism prevailing in the community; and attitude of elite and availability of literature in the language, respectively' (Khubchandani, 1992: 81).

Marathi was widely used in imparting instruction before Liberation. The MGP encouraged the tradition of imparting primary education in Marathi in which the majority of population illustrated themselves before 1961. The colonial masters were responsible for artistic and intellectual degradation of the masses. Interestingly, the advocates of Konkani argued that a child from Bhil community should be taught in his own mother tongue. They stressed on imparting the primary education in Konkani rather than literary Marathi.

In 1963-64, 47,483 (95.65) per cent students at primary stage opted for Marathi and 2,161 (4.35) per cent for Konkani. In 1973-74, Marathi 76,119 (97) per cent and Konkani 2,358 (3.0) per cent. In 1983-84, Marathi 82,400 (99.23) per cent and Konkani 840 (0.77) per cent. In 1984-85, Marathi 76,994 (99.47) per cent and Konkani 410 (0.53) per cent, respectively (MRBPS), 1985, p.5).

The majority of the students at the primary stage were enrolled in the Marathi medium schools, since Liberation. On the eve of official language controversy, the enrolment of the students at the primary stage shot up from 95.65 per cent in 1963-64 to 99.47 in 1984-85 in Marathi. The enrolment of students in Konkani at primary stage declined from 4.35 per cent in 1963-64 to merely 0.53 in 1984-85.

The enrolment of students in the Marathi medium primary schools continues to be higher i. e. 9,967 in Marathi as against 664 in Konkani, Kannada 458, Urdu 380, Hindi 127 and others 15 in the State (Tarun Bharat, Goa, 17-07-1999). Thus, after twelve years after recognition of Konkani as the official language, the medium of instruction at primary level continues to be in Marathi.

The percentage of Marathi medium schools at primary stage accounted for 84.55 per cent followed by Konkani 7.58 per cent, English 3.26 per cent and others 4.61 per cent. In case of middle schools, Marathi 65.33 per cent followed by English 16.33 per cent, Konkani / English 8.16 per cent and others 9.18 per cent. In case of high schools, English 57.18 per cent followed by Konkani / English 30.42 per cent, Marathi / English 9.86 per cent and others 2.53 per cent respectively (Government of Goa, List of Recognised Educational Institutions in Goa-1998-99, Goa: Directorate of Education, Panaji, 1999). Interestingly, the enrollment of students in the Kannada medium primary schools in Mormugao taluka has increased due to influx of labour from the adjoining states. The enrollment of the students in the industrial city of Vasco-da-Gama out of total 3265 students in 20 government primary schools were— 1544 i.e. 47.28 per cent in case of Kannada followed by Marathi 905 (27.71); Urdu 372 (11.39); Konkani 237 (7.25) and Hindi 207 (6.33), respectively (Tarun Bharat: 23-06-01)

In the USA, 'the primary purpose of bilingual programs in elementary and secondary schools, which use both English and a child's native language to teach all subjects, is to develop proficiency in English and, thus, facilitate the child's transition to all-English instruction. Although debate about this approach continues, the latest studies show that bilingual education definitely enhances a child's ability to acquire the second language. Some studies even show that the more extensive the native language instruction, the better students perform all around, and that the bilingual method engenders a positive self-image and self-respect by validating the child's native language and culture' (American Civil Liberties Union (ACLU), New York, 1996).

Tanaji Halarnkar argued: "The dominant position taken by English in the country has driven the national languages to acquire a backseat. The replacement of English by any other language will broaden the scope of regional languages. The role of regional languages should not be limited to cultural plane alone. The in-built potential of the regional language should be developed and be made useful to meet timely challenges of the society. Unfortunately, the regional protagonists have not taken even a primary step towards this line" (Halarnkar: Interview: 5-5-1998).

Naguesh Karmali stated: "Every language has its limitation and it has to work within those limitations. The tiny size of state, multiplicity of scripts and scattered linguistic population affects the speedy development of the Konkani language. There is no possibility of any linguistic conflict in the State after inclusion of Konkani in the Eighth Schedule to Constitution of India" (Karmali: Interview: 28-4-99).

Thus, Konkani suffers from inherent limitation as the language of medium of instruction from primary to university level. The advocates of Konkani have paid lip service to produce soul-satisfying literature in the language. The basic education continues to be imparted through the Marathi language. Moreover, English and not the regional languages are gaining importance amongst the elite enjoying power, culture and money. The continued use of English in the administration is technique to avoid choosing between the regional languages. Konkani is given a lip service to qualify for the state grants in the State. The official status to Konkani under the Congress regime brought no change in its use at the practical plane.

The state government has failed to arrive at a clear-cut language policy or implement the Official Language Act, 1987. The Government of India gave recognition to Konkani in order to satisfy the pressure groups. English continues to enjoy the dominant position irrespective of the official language policy in the State. Section 3 of the Official Language Act, 1987 provides — (1) with effect from such date as the Administrator may, by notification, appoint, Konkani language shall, subject to the provisions contained in section 34 and 35 of the Government of Union Territories Act, 1963 (Central Act 20 of 1963), be the official language for all or any of the official purposes of the Union territory, and different dates may be appointed for different official purposes: Provided that the Administrator may, by a like notification, direct that in case of Goa District, the Marathi language, and in the case of Daman & Diu Districts, the Gujarati language, shall also be used for all or any of the official purposes and different dates may be appointed for different official purposes. Provided further that nothing contained in this sub-section shall be deemed to affect the use of the Marathi and Gujarati languages in educational, social and cultural fields: - Provide further that the Government shall not, in granting aid to any educational or cultural institution, discriminate against such institution only on the ground of the language. (2) Nothing contained in sub-section (1) shall preclude any person from submitting any representation for the redress of any grievances to any officer or authority of the Union territory in any of the languages used in the Union territory. Further Section 4 provides: Notwithstanding anything contained in the section 3, the English language shall continue to be used in addition to the languages specified in that section for all or any of the official purposes of the Union territory (See Appendix-4).

In its landmark judgement, the High Court of Judicature at Bombay, Panaji Bench in Sesa Goa Ltd V/s State of Goa case on June 28, 1989 stated: "The proviso to Section 3 of the Goa, Daman and Diu Official

Language Act, 1987 (Act 5 of 1987) states that the Administration may direct in case of the Goa District the Marathi language shall also be used for all or any of the official purpose. The recognition of Marathi as a language for official purposes is dependent upon, as the language of Konkani is dependent upon, the Notification to be issued in that regard by the administration.

In exercise of the powers conferred by Section 3 of the Act 5 of 1987, the Government of Goa has appointed the 19th day of January 1987 as the date from which Konkani language shall be the official language for the purpose of the replies by the Government whenever communications are received in Konkani. Similarly, a Notification was published on the 15th December, and the same manner it has been provided that the 19th day of December 1987 will be the date on and from which Marathi language shall be used for replies from the Government whenever communications are received in Marathi language. In other words, both Konkani and Marathi languages have been recognised as official languages from the same date and for the same official purposes" (Para 8).

Further, In the affidavit-in-reply sworn by under-secretary (Revenue) Government of Goa, on March 18, 1989 stated: "I say that Marathi language satisfied the requirement as a regional language for the purpose of Land Acquisition Act in the State of Goa, I also say that Goa, Daman and Diu Official Language act, 1987 also provides a clue to the acknowledgement of the fact that the Marathi language is one of the regional languages in the State of Goa" (Para 10).

The above judgement of the High Court strengthened the argument that both regional languages— Konkani and Marathi enjoy equal status in the State. It boosted the morale of the advocates of Marathi. The advocates of Konkani did not challenge the verdict of the High Court. Thus, the bi-lingual policy to accommodate the interests of the Marathi language temporarily shelved the language controversy in the State. The advocates of Konkani the Official Language Act, 1987 is ambiguous and gives scope for entry of Marathi from the back door.

The situation in Goa is not simply one of conflict between Konkani and Marathi. It is complicated further by the fact that the elite enjoying power and culture and money use English in the domains of power more than they use any of the regional language. The anti-integration groups used Konkani as a tool to keep Goa separate. They evoked atma gaurav or regional pride rather than rashtra gaurav or national pride. The struggle for recognition of Konkani reflects sub-national sentiments and sub-national competition, which has taken form of linguistic rivalries in the

State. The Congress party adopted policy of appeasement of the anti-integration groups who attempted to deny the rightful position enjoyed by the Marathi language and literature in the socio-cultural milieu in the State. The advocates of Konkani have perpetuated idea that Konkani identity is restricted to Goa alone. In fact, it extends to whole of Konkan Kshetra.

Revival of Official Language Controversy in 2000

The language controversy rocked the State of Goa over the judgement of the Panaji Bench of Bombay High Court on March 30, 2000 in the Writ Petition No. 288/1996, filed by the Marathi Rajya Bhasha Prasthpan Samiti and Marathi Akademy versus the State of Goa.

The High Court in its judgement stated: "There is no substance in the argument that the bilingual situation warranting equal status to both languages— Konkani and Marathi. Undisputedly Konkani is the official language. Mere use of Marathi language for official purposes to reply the communication received in Marathi language by itself cannot afford the status of official language to Marathi or equal status with the official language Konkani. The fact stated on the oath that 95 per cent of the people of Goa speak Marathi is not in dispute. Apparently it is the language of majority to the extent of 90 per cent of the people of Goa. Faint attempt was made to some answers given by the Minister in the Assembly to derive support to the contention of need for equal status to both the languages. Moreover, in our considered opinion the material placed on record do not suggest in any manner that both the languages are granted equal status under the Official Language Act in force in the State" (Para 13).

The Konkani literary activists in a Memorandum (24-04-2000) stated: "We, the writers, artistes and activists, serving in the cause of Konkani in our respective fields, have noted with satisfaction the correct interpretation of the Official Language Act contained in the recent decision of the Panaji Bench of the Bombay High Court... It is our firm belief that the Official Language Act is an instrument that can protect the interest of Goan youth and contain unemployment of the sons of the soil if properly implemented. Making Marathi the official language will destroy that advantage opening the gates of employment to crores of people from the neighbouring Marathi speaking state. As we all know, mere domicile stipulation cannot check the job opportunities to outsiders. The Official Language Act, as it is, provides, the use of Marathi for official purposes. That provision is more than its due considering the status of Marathi in Goa. It was, in fact, with reservation that we had accepted it. As a measure to accommodate the sentiment regarding Marathi prevailing among certain sections of people. But, we will not tolerate, under any circumstances, any amendment to the

Official Language Act. It is our firm resolve to fight any such attempt tooth and nail to safeguard the Goan identity and thwart the sinister plan to pave way for Goa's merger with Marathi-speaking areas… We solemnly declare that we shall spare no efforts to give the final effective blow to these betrayers who have again raised their ugly heads to divide and destroy Goa" (The Navhind Times: 24-04-2000).

On April 30, 2000, the 75th Akhil Bharatiya Marathi Sahitya Sammelan (ABMSS) held at Belgaum district of Karnataka, unanimously passed resolution that Goa government should take into consideration the sentiments of the majority of the population and also accord the official status to Marathi. In a joint meeting of Goa Pradesh Congress (GPCC) and Congress Legislature Party (CLP), former Chief Minister and GPCC President Luizinho Faleiro stated that the issue of Official Language Act was already resolved by the people of Goa and the will of the people was expressed through the Act, 1987 (The Navhind Times: 24-04-2000). Chief Minister Fransisco Sardinha argued that his Goan People's Party (GPP), the splinter group of the Congress party, favoured the sole official status to Konkani. He asserted that due place has been given for use of Marathi for the official purposes under Act (The Navhind Times: 12-05-2000).

The Bharatiya Janata Party, the alliance partner of the Fransisco Sardinha led coalition government, in its fifth state-level convention held on May 14, 2000 at Mhapsa, reiterated its commitment to accord the equal status to Marathi without altering the basic structure of the Act and keeping the status of Konkani intact. The resolution stated 'the recent judgement of the Panaji Bench of Bombay High Court has clearly spelt out that the Official Language Act had not accorded equal status to Konkani and Marathi. The High Court order had exposed the crafty politicians in the State who were professing that the Act had conferred the equal status on Konkani and Marathi. The politicians are bowing to public sentiments, thereby, avoiding the core issue of language. The controversy over the sister languages had granted undue importance to English in the State' (The Navhind Times: 15-05-2000).

Advocate Uday Bhembre wrote: "If Marathi is made official language on par with Konkani, interest of local people will be jeopardised, especially in the matter of jobs and employment. Secondly, an erroneous impression will be created that Goa is a bilingual State making Goa's political status a subject of dispute and controversy once again. No Goan will like to be troubled by these problems any more (The Navhind Times: 14-05-2000)… I have not the slightest hesitation to say that it (Konkani) is the widely spoken language or the language spoken by the largest group that can legitimately claim to be the official language of a state. Marathi is not spoken by Goans. Neither any section of the people nor any part of Goa is Marathi speaking. It is used in certain spheres of the life by the educated section of Hindus who may constitute the most 30 per cent of the population of Goa. Under no circumstances it can justifiably lay any claim to be the other official language of Goa...Konkani, the language of the masses is the official language. There is absolutely no need to have another official language to accommodate the language of a learned coterie" (The Navhind Times: 23-07-2000).

Arun Sinha, in his editorial in 'The Navhind Times' wrote: "...There is also no dispute that the official language status to Konkani has brought no effective change in the way official business is conducted in the offices of Goa government. Neither had the supposedly equal status to Marathi brought any discernible change in the communication within the government or between the government and public. English continued to be the sole official language of Goa. Even at the lower level that is at popular levels, like panchayats the government communication was done in English, rather than in Konkani or Marathi. English continued to dominate in the primary schools, too but that is also another question. As far as the official business was concerned, the government remained indifferent to the implementation of the Official Language Act. The government must take initiative to implement the legislation in letter and spirit, or improve it, without denying the legitimate interests of Marathi (The Navhind Times: 20-05-2000).

In the background of the High Court judgement various gram panchayats and municipalities passed resolutions urging the state government to accord the official status to Marathi along with Konkani. These include— Mhapsa Municipal Council (05-05-2000), Canacona Municipal Council (12-05-2000), Bicholi Municipal Council (01-06-200), and Mormugao Municipal Council (19-06-2000) amongst others. The majority of the village panchayats stood for official status to Marathi in the State. Dr. Wilfred De Souza former chief Minister and the leader of Nationalist Congress Party (NCP) stated that the language issue is dead and gone. Interestingly, 'Dr. De Souza a staunch supporter of sole official status to Konkani demanded that the medium of instruction at primary stage should be in English rather than in the regional languages, (The Navhind Times: 24/23-05-2000).

Pandurang Raut, the MGP legislator without consulting the party office bearers, proposed amendment to the Official Language Act, 1987 to accord the official status to Marathi. The Bharatiya Janata Party (BJP) proposed an amendment to the Act to accord equal status to Marathi. The BJP amendment to Section 3 stated: (i) with effect from such date as the

Government of Goa may, by notification, appoint, Konkani language shall be the official language for all or any of the official purposes of the State of Goa, and different dates may be appointed for different official purposes. Further, (ii) the Government of Goa, shall, by notification, declare that in the State of Goa, Marathi language shall be also used with equal status, for all the official purposes, as and whenever notified under the sub-section (1), with effect from the same date or dates, as appointed under sub-section (1).

The Section 4 provided for continued use of English language. Simultaneously, the BJP proposed the amendment to the Section 4 that English language may continue to be used in addition to the languages specified in that section for all or any of the official purposes of the State of Goa. The BJP claimed that the official language policy is no measure to protect the employment opportunities of the local youth and the domicile criterion can effectively safeguard the interest of Goans.

The Konkani Porjeach Awaz (KPA) and Goa Hitrakhan Manch (GHM) opposed the amendments to the Official Language Act, 1987. The advocates of Konkani argued that any change in the official language policy will affect the employment opportunities of local youth and the BJP and the MGP are trying to put forth the Vishal Gomantak idea from the back-door (The Navhind Times: 22-06-2000). The Herald in its editorial commented that 'the High Court order purely relates to employment opportunities for Goan youth and has no bearing what so ever on the relative status of Konkani and Marathi…The official language policy is linked to local identities and pride in an ethnic culture, (Herald 21-06-2000).

Kashinath Jalmi, the MGP leader, wrote: 'It is to make good for these deficiencies, also to provide for official status to the language of majority use that is Marathi and bring the text of the Official Language Act, 1987 in complete conformity and consonant with the text of Article 345 of the Constitution of India and the national language policy, a drastic amendment or a new Official Language Act is needed (The Navhind Times: 02-07-2000).

The political parties tried to derive maximum mileage out of language issue. A faction of MLAs within Congress party including Adv. Ramakant Khalap, Prakash Velip, Sanjay Bandekar, Babu Azgaonkar and Jitendra Deshprabhu argued in favour official status to Marathi out of constituency pressure. Apparently, the Bill introduced by the BJP rather than the MGP had more support of thc legislators in the House. On 21-07-200, Pratapsing Rane, the Speaker of the House stated that although the majority of the population of the State understands Marathi, the Christians who constitute 30 per cent are not conversant with the language. Rane argued that the Bill, if passed, involved financial implications and therefore was referred to Governor of the State. In the mysterious circumstances, the House skipped its responsibility to decide the fate of the Bill.

The judgement of the Panaji Bench of Mumbai High Court led the Marathi protagonists to mobilise public opinion to amend the Official Language Act, 1987 to accord official status to Marathi by the Gomantak Marathi Akademy (GMA) and Marathi Rajya Bhasha Prasthapan Samiti (MRBPS). Simultaneously, they challenged the judgement of the High Court on July 10, 2000 in the Supreme Court. The MRPBS stated that the apex court did not entertain the petition on 01-08-2000 on the technical ground. The earlier petition in the High Court had challenged provision under Article 309 making the knowledge of Konkani essential and Marathi desirable for regulating the recruitment and conditions of service of persons appointed to state services. It had not raised the issue of Article 345 of the Constitution dealing with adoption of any one or more of the languages in use in the State or Hindi for all or any of the official purposes in its appeal to the Supreme Court. Thus, after enactment of the official language act in 1987, the political masters have failed to implement the Act or to accommodate the legitimate interests of Marathi by according equal official status to both the regional languages.

'Chief Minister Manohar Parrikar appeared firm on his stand and obviously did not want any immediate change in the Act since the BJP MLA's themselves were divided on the issue' (Times of India, Bangalore: 14-03-2001). Mr. Parrikar stated that 'he accords equal importace to both the languages and called upon the advocates of Konkani and Marathi to unitedly halt the trend of English gaining popularity in the State' (Gomantak: 23-04-2001).

At 15th All India Konkani Sahitya Sammelan held on April 21-22, 2001 (Parvari, Goa) stressed the need to produce intellectual literature in the Konkani language. Fr. Freddy D' Costa lamented the fact that 'Goan Christians prefer English to their mother tongue. The trend of celebration of mass in English is steadily moving to the villages' (Herald: 23/04/2001). Advocate Uday Bhembre called upon 'the Konkani speakers to popularise use of Devanagari script for Konkani' (Gomantak: 23/04/2001). Mr. Chandrakant Keni stated that 'Konkani has been included in the Eighth Schedule, however, the advocates of Konkani have to be alert. The Marathi language movement has come to an end. The advocates of Marathi may grab opportunity to rake up the issue in the court on pro-Marathi people entering the institution of judiciary in the State' (Sunaprant: 23-04-2001).

The BJP-led government decided in April, 2001 to privatise 48 Marathi including three Konkani and one Urdu primary schools due to falling number of students in the villages. In these primary schools the strength of the students was below six students in eight schools; below ten students in 27 schools and below 12 students in 16 schools, respectively. The state government asked the private bodies at the local level to take over these schools. The Rashtriya Swayamsevak Sangh backed Vidya Bharati took lead in reviving these Marathi schools. 'Principal Subhash Bhaskar Velingkar argued that Marathi represents the cultural heritage and vested political interests are pitted against the dominance of Marathi language in the socio-cultural milieu in Goa' (Gomantak: 10-06-01).

Interestingly, the Konkani groups backed the Committee to Protect Government Primary Schools, which opposed the decision of the state government. The protagonists of Marathi, however, were divided over the decision of the state government. Mrs. Nirmala Sawant, President of Goa Pradesh Congress Committee and Dr. Wilfred D' Souza labelled the move as an attempt to saffronise the education system in the State. (The Navhind Times: 08-06-2001). The cricket scam tainted former Deputy Chief Minister Dayanand Narvekar who had vowed to dislodge Parrikar Ministry opposed the decision of the state government to derive political mileage. Mr. Devendra Kandolkar, a socio-educational activist, resorted to hunger strike to re-open four government primary schools in the North Goa where strength of the students went up to 12 (The Navhind Times: 07-07-2001). Thus, the issue of amalgamation of 50 and odd unviable primary schools became a tool to embarrass the Ministry headed by Mr. Manohar Parrikar. The state government decided to monitor 40 Marathi primary schools handed over to private bodies in the State. The three-day 24th Gomantak Marathi Sahitya Sammelan held at Quepe in South Goa passed resolution on 11-11-2001 that the state government and the cental government should take steps to accord the official status to Marathi language. Chief Minister Manohar Parrikar in his inaugural address on 9-11-2001 had stated that at appropriate time his government would accord the official status to Marathi. (Gomantak: 12-11-2001).

Language is not a major symbol of political identity in case of Goa. The month-long Census ernumeration in February 2001 pitted the Marathi and Konkani protagonists against each other. President of Gomant Marathi Akademy, Gopalrao Mayenkar, argued that 'the recognition to so-called Konkani of upper caste communities hailing from Goa and Udipi-Mangalore belt, all the other Konkani-speaking population including Christians using Roman scripts are pushed to secondary position...There is powrless paper supremacy of Konkakni whereas the position of Marathi has remained unchanged inspite of political set backs received by it' (The Navhind Times: 29-04-2001). According to 1991 Census the Konkani speaking population constituted 51.52 per cent whereas Marathi 33.36 per cent *(Ibid)*. The word mother tongue was defined in Census of 2001 as the language spoken in childhood by person's mother to the person. The Marathi protagonists claimed Konkani as a form of Marathi and asked the people to enumerate Marathi as the mother tongue. If, we substitute word mother tongue by regional language then it would end the language chaos during the census operations.

The political parties used language as a tool to mobilise masses politically. The Marathi enjoyed dominant position in the socio-cultural milieu. The Marathi language movement received a set back due to vested political interests. The BJP tried to distance itself from the language controversy. Chief Minister Manohar Parrikar stated that the language issue is so serious that it can bring down the coalition government. 'Moreover, the BJP is committed to policy of according equal status to Marathi keeping intact the status of the Konkani language' (Gomantak: 21-01-2001, 1&6).

In 1987, the ruling Congress-I party had introduced the amendment to accommodate the legitimate interests of Marathi. The judgement of the Panaji Bench of Mumbai High Court in its judgement (1989) had pointed out that both Konkani and Marathi are the official languages whereas the same court in its ruling (2000) stated that Konkani is the sole official language. The former ruling dealt with the land acquisition whereas the later dealt with the employment policy of the state government.

Emerging Trends in State Politics

The small size of the State and political opportunism led to political instability after Statehood in 1987. Goa's financial dependency on the Centre is on the rise. The central assistance is in form of 30 per cent subsidy and 70 loans. The allocation of resources under Gadgil-Mukherjee formula where 7.5 per cent of assistance is given on the performance of the state and 7.5 per cent as discretionary quota and 85 per cent on the baiss of population and poverty is working against the smaller states. Only 4.04 per cent population is under below poverty line as compared to 26.01 per cent at all-India level. The per capita income is highest in India in 2002. The small states are favoured for better governance in the country. But, the idea can be a failure, if the political class lacks vision and code of conduct to manage the affairs of the State. The political class showed lack of commitment or moral code of conduct in running the affairs of the

State. Norman Dantas argued 'the infirmity and its consequences were reflected most sharply in the state politics— the lack of clarity, the uncertainty of choice and commitment about which way and how Goa should be' (Dantas 1999 (a): 1).

The political parties are the major agents of transforming society. Nevertheless, when presented with an opportunity to aggrandise power and influence, they tend to succumb to parochial loyalties at the cost of democratic governance. The defection factor has affected the Goan polity. The state's defection rate is highest in the country and probably in the world. In 1994 assembly elections, the total electorate constituted 8,68,138. The INC bagged 18 seats followed by the MGP 12 seats, the BJP 4 seats, the United Goans Democratic Party (UGDP) three seats and the independent three seats, respectively (Assembly Elections Ready Reference-1999). The BJP was the new entrant in the State. The BJP adopted policy of encouraging both the regional languages. It had played no major role in the language issue in 1985-87. The advocates of Marathi claimed that the top-leadership of the BJP had ignored the cause of Marathi for political gain whereas the BJP maintained that it does not consider the language as a serious issue.

The political opportunism at the state level has given an edge to the BJP to make inroads in the State. Ironically, the Christian community in the South Goa was alienated from the Congress party in 1999 Lok Sabha elections. The eleven Congress MLAs broke away to form coalition government with the support of the BJP in November 1999. The Congress government led by Luisinho Faleiro had to resign after six months in the office. Faleiro attributed the fall of his government to a section of the upper castes wielding influence within the party and the Church.

Former Chief Minister Dayanand Bandodkar of the MGP held office from 20-12-1963 to 02-12-1966 and from 05-04-1967 to 23-03-1972 whereas his daughter Shashikala Kakodkar held office from 12-08-1973 to 07-06-1977 and from 07-06-1977 to 24-07-1979. Mr. Pratapsinh Rane held office from 16-01-80 to 07-01-1985 and from 30-05-1987 to 27-03-1990. Mr. Churchill Alemao held the office from 27-03-1990 to 14-04-1990. Mr. Luis Proto Barbosa from 14-04-1990 to 14-12-1990. Mr. Ravi Naik from 25-01-1991 to 18-05-1993. Dr. Wilfred D'Sousa from 16-05-1993 to 02-04-1994. Mr. Ravi Naik from 02-04-1994 to 08-04-1994. Dr. Wilfred D' Sousa from 08-04-1994 to 16-12-1994. Mr. Pratapsinh Rane from 16-12-1994 to 29-07-1998. Mr. Luisinho Faleiro from 26-11-1998 to 10-02-1999 and from 09-06-1999 to 24-11-1999. Mr. Fransisco Sardinha from 24-11-1999 to 21-10-2000 whereas Chief Minister Manohar Parrikar assumed office on 24-10-2000 till date, respectively.

The total electorate was 9,09,018 in the assembly elections held in May 1999. The INC cornered 21 seats with 38.55 per cent vote share; the BJP 10 seats wit 26.19 per cent vote share; the MGP four seats with 14.03 per cent vote share; the UGDP two seats, Goa Rajiv Congress two seats (vote share N.A.) and the independent one seat with 21.23 vote share, respectively (Assembly Elections Ready Reference-1999). The INC polled 38.55 per cent votes followed by BJP (26.19), the MGP (14.03), independents, and others (21.21), respectively. The MGP's vote share declined to 14.03 per cent in 1999 from 39.52 per cent in 1989. The BJP's vote share has increased to 26.19 per cent from 0.47 per cent for the corresponding period for assembly polls in the State.

In Lok Sabha Elections-1999, the Bharatiya Janata Party wrested both the Lok Sabha seats from the INC. The percentage of votes secured by the BJP is 51.47 per cent followed by the Congress party 38.99, independents, and others 9.54, respectively. In Mormugao Parliamentary Constituency, the BJP's vote share recorded 48.46 per cent followed by the Congress party 41.85 per cent, independents, and others 9.69 per cent, respectively. In Panaji Parliamentary Constituency, the BJP's vote share recorded 54.92 per cent followed by the Congress party 35.70 per cent and others 9.38 per cent, respectively. The total votes secured by the BJP in both Mormugao and Panaji parliamentary constituency were 2,18,851 and 1,91,093, respectively (Adapted from Office of the State Election Commissioner, Panaji, 1999).

The State faces political instability, financial crisis and corruption eating its vitals of the society. The Congress party witnessed again split on August 15, 2000 after five MLAs Shaikh Hassan Haroon, Prakash Velip, Suresh Parulekar, Filipe Neri Rodriguese and Jose Phillip De Souza broke away from the parent party. Subsequently, the BJP withdrew the support to the Sardinha Government and formed the another coalition government headed by Manohar Parrikar on October 24, 2000. The breakaway factions of the Indian National Congress led by Shaikh Hassan Haroon and the Opposition leader Ravi Naik with four MLAs each joined the BJP. The strength of the BJP rose to 20 and its allies stood at 26 (BJP 20, GRCP (Dessai)- 2, MGP- two, Shaikh Hassan Haroon Congress and independent one each) whereas GRCP–7, INC-6 including speaker and NCP- 1 in the 40-member House. After collapse of Sardinha government four MLAs of GRCP Somnath Zuarkar, Subhash Shirodkar, Victoria Fernandes and Francis D' Souza broke-away and re-joined Congress party. Interestingly, Fransisco Sardinha and Mauvin Godinho were re-admitted into the Congress-I party fold on April 5, 2001. The BJP admitted Suresh Parulekar MLA from Calangute constituency into party in the wake of the visit of Mr. Kamal Nath, AICC general secretary, in charge of Goa desk followed by re-admission of Mr. Dayanand Narvekar into the Congress party on 27-08-2001. Thus, the strength of the BJP went upt to 23, Congress 14, MGP two and Nationalist Congress Party one in the forty member House Chief Minister Manohar Parrikar dissolved the Ministry on February 28, 2002 for seeking fresh mandate from the people. On the language issue, the BJP election manifesto 2002 declared that 'We are committed to ensure development of Konkani as the official language and Marathi with equal status. The BJP has already substantially increased assistance to the institutions working in the field of Konkani and Marathi'. The M. G. Party who had forged alliance with the United Goans Democratiic Party stated in its election manifesto that, 'M. G. Party will strive for the recognition of Marathi language on par with Konkani as the official language and shall achieve this goal by making a cogent case and obtaining support of all sections of our population'. The UGDP declared that, 'It stands for Konkani alone though it is not opposed to government giving grants to Marathi also'. In the assembly polls held on May 30, 2002, the BJP wrested 17 seats, the INC 16, UGDP three, MGP two, and Nationalist Congress Party and independent one each, respectively. The BJP managed to form the governmet with support from the UGDP, MGP and independent candidate supported by the BJP in the State.

Dr. Subhash Bhende, President of the 76th Akhil Bharatiya Marathi Sahitya Sammelan held in January, 2003 in Karad, Maharashtra, raised the demand for equal official status to Marathi in Goa. The 8th Konkan Marathi Sahitya Sammelan, held in Panaji, Jan-Feb, 2003 also reiterated demand for equal official status to Marathi, but Chief Minsiter stated that the BJP government needs more time to solve 42-year old language issue, which dates back Liberation of Goa. The Konkani protagonists raise the bogey of influx of Maharashtrians in the State. However, the migrant population from Maharashtrians is negligible compared to adjoing State of Karnataka. The protagonists of Konkani attempted to woe the sizable section of migrants from Karnataka (Kannad Samaj) who have drastically altered the demographic profile to support the cause of Konkani in the State. Former Chief Minister and MGP turned Congress leader Ramakant Khalap actively participated for the success of the Marathi literary activity in the State. Dr. Wilfred D'Souza of the Nationalist Congress Party criticized the Ramakant Khalap for supporting the cause of Marathi. Chief Minister Manohar Parrikar provided financial support for the literary activity.

MEDIUM OF INSTRUCTION DEBATE IN GOA

The United Nations Educational, Social and Cultural Organization (UNESCO) goal is to promote linguistic diversity and multilingualism. The UNESCO statement on linguistic diversity and multilingualism reads:

Languages, with their complex implications for identity, communication, social integration, education and development, are of strategic importance for people and the planet. There is growing awareness that languages play a vital role in development, in ensuring cultural diversity and intercultural dialogue, but also in attaining quality education for all and strengthening cooperation, in building inclusive knowledge societies and preserving cultural heritage, and in mobilizing political will for applying the benefits of science and technology to sustainable development.

It is thus urgent to take action to encourage broad and international commitment to promoting multilingualism and linguistic diversity, including the safeguarding of endangered languages. In the global and local context the indigenous languages play important role in promoting equity, access and quality in educational system. The Queen's tongue has assumed so much importance mainly amongst the middle class in post-colonial India that academic debate of indigenous languages has become less important. There are The Anglo-Saxon bull-dozer view of globalization is attempting to wipe out the indigenous languages all over the world with rapid pace. The standardization is replacing diversity in global market. Truly, globalization refers to free flow of ideas. In fact, diversity should replace standardization. The enchanting phrase of 'global family' is being threatened by profit-driven 'global market' phrase. The rise of English as medium of instruction from primary to university stage is a portrait of distorted version of globalization.

The Christian missionaries set up primary schools in 1813 with local languages as the medium of instruction in India. Later, adopted English at secondary stage and set up universities in 1857 in the port cities. The colonial rulers set up educational/economic infrastructure not to develop India, but to exploit the resources of colonies in a more systematic manner. In free India, access, equity and quality of basic education continues to affect the human, cultural, developmental objectives.

The Right to Education Act, 2009 aims at providing free, compulsory and quality education to children from age of six to fourteen years. The access and quality are the twin-issues affecting educational system in India. The problems of education have no quick-fix solutions based on imported models, designs or theories. We have to draw out our own concepts, plans and strategies to revive primary to university the education in the country.

The need id stressed to integrate various branches of knowledge and stages of learning. Primary education is most vital component of the entire superstructure of the educational system and most neglected one for centuries in the country. The examination-oriented education system works against access, quality and relevance. The education needs to be made active, creative and inclusive by redefining, restructuring, re-locating the examination system.

The academic authority while laying down the curriculum, according to Clause 2 Section 29 of the RTE Act 2009, shall take into consideration:

(a) conformity with the values enshrined in in the Constitution of India;
(b) all-round development of the child;
(c) building up child's knowledge, potentiality and talent;
(d) development of child's physical and mental abilities to the fullest extent;
(e) learning through, activities, discovery and exploration in child-friendly and child-centered manner;
(f) medium of instruction shall, as far as practicable, be in child's mother tongue;
(g) make the child free of fear, trauma and anxiety and helping the child to express freely;
(h) comprehensive and continuous evaluation of child's understanding of knowledge and his or her ability to apply the same.

The medium of instruction controversy at primary stage of learning was raked up in 1990-91 when the state government adopted a policy to provide grants to Indian languages (Konkani, Marathi, Kannada, Urdu and others) primary schools. In 2011, the Forum for the Rights of Children's Education (FORCE) demanded the grants-in-aid to English medium primary schools. There are 1252 primary schools with strength of 101523 students in 2010-11. There are 1252 primary schools with strength of 101523 students in 2010-11. 139495 or 9.57 per cent persons are in the age group of 0-6 years out of total population 1457723 in 2011. 1152117 or 87. 4 per cent persons above seven years can read and write in any language as per Census of India 2011. The major contention of the FORCE is that the poor should not be denied access to English at primary stage. The parents should decide the medium of instruction at primary stage. The experts/ educationists should not have any say over the matters related to choice of language (Herald, Goa: 14/04/2011). The pro-English lobby refuses to take legal opinion over state aid to English medium primary schools and opted for pressure tactics to resolve the issue at political plane.

The Bharatiya Bhasha Suraksha Manch (BBSM) or Forum for Protection of Indian Languages argued that the state government should maintain the status of Indian languages (Konkani and Marathi) at primary school level and should not give grants to English medium primary schools. Goa needs state-funded primary education only in Indian languages, according the Manch. The BBSM urged upon the state government to refuse recognition to English private medium primary schools as well as ban play schools and to shift the registered English medium primary schools to Indian languages within a time-frame. (Times of India, Goa: 07/04/2011).

The demand for state-funding of English primary education is contrary to Constitutional provisions. English is not the mother tongue of those who favour state grants to primary schools in Goa. Strangley, the Government of India is not averse to consider the demands for state grants to English primary education in Goa and elsewhere in the country. The proficiency in English does not mean that the Indian languages should be replaced by English at primary stage. The mother tongue based education at formative stage weighs in favour of equity, access and quality. All languages are equally creative and innovative. The people have to nurture the native languages. The strength of a tree lies in its roots and not in fruits.

The failure to implement the Official Language Act, 1987 has led to increased hold of English in secular spheres of life and local languages are used at cultural plane. Konkani is the spoken medium of expression whereas Marathi represents the literary culture of the majority of Goan people. The Official Language Act, 1987 have inherent defects. The state legislature under Article 345 of the Constitution is empowered to accord the official status to the languages in use. It is the constitutional responsibility of the state government to accommodate the legitimate interests of Marathi by amending the Act. The protagonists of Marathi were in favour of official status to Konkani— the spoken language. The Konkani protagonists propagated a myth that Marathi was foisted from outside to deny official status to Marathi— the language in use in Goa. In fact, Konkani is not the sole marker of identity in Goa. It is not the symbol of political identity, too.

The Official Language Act, 1987 gives the sole official status to the Konkani language in Devanagari script. In fact, Konkani has evolved as a modern literary language. The Roman Catholic Church has scoffed at the native Devanagari script to keep its flock away from the mainstream of national languages.

Chapter–VI

CONCLUSION

Language has turned out to be a major source of identity in the post-colonial history of India. It has been legitimised as a marker of sub-nation identity. Its elevation at the political plane exhibits sub-national sentiments and sub-national competition, which often takes the form of language rivalries. The linguistic reorganisation of the states has encouraged the anti-integration forces that work against the national unity. The Congress party followed a policy of appeasement of the anti-integration forces most hostile to integration of Goa. The demand for recognition of Konkani lacked demonstrably popular support and it was not a clearly distinct language from Marathi. The Government of India accorded the official recognition to Konkani, despite its inherent limitations under the pressure from the vested political interests.

Goa has no separate socio-linguistic identity. Culturally, it is a part of the Konkan Kshetra. Konkani had entirely an oral tradition in the entire Konkani Kshetra. The anti-integration groups who faced problem of reintegrating with the mainstream culture attempted to carve out separate identity and cultivate pride in so-called ethnic culture. They tried to glorify the influences of Portuguese rule rather than the mainstream culture. There is no historical evidence that literature in Konkani flourished at any point of time. The Portuguese regime destroyed the literature in Sanskrit and Marathi in the wake of infamous Inquisition in the tiny island of Goa. The Marathi language and literature had profound impact on Goa, which was known as Konkan Kashi— one of the holiest places of pilgrimage in the West Coast of India.

THE PRE-LIBERATION PHASE

The Portuguese precisely chose Goa for strategic, commercial consideration and evangelisation. The Portuguese were unaware of the language called Sanskrit that existed in Goa. They believed that Apostle Thomas had converted India. They adopted repressive measures to impose the Portuguese language, religion, and culture on the native population. They failed to achieve their end despite 451 years of the colonial rule. The native population nurtured Marathi language and literature. The Portuguese conquered Goa in a phased manner. They occupied tiny island of Tiswadi Mahal in 1510 A. D. and Bardez Mahal and Salcete Mahal in 1543 A. D. It took over 250 years to consolidate their power in the entire territory. The natives in the Old Conquest areas of Tiswadi, Bardez, and Salcete became targets of the barbaric atrocities unparalleled in the history of colonialism in the world. The Portuguese adopted the most repressive measures to alienate the masses from the mainstream culture. The Portuguese propaganda of the superiority of their blood, religion and culture made the native population to disown their own cultural heritage.

The unholy Inquisition altered the socio-cultural identity of the Velhas Conquistas part of the region. The people migrated in the adjoining areas of Konkan Kshetra to escape persecution of their language, religion and culture. Those who migrated to the neighbouring Marathi-speaking areas assimilated and enriched the Marathi language and literature. In the South, the Konkani-speaking population retained their cultural identity, as the spoken Konkani had no affinity with the regional languages. The Konkani-speaking population adopted the literary languages of the region at the practical plane. The Kannada language moulded the spoken Konkani language in adjoining areas of former Bombay Province. Konkani adopted various scripts of the regional languages. The Christian community adopted the Roman script for the native languages, where Christianity was the major force. The Christian missionaries asked the non-Brahmins in the Madras Province to get rid of non-Tamil word especially Sanskrit to refine and raise the purity of the Tamil language. They evoked regional pride by arguing that the Tamil-speaking people are the inheritors of the so-called ethnic culture. In Goa, they attempted to create pride in the Konkani language by alienating it from the literary Marathi language and literature. Interestingly, in Indian tradition, both literary and oral culture played important role in the life of the people.

CHRISTIAN MISSIONARIES AND NATIVE LANGUAGES: The Christian missionaries cultivated interest in the native regional languages—the literary Marathi language and spoken Konkani language for effective evangelisation. It was part of the policy of the church 'to be where laity is'. Revered Father Thomas Stephen wrote Christ Puran in Portuguese and later rendered its Marathi version for the parishes. The Christian missionaries unconsciously or deliberately argued that Konkani is a separate language. A section of upper caste from in Hindu and Christian community propagated this theory for their parochial end. The Christian masses steeped in semi-literacy, poverty and ignorance supported them under the influence of the powerful Roman Catholic Church. The Christian missionaries abandoned Marathi to produce religious literature Konkani. They attempted to raise the spoken language to a polished medium of literary __expression through the Roman script. The Roman script was used to alienate the masses from the literary Marathi language. The change in script affected the intrinsic beauty of the spoken language. The use of the Roman script gave rise to communal divide and sequestered Konkani from Marathi. The Christian missionaries also abandoned Konkani, when it became hurdle in the colonial design.

MARATHI LANGUAGE UNDER PORTUGUESE RULE: In Goa, the Marathi language and literature flourished under the Varkari sect in the thirteenth century. The native population enriched the Marathi language and literature. It was not imposed from outside. It fostered nationalist sentiments and drew the masses closer to the mainstream culture. The Portuguese encouraged Marathi as the medium of instruction at primary state, but also viewed Marathi as the foci of nationalist sentiments. The Portuguese regime and the Roman Catholic Church conspired to undermine the dominant position enjoyed by Marathi in the socio-cultural milieu in the territory. They always attacked the Marathi language and literature as a symbol of national identity and mainstream culture. The Marathi press in Goa forged nationalist sentiments amongst the native population during India's freedom struggle. The Partition of Bengal in 1905 was closely followed in Goa through Marathi press, especially Kesari of Lokmanya Bal Gangadhar Tilak. The Konkani press was used by the Roman Catholic Church to foster anti-India propaganda. It evoked sectarian sentiments.

The All India Congress Committee in its session (1916-1931) accepted Marathi as the vernacular medium of the territory. Eminent Goan thinker T. B. Cunha asserted that Marathi was cultural language through which more than half of the population of the territory illustrated itself. The Portuguese regime could not create a desired ambience of the Portuguese, despite severe repressive measures to impose it. The anti-integration groups used Konkani as a tool to assert the separate identity and mobilise the masses, politically. In fact, Konkani was spoken in the entire Konkan region. The idea of distinct identity of territoy did not gain ground during Goa's freedom struggle. Both, Konkani and Marathi were allied languages. The anti-integration groups banked upon the distinct identity of territory. They claimed that Konkani is a separate language independent of Marathi primarily to keep Goa separate.

THE POST-LIBERATION PHASE

The Bahujan Samaj supported the MGP to counter the forces that were opposed to integration of Goa. The MGP sided with the advocates of Marathi. It did not subscribe to the theory of separate identity of Goa. They considered Konkani as a dialect rather than a separate language. A section of upper caste in Hindu community and Christians sided with the United Goans to keep Goa separate. The United Goans had played no worthwhile role in the Liberation of Goa. These communal elements within and outside Goa forged proximity to the Congress leaders at the Centre. They persuaded Premier Jawaharlal Nehru to include Konkani in the Eighth Schedule to the Constitution. Interestingly, Pandit Nehru expressed doubts over the development of into a separate language.

ANTI-INTEGRATION FORCES: A section of upper caste in Hindu community and Christians in the Goan society share common historical and geographical roots in the Velhas Conquistas areas, which came under the spell of the unholy Inquisition. The urge for separation of Goa from the mainstream culture came from these areas. They exhibited sub-national sentiments and sub-national competition, which took the form of linguistic rivalries. These sectarian groups enjoyed power, pelf and patronage in the political set-up before and after Liberation. The masses of people frowned upon whatever they stood for. The Opinion Poll verdict in 1967 went in the favour of the status quo over the future of the territory. The Indian National Congress was opposed to merger of Goa with the Marathi-speaking areas of neighbouring State of Maharashtra. The Congress High Command adopted anti-Samyukta Maharashtra posture in 1955-60. The Samyukta Maharashtra movement harped upon the cult of linguistic nationalism in the Marathi-dominated areas of the former Bombay Province. The linguistic boundaries of Goa are not fixed. Goa is squeezed between the powerful neighbours— Maharashtra and Karnataka. Both, laid claim over the tiny territory. Pandit Nehru claimed that Goa had a distinct identity on his erroneous impression of the colonial rule. In fact, Goa had no separate identity. It was integrated with mainstream culture for centuries. Interestingly, the Congress and leftist parties sided with the anti-integration forces that wanted to keep Goa separate.

The mine owners in Goa opposed the merger of Goa with Maharashtra to safeguard their corporate interests. Barring one or two mine owners, all others engaged in the anti-merger activity. They supported the advocates of Konkani to promote their sectional interests. Former Chief Minister Dayanand Bandodkar, mine owner- turned-politician, soft-pedalled on the merger issue. The advocates Konkani scattered in Goa, Kerala and

Karnataka urged the Government of India to declare Konkani as a separate language. Konkani had no worthwhile literature. It was written in five different scripts. The interpersonal and journalistic writings in Konkani were scattered and diffused. The linguists were of the opinion that Konkani needs a great genius of the rank of Kalidas or Tagore to raise it to the level of a polished literary medium.

The advocates of Konkani attempted to recognise Konkani as a separate language for more material than linguistic end. Konkani was declared as an independent language in the Census of 1961. It was a tentative re-classification and its position was considered open to further verification and research, since a section of scholars were inclined to agree with the old classification in the Linguistic Survey of India. The opinion among linguists differed over status of Konkani. However, as far as Nehru Government was concerned it was an independent language. After 1964, the Congress party toed the Nehruvian doctrine. The General Council of the Sahitya Akademi (1975) approved Konkani as a modern literary language by eight votes in favour of the resolution and four against out of total 20 members of the Board. Interestingly, eight members abstained. The politically motivated decision of the Government of India to accord separate status to Konkani boosted the morale of the anti-integration groups. It carried political significance and opened up avenues for funds to Konkani literary institutions and figures. The Congress party followed a policy of appeasement of the feudal, reactionary and anti-national forces that were opposed to integration of Goa.

INTEGRATION FORCES: In the past, Marathi was used, as the literary language whereas Konkani remained a spoken language in the Konkan Kshetra of which Goa is a part. The masses spoke Konkani but enrolled their children to the Marathi medium schools run on the private initiative before 1961. The Marathi language remained as the language of domains of intellectual exchange and medium of written __expression of the majority of the population. It is the language of art and culture and freedom struggle. It was used by the masses in various official and non-official communications and influential section of media. The MGP encouraged basic education in Marathi for socio-cultural and economic regeneration of territory. The anti-integration groups opted for Portuguese and later English rather than Konkani in the domains of power. It was a technique to avoid choosing between Konkani and Marathi. The use of English language in the domains of power after 1961 encouraged the elite bias. It provided opportunity to Luso-Indians to re-integrate with the mainstream of the country after 1961.

In the history of literature, Konkani was not used as a written medium of_expression. The Konkani literary activities began to flourish only after 1961 where as Marathi was the language in use for centuries. The Praja Socialist Party, Bharatiya Jana Sangh and Hindu Mahasabha supported the merger to enhance national identity of territory. The MGP used merger of territory with Maharashtra to counteract the sub-nation theory propounded by the anti-integration forces after. It took no major initiatives to accord the official status to Marathi after 1967. It allowed English to continue as the official language in the territory. In the mysterious circumstances, the MGP allowed the Sahitya Akademi to take its own course over the issue of declaration of Konkani as a separate language. In fact, the MGP facilitated the recognition of Konkani by Government of India.

LANGUAGE ROW IN GOA: The Official Language Bill, 1986 was introduced in the Legislative Assembly of Goa to accord the sole official status to Konkani. The Congress party resorted to appease the anti-integration groups for political gain. It tried to expand anti-Marathi tendencies rather than to counteract it. A faction of Congress party legislators apparently adopted pro-Marathi stand and demanded for accommodation of the legitimate interests of the Marathi language. The state-level leadership of the Congress party toed the appeasement policy followed by the party high command. The advocates of Konkani sided with the Congress party. The regional outfits like Goa Congress and others stood for the sole official status to Konkani. The Official Language Act, 1987 apparently provided equal status to both the regional languages. The compromise formula did not satisfy the advocates of Konkani groups. They were aware of the fact that Konkani cannot stand on its own as the sole official language. The Konkani language group lacked demonstrably popular support. They resorted to violent tactics to pressurise the Government of India to accord the official status to the Konkani language. The Christians and a section of upper caste in Hindu community formed an alliance to advance a political demand for promotion of Konkani and keep Goa separate. The masses were used politically by the elite enjoying power, culture and money for their selfish end. The advocates of Konkani labelled the amendment to the Official Language Bill, 1986 as the black mail of the people who wanted to merge Goa with Maharashtra and that the Government had succumbed to it. They argued that the passage of the Bill would hardly facilitate the use of Konkani as the official language. The advocates of Marathi, however, labelled it as the betrayal of the people.

THE POST-STATEHOOD PHASE

The number of the states has shot up from 14 in 1956 to 28 in 2000. The states under the federal set up share a common legal-constitutional framework and administrative structures as well. The internal political patterns vary considerably in the states. The state's own social, economic, and historical environment shapes the sequence of political development. Goa has enhanced its national identity after the attainment of the statehood in 1987. Ironically, Goa's identity has under gone a sea change. The lusitanian culture is preserved only to promote tourism. The integration of Goa with rest of India was a tortuous course in the political history of the territory. The anti-integration groups argued that the full-fledged statehood alone could promote Konkani language. The advocates of Konkani attempted to include Konkani in the Eighth Schedule to further their political and material interests. The recognition given to Konkani reflects the vested political interests rather than the literary merit of the language. The Government of India has not laid any definite standard for inclusion of the languages in the Eighth Schedule. The inclusion of Konkani in the Eighth Schedule in 1992 was had political undertones. It has no material gain. The only important Articles are Article 344(1) which allows to have a member in the official language commission constituted by the President and Article 351 considers the language specified in the Eighth Schedule for enrichment of the Hindi language.

The Maithili language is recognised by the Sahitya Akademi in 1965. It is spoken by three crore population in 18 districts of State of Bihar and yet to be included in the Eighth Schedule. There are over 44 lakhs each Bhili-speaking and Santhali-speaking people in India. Interestingly, Malvani-speaking people in Konkan region are vying for a separate status to their language, which is a dialect of Marathi. There is no backing of political will to accord the official status to these languages. The demands are put forth to accord status of language to Chhatisgrhi dialect after creation of the State of Chhatisgarh. But, the people favour Hindi as the state language. Language is no longer a criterion to create new states after 1956. The recognition to one or more than one languages can hardly jeopardise the political status of constituent units. The economic viability, democratisation, administrative convenience takes edge over the linguistic, tribal or ethnic affiliations in the reorganisation of the states.

It is important to note here that Konkani does not originate in Goa. As the name suggests, it is the language, which originates in Konkan region. Every spoken language becomes a written language in the course of time. Amazingly, Konkani seems to be an exception. The linguists argue that in terms of time Konkani is as old as Marathi. Nevertheless, Konkani did not become a written language until the anti-integration groups resorted to agitation in its favour in 1985-87. It can fairly be assumed that, every spoken language becomes a written language. If the assumption is valid then, it follows that literature in the Konkani language was destroyed during the Portuguese rule. Therefore, research is necessary to know the truth. Who destroyed Konkani literature, which must have been existed in the entire Konkan, which includes Goa?

Those who were opposed to the integration of Goa with India adopted Konkani as a tool to keep Goa separate. The MGP stood for merger to counteract the traditional elitist bias in the Goan society. It opted for integration rather than separate identity of the region. The MGP's ideology, however, clashed with the rival groups that stood for separate identity of Goa. The sub-national sentiments and sub-national competition took the form of linguistic rivalries in the course of time. The Congress party attempted to woo the regional parties in its bid to create a political base. It encouraged large-scale defections in the regional parties, since 1980. After 1984, the Congress party used Konkani and statehood to derive political mileage. The official recognition given to the Konkani language is on the political consideration rather than on its literary merit. Konkani is not a separate language because it does not satisfy basic attributes of a language. Yet, it is recognised by the Government of India to satisfy the pressure groups in Goa determined to prevent Goa's merger with Maharashtra. These groups have succeeded because Goa is granted a full-fledged statehood in 1987. The movement to define separate identity of region has undermined the cause of Marathi at political plane. The MGP, which swore by Marathi, failed to uphold the legitimate interests of Marathi in the State. The only course open to the advocates of Marathi is to mobilise public opinion with strong organisational and financial backing to bent the political will in their favour. Nevertheless, the dual language policy can only reinforce the cultural and national integration in the State.

Even after Konkani became an official language in Goa, there were practical difficulties in separating Konkani from Marathi. The roots of Konkani lay in Marathi. The so-called development of Konkani by Jesuit priests sequestered the spoken tongue from Marathi. The advocates of Konkani are yet to develop the language. The government and literary institutions both have failed to implement the Official Language Act of 1987. This confirms the contention that, even to supporters of the Konkani language, it is not a language, which can stand independently on its own. The Panaji Bench of Mumbai High Court in its ruling (30-03-2000) upheld the employment policy of the state government making the knowledge of the Konkani language essential and Marathi language desirable for recruitment of government servants. Interestingly, Konkani speakers are scattered from Kerala to southern tip of Maharashtra. Language is no measure for economic gain. The state government is yet to discharge its constitutional responsibility to amend Official Language Act, 1987 to accommodate the legitimate interests of Marathi in the State. There are recurring demands to amend the Official Language Act, 1987 to accord official status to Konkani in Roman script, too.

The Official Language Act, 1987 provides that Konkani shall be the official language and Marathi shall be used for all or any of the official purposes. Konkani has evolved as a modern literary language. Devanagari script is a popular, distinct and natural script of Konkani. The official status to any language need not reflect its literary merit but it paves the way for growth of national languages in the mainstream of the country. The demand for Roman script for Konkani is a weapon to alienate the Christian community from native culture, identity and deeply ingrained spirit of nationalism in Goa.

APPENDICES

Appendix–1

List Of Persons Interviewed / Consulted (1998-1999)

Bhembre, Uday Editor, Konkani daily *Sunaprant&*, President, Goa Konkani Akademi, Alto-Parvari, Goa (14-05-1998)

Dr. Doctor, A.H, Former Head, Department of Political Science, Goa University, Taleigao, Goa. (12-01-1998)

Dr. Halarnkar, Tanaji, Editor, Konkani Encyclopaedia, Goa University, noted Konkani writer, Parvari, Goa. (05-05-1998)

Dr. Jalmi, Kashinath, Maharashtrawadi Gomantak Party leader & former Law Minister, Marcela, Goa (14-12-1999)

Kakodkar, Shashikal, former Chief Minister of Goa, Daman & Diu & Maharashtrawadi Gomantak Party leader, Panaji, Goa. (13-10-1999)

Karmali, Naguesh, Konkani writer, freedom fighter, Konkani activist, Chimbel, Goa (28-04-1999)

Kelekar, Ravindra, Writer, freedom fighter, Konkani activist, Priol, Ponda, Goa. (13-05-1998)

Khalap, Ramakant, former, Union Law Minister & Former Maharashtrawadi Gomantak Party leader and now Congress Party leader, Mhapsa, Goa (03-10-1999)

Mayenkar, Gopalrao, ex-Member of Parliament, former leader of Maharashtrawadi Gomantak Party, President, Gomantak Marathi Akademi, Panaji, Goa (27-11-1999)

Naik, Pundalik, Konkani writer, activist and former Convenor, Konkani Porjeacho Awaz, Volvoi, Ponda, Goa (10-10-1999)

Pai Angle, Bhiku, Marathi write, Marathi protagonist, Margao, Goa. (11-06-1998)

Rane, P. R, Former Chief Minister of Goa & Speaker, Goa Legislative Assembly, Panaji, Goa. (28- 10-1999)

Rane Jaisingrao, Reedom fighter, Marathi writer, ex-MLA, Marathi activist, Mapsa, Bardez, Goa (01-06-1998)

Shirodkar, P.P, the first speaker of Legislative Assembly of Goa, Daman & Diu, Parvari, Bardez, Goa (10-03-1998)

Tilak, Jayantrao, Ex-Speaker of Maharashtra Legislative Council, freedom fighter, former editor of Marathi daily Kesari, Pune (10-02-1999)

Appendix–2

List Of Responses of Language Choice by Legislators in Goa

Alemao, Joquim, MLA, (18-03-1998)
Dr. Amonkar, Suresh, MLA, (25-10-1999)
Amshekar, Mohan, ex-MLA, (30-03-1998)
Asnodkar, Ulhas, MLA, (28-09-1999)
Bandekar, Shambu Bhau, MLA, (28-03-1998)
Bakal, Pratap, ex-MLA, (07-04-1998)
Cardozo, Tomazinho, ex-Speaker, (17-03-1998)
Cardozo, Alex Luis, Minister of State for Panchayat, March, 1998
Naique Desai, Dattaram Deu, ex-MLA, (07-04-1998)
Desai, Ramrao, MLA, (03-09-1999)
De Souza, Arecio, MLA, (17-03-1998)
De Souza, Francis, MLA, (30-09-1999)
De Souza, Wilfred, Deputy Chief Minister of Goa, (02-04-1998)
De Souza, Simon, ex-MLA, (27-03-1998)
Dhavalikar, Sudin, MLA, (25-09-1999)
Dourado, Herculano, ex-MLA, (27-03-1998)
Fadte, Prakash, MLA, (03-09-1999)
Fernandez, Domnic, Minister for Law & Justice (March, 1998)
Ferandez, Victoria, MLA, (19-03-1998)
Gaonkar, Prabhakar, MLA, (03-09-1999)
Gonsalves, Victor, ex-MLA, (04-04-1998)
Haldankar, Narhari, MLA, (24-03-1998)
Jalmi, Kashinath, MLA, (17-03-1998)
Kadkade Kusumkar, ex-MLA, (13-04-1998)
Kakodkar, Shashikala, ex-Chief Minister of Goa, (19-03-1998)
Kamat, Digambar, MLA, (17-03-1998)
Khalap, Ramakant, MLA, (03-10-1999)
Kotkar, Parshuram, MLA, (April, 1998)
Lima Leitao, ex-MLA, (April, 1998)
Malik, Sadanand, MLA, (19-03-1998)
Naik Sripad, Yesso, MLA, (17-03-1998)

Naik, Vishnu, ex-MLA, (09-04-1998)
Naik, Kashinath Baburao, ex-MLA, (12-06-1998)
Naik, Jaikrishna, ex-MLA, (27-03-1998).
Naik, Shantaram, ex-MP, (27-03-1998)
Naik, Anant Narciva, ex-MLA, (27-03-1998)
Mandrekar, Dayanand, MLA, (27-09-1999)
Neogi, Shyamsunder, ex-MLA, (27-03-1998)
Parrikar, Manohar, MLA, (13-03-1998)
Parulekar, Suresh, ex-MLA, (02-04-1998)
Pereira, Rocque Santan, ex-MLA, (27-03-1998)
Prabhu, Vishnu, MLA, (19-03-1998)
Rane, Jaisingrao, ex-MLA, (03-04-1998)
Rodrigues Filipe Neri, MLA, (27-09-1999)
Satarkar, Vishwas, MLA, (26-09-1999)
Sawant, Nirmala, ex-Minister for Power, (23-09-1999)
Shirodkar, Subhash, ex-Minister for Education (29-09-1999)
Shaba K. D, ex-MLA, (11-04-1998)
Sirsat, Surendra, MLA, (April, 1998)
Tople, Raghunath, ex-MLA, (27-03-1998)
Usgaonkar, Atchut, ex-MLA, (March, 1998)
Vaz, John Manuel, MLA, (19-03-19198)
Velip, Prakash, MLA, (19-03-1998)
Verenkar, Shivdas, MLA, (17-03-1998)
Zuwarkar, Somnath, Minister for Cooperation (14-05-1998)

Appendix-3

The Goa, Daman & Diu Official Language Bill, 1986

Official Gazette, Government of Goa, Daman and Diu, July 24, 1986, Series I, No. 17

Legislative Assembly of Goa, Daman & Diu

LA/B/1637/86

The following Bill, which was introduced in the Legislative Assembly of Goa, Daman and Diu on 17th July 1986, is hereby published for general information in pursuance of the provisions of Rule-136 of the Rules of procedure and Conduct of Business of the Legislative Assembly.

The Goa, Daman & Diu Official Language Bill, 1986.

(Bill No. 26 of 1986)

A BILL

to adopt the official language for official purposes of the Union territory of Goa, Daman & Diu.

BE it enacted by the Legislative Assembly of Goa, Daman & Diu in the Thirty-seventh Year of the Republic of India as follows: -

1. Short title, extent and commencement
   - (1) This Act may be called the Goa, Daman & Diu Official Language Act, 1986.
   - (2) It extends to the whole of the Union territory of Goa, Daman & Diu.
   - (3) It shall come into force at once.
2. Definitions

   In this Act, unless the context otherwise requires,
   - (a) "Administrator" means the Administrator of the Union territory of Goa, Daman & Diu appointed by the President under Article 239 of the Constitution;
   - (b) "Government" means the Government of Goa, Daman & Diu;
   - (c) "Konkani language" means Konkani language in Devanagari script;
   - (d) "Notification" means a notification published in the Official Gazette.
   - (e) " Official Gazette" means the Official Gazette of Government of Goa, Daman & Diu;
   - (f) "Union territory" means the Union territory of Goa, Daman & Diu.

3. Official language of the Union territory

(1) With effect from such date as the Administrator may, by notification, appoint, Konkani language shall, subject to the provisions contained in section 34 and 35 of the Government of Union Territories Act, 1963 (Central Act 20 of 1963), be the official language of the Union territory, and different dates may be appointed for different official purposes:

Provided that the Marathi language shall be used ——

(a) in correspondence with persons communicating with the Government in that language; and

(b) in Government publications:

Provided further that nothing contained in this sub-section shall be deemed to affect the use of the Marathi and Gujarati languages in educational, social and cultural fields:

Provide further that the Government shall not, in granting aid to any educational or cultural institution, discriminate against such institution only on the ground of the language:

Provided also that the Gujarati language shall be used in the districts of Daman and Diu for such official purposes and subject to such conditions as the Administrator may, by notification, specify.

(2) Nothing contained in sub-section (1) shall preclude any person from submitting any representation for the redress of any grievances to any officer or authority of the Union territory in any of the languages used in the Union territory.

4. Continued Use of English Language

Notwithstanding anything contained in the section 3, the English language shall continue to be used in addition to the languages specified in that section for all or any of the official purposes of the Union territory.

5. Laying of notification before the Legislative Assembly

Every notification issued under this Act shall be laid, as soon as may be after it is issued, before the Legislative Assembly while it is in session for a total period of fourteen days which may be comprised in one session or in two successive sessions, and if before the expiry of the session in which it is so laid or the session immediately following, the Legislative Assembly agree in making any modification in the notification or agree that the notification should not be issued, the notification shall thereafter have effect only in such modified form or be of no effect as the case may be; so, however, that any such modification or annulment shall be without prejudice to the validity of anything previously done under that notification.

Statement of Objects and Reasons

Section 34 of the Government of Union territories Act, 1963, empowers the Legislative Assembly of a Union territory to adopt by law any one or more of the language in use in the Union territory or Hindi as the official language or languages to be used for all or any of the official purposes of the Union territory.

The Legislative Assembly of Goa, Daman and Diu has not so far enacted any such law. Although English continues to be the official language of this Territory, it is high time that people's language must replace the English language as official language of the Territory. Since 95 per cent of the people speak Konkani, it is but obvious that the same is adopted as the official language of this Territory.

A substantial section of our population has studied through the medium of Marathi language and may desire to communicate with the Government in that language. Therefore, the Bill, while providing that the Konkani language shall be used as the official language for Goa District and Gujarati language for Daman and Diu Districts, it has given liberty to those who would like to communicate with the Government in Marathi language to do so, so that it has also been made mandatory for the Government to correspond with such people in that language; Besides the right to use of Marathi language in social, educational and cultural fields has also been assured.

The Bill seeks to achieve the above objects.

Financial Memorandum

to Clause 3 of the Bill provides for Konkani language be adopted as official language for Goa District and Gujarati for Daman and Diu Districts, for the first time. The Bill if enacted will involve and expenditure of about Rupees 50 lakhs for purchasing printing machinery, Devanagari typewriters and allied items.

Memorandum of Delegated Legislation

Section 3 of the Act contemplates that, the Administrator may, by notification appoint such date on which the Konkani language shall be the official language for all or any of the official purposes and he has been further empowered to appoint different dates for different official purposes.

The Administrator has also been further empowered to notify the use of Gujarat language in the districts of Daman and Diu for such purposes and subject to such conditions as he may specify. This delegation is of normal character.

PRATAP SINGH RANE
(Chief Minister)
Panaji- Goa
15th July 1986.

M.M. NAIK
Secretary to the Legislative Assembly of Goa, Daman & Diu
Assembly Hall, Panaji
16th July 1986.

Appendix–4

The Goa, Daman & Diu Official Language Act, 1987
(Act No. 5 of 1987)
14/4/1987
AN ACT
to adopt the official language for official purposes of the Union territory of Goa, Daman & Diu.

Be it enacted by the Legislative Assembly of Goa, Daman & Du in the Thirty-eighth year of the Republic of India as follows: —

1. Short title, extent and commencement
   (i) This Act may be called the Goa, Daman & Diu Official Language Act, 1987.
   (ii) It extends to the whole of the Union territory of Goa, Daman & Diu.
   (iii) It shall come into force at once.
2. Definitions

   In this Act, unless the context otherwise requires,
   (a) "Administrator" means the Administrator of the Union territory of Goa, Daman & Diu appointed by the President under Article 239 of the Constitution;
   (b) "Government" means the Government of Goa, Daman & Diu;
   (c) "Konkani language" means Konkani language in Devanagari script;
   (d) "Notification" means a notification published in the Official Gazette.
   (e) " Official Gazette" means the Official Gazette of Government of Goa, Daman & Diu;
   (f) "Union territory" means the Union territory of Goa, Daman & Diu.
3. Official language of the Union territory
   (1) With effect from such date as the Administrator may, by notification, appoint, Konkani language shall, subject to the provisions contained in section 34 and 35 of the Government of Union Territories Act, 1963

(Central Act 20 of 1963), be the official language for all or any of the official purposes of the Union territory, and different dates may be appointed for different official purposes:

Provided that the Administrator may, by a like notification, direct that in case of Goa District, the Marathi language, and in the case of Daman & Diu Districts, the Gujarati language, shall also be used for all or any of the official purposes and different dates may be appointed for different official purposes.

Provided further that nothing contained in this sub-section shall be deemed to affect the use of the Marathi and Gujarati languages in educational, social and cultural fields:

Provide further that the Government shall not, in granting aid to any educational or cultural institution, discriminate against such institution only on the ground of the language.

(2) Nothing contained in sub-section (1) shall preclude any person from submitting any representation for the redress of any grievances to any officer or authority of the Union territory in any of the languages used in the Union territory.

4. Continued Use of English Language

Notwithstanding anything contained in the section 3, the English language shall continue to be used in addition to the languages specified in that section for all or any of the official purposes of the Union territory.

5. Laying of notification before the Legislative Assembly —

Every notification issued under this Act shall be laid, as soon as may be after it is issued, before the Legislative Assembly while it is in session for a total period of fourteen days which may be comprised in one session or in two successive sessions, and if before the expiry of the session in which it is so laid or the session immediately following, the Legislative Assembly agree in making any modification in the notification or agree that the notification should not be issued, the notification shall thereafter have effect only in such modified form or be of no effect as the case may be; so, however, that any such modification or annulment shall be without prejudice to the validity of anything previously done under that notification.

M. RAGHU CHANDER

Secretary to the Government of Goa, Daman Dated: 23 April, 1987 & Diu, Law Department, (Legal Affairs)

Secretariat, Panaji-Goa

Appendix–5

Notifications

Legal Department, Legal Affairs Branch

Notification (7-2-37/LA)

The Goa, Daman and Diu Official Language Act, 1987 (Act 5 of 1987), which has been passed by the Legislative Assembly on 4-2-1987 and assented to by the President of India on 14-4-1987, is hereby published for the general information of the public.

P. V. Kadnekar, Under Secretary (Drafting)

Panaji, 23rd April, 1987

Government of Goa, General Administration and Coordination Department, Official language and Public Grievances Cell

Notification

1-1-1987 (OL/PG)

In exercise of the powers conferred by sub-section (1) of section 3 of the Goa, Daman & Diu Official Language Act, 1987 (Act No. 5 of 1987), the Government of Goa hereby appoints the 19th day of December, 1987 as the date from which Konkani Language shall be the official language for the purpose of replies by the Government whenever communications are received in Konkani language.

By order and in the name of the Governor of Goa.

Suresh Bhosle, Under Secretary to the Government.

Panaji, 15th December 1987.

Notification

1-1-1987 (OL/PG)

In exercise of the powers conferred under the first proviso to sub-section (1) of section 3 of the Goa, Daman & Diu Official Language Act, 1987 (Act No. 5 of 1987), the Government of Goa hereby appoints the 19th day of December, 1987 as the date from which Marathi shall be used for the purpose of replies by the Government whenever communications are received in Marathi language.

By order and in the name of the Governor of Goa.

Suresh Bhosle, Under Secretary to the Government.

Panaji, 15th December 1987.

Appendix–6

The Goa Official Language (Amendment) Bill, 2000

(Bill No.___ of 2000)

A BILL

Further to amend The Goa, Daman and Diu Official Language Act, 1987.

Be it enacted by the Legislative Assembly of Goa in the Fifty-first year of the Republic of India as follows:-

1. Short title and commencement: (1) This Act may be called the Goa Official Language (Amendment) Act, 2000. (2) It shall come into force at once.
2. Amendment of Section: In Section 1 and in other sections of the Goa, Daman and Diu Official Language Act, 1987 (Act No. 5 of 1987 hereinafter referred to as the 'Principal Act') in the long and short title, the figure and words 'Daman' and 'Diu' wherever it occurs, shall be omitted.

for the _expression 'Union Territory' and 'the Union Territory of Goa, Daman and Diu', wherever they occur, the _expression 'The State of Goa' shall be substituted.

Amendment of Section 2: In section 2 of the Principal Act, Clause (a) and (f) shall be omitted i) Clauses (b), (c), (d), and (e) shall be restructured as clauses (a), (b), (c) and (d), respectively ii) After restructured clause (d), new clause (e) shall be inserted as follows (e) 'Marathi language' means Marathi language in Devanagari script

Amendment of Section 3: In Section 3 of the Principal Act: - i) With effect from such date as the Government of Goa may, by notification, appoint, Konkani language shall be the official language for all or any of the official purposes of the State of Goa, and different dates may be appointed for different official purposes. ii) Existing first proviso shall be omitted; iii) A new sub-section (2) shall be inserted after sub-section (1) as follows: - (2) The Government of Goa, shall, by notification, declare that in the State of Goa, Marathi language shall be also used with equal status, for all the official purposes, as and whenever notified under sub-section (1), with effect from the same date or dates as appointed under sub-section (1). iv) In the second proviso, the expression and Gujarati shall be deleted. v) In the same second proviso, for the expression 'Languages' the expression 'language' shall be substituted. vii) Existing sub-section (2) shall be renumbered as sub-section (3) vii) In the renumbered sub-section (3), after the expression, 'in sub-section (1), the expression; and sub-section (2)' shall be inserted.

5 Amendment of Section 4:In section 4 of the Principal Act: -

The expression 'Notwithstanding anything contained in section 3', shall be omitted.

For the word 'shall', word 'may' shall be substituted.

For the expression 'that section', the expression 'in Section 3'shall be substituted.

STATEMENT OF OBJECTS AND REASONS

The Goa, Daman and Diu Official Language Act, 1987, has conferred a status of Official language on Konkani language. However, the said Act was also enacted with an intention and desire to give equal status to Marathi language for its use for all the official purposes for which Konkani language is used. Whereas, the Honourable High Court of Bombay at Goa in its judgement dated 30-03-2000 passed in Writ Petition No. 286/96 has held that both, the Konkani and Marathi languages do not enjoy the equal status, the present Bill is being introduced to remove said lacunae and to achieve and give effect to the original intention as referred to above so to make it express and explicit. The Bill also seeks to encourage the people to use the Konkani and Marathi languages for the official purposes of the state of Goa.

FINANCE MEMORANDUM

No financial implications are involved towards the implementation of the provisions of the Bill.

Panaji, 14 June, 2000 (Manohar Parrikar)

Bharatiya Janata Party, MLA

Appendix–7

Survey-I: Percentage of advertisement space covered in Vernacular and English newspapers published in Goa

The Sample Survey-I was conducted to find out the percentage of space covered by advertisement to the total space in the local editions of the vernacular (Konkani & Marathi) and the English newspapers in the State. It included three Marathi dailies *Gomantak*, *Navprabha* and *Rashtramat*, *Sunaprant*— the sole *Konkani* daily (now publication suspended) and three English dailies— *The Navhind Times*, O *Heraldo* and *Gomantak Times*, respectively. The percentage of the space covered was taken for the advertisement appeared in the newspaper for a period of one month (January, 1997) in each case in the calendar year 1997. The national dailies and those Marathi dailies published from outside Goa were not covered in the Survey including Marathi daily *Tarun Bharat* of Belgaum.

Table–1: Per cent of space covered by advertisement to total space (percentage) in the local editions of the vernacular (Konkani & Marathi) and the English press in 1997 in Goa. Three Marathi, one Konkani and three English dailies were covered in the Survey-I.

Marathi	**%**
Gomantak	23.20
Rashtramat	10.00
Navprabha	07.60
Konkani	
Sunaprant	11.00
English	
The Navhind Times	32.90
OHeraldo	18.70
Gomantak Times	18.10

(Source: Survey-I, January 1997)

In the Survey-I conducted for percentage of advertisement cornered by the local newspapers in the State in January 1997, reveals that the English press cornered the highest percentage of the advertisement in the State. The leading English daily The Navhind Times covered 32.90 per cent of advertisement to the total space covered which has wider readership with highest circulation. The other

English dailies Herald cornered 18.70 per cent whereas Gomantak Times cornered 18.10 per cent of the total advertisement for the corresponding period. The prominent Marathi daily Gomantak cornered 23.20 per cent of the advertisement followed by Rashtramat 10 per cent and Navprabha 7.6 per cent, respectively. The Konkani daily Sunaprant has 11 per cent advertisement coverage. The English press continues to dominate the advertisement space. The sole Konkani daily Sunaprant ranks after the Marathi dailies, which have wider readership in Goa, since the Liberation.

Appendix–8

Survey-II: Use of language(s) preferred by Members of Legislative Assembly in Goa.

The Sample Survey-II was conducted in March, 1998 to November, 1999 by collecting data based on the structured questionnaire. The structured questionnaire was used to elicit opinion and collect data from - (i) Members of Legislative Assembly (MLAs) of Goa and Members of Parliament (MPs); (ii) Members of municipalities; and (iii) Members of Village Panchayats in the State. The purposive sampling method was employed in three categories viz. the members of state assembly; municipal councils and village panchayats in the State.

The respondents were asked to state the language of their choice in the domain of the legislature, judiciary, administration, intellectual exchange and commerce. In the Sample Survey-II, 21 out of 40 elected members of the legislative assembly (MLAs), 34 ex-MLAs of the State of Goa including two members of Parliament (MPs) responded to the questionnaire. There were 49 out of 155 members of the municipal councils of Mhapsa, Panaji, Bicholi, and Perne of North Goa district and Ponda, Mormugao, Margao of South Goa district. They belonged to 13 municipal councils in the State. In Goa, there are 188 village panchayats and 1428 their elected members. Out of which 56 members were interviewed by using structured questionnaire.

Table-II: Language(s) preferred (percentage) for domain of Legislature by Members of Goa Legislative Assembly:-

Language(s)	**%**
Konkani	23.64
English	20.00
Marathi & Konkani	16.36
Marathi, Konkani & English	16.36
English	12.73
Marathi	05.45
Marathi & English	01.81
Hindi	01.81
Others	01.84

(*Source: Survey-II, 1998-1999*)

The findings of the Survey-II reveal that 23.64 per cent of the legislators favoured the use Konkani in the legislative assembly for conduct of the business of the House. Konkani & English is preferred by 20 per cent followed by Marathi, English & Konkani 16.36 per cent; English 12.73 per cent; Marathi alone 5.45; Marathi & English 1.81 per cent; Hindi 1.81 per cent and Others 1.84 per cent, respectively. The legislators favoured primarily the use of Konkani and secondarily English and both the regional languages in the domain of legislature.

Table-III: Language(s) preferred (percentage) for domain of Judiciary by Members of Goa Legislative Assembly:-

Language(s)	%
English	54.54
Konkani	09.09
English & Konkani	09.09
Marathi & Konkani	07.30
Marathi & English	05.45
Marathi	03.64
Marathi, Konkani & English	03.64
Hindi	01.81
Others	05.44

(*Source: Survey-II, 1998-1999*)

In the domain of judiciary, the use of English is preferred by 54.54 per cent legislators followed by Konkani 9.09 per cent; English & Konkani 9.09 per cent; Marathi & Konkani 7.3 per cent; Marathi & English 5.45 per cent; Marathi alone 3.64 per cent; Marathi, Konkani & English 3.64 per cent; Hindi 1.81 per cent and Others 5.44 per cent, respectively. The majority of the legislators favoured the use of English in the domain of judiciary.

Table-IV: Language(s) preferred (percentage) for domain of Administration by Members of Goa Legislative Assembly:-

Language(s)	%
English	29.09
Konkani	16.36
Marathi & English	14.54
English & Konkani	14.54
Marathi	09.09
Marathi, Konkani & English	03.64
Hindi	03.64
Others	09.10

(*Source: Survey-II, 1998-1999*)

In the domain of administration English is preferred by 29.09 per cent of the legislators followed by Konkani 16.36; Marathi & English 14.54 per cent; English & Konkani 14.54 per cent; Marathi, Konkani & English 3.64 per cent; Marathi 9.09 per cent; Hindi 3.64 per cent and Others 9.1 per cent, respectively. The legislators favoured primarily the use of English and secondarily the regional languages in the domain of administration.

Table-V: Language(s) preferred (percentage) for domain of Intellectual Exchange by Members of Goa Legislative Assembly:-

Language(s)	**%**
English	40.00
English & Konkani	14.54
Konkani	12.73
Marathi & English	10.91
Marathi	05.45
Marathi, Konkani & English	03.64
Marathi & Konkani	03.64
Hindi	01.81
Others	07.28

(*Source: Survey-II, 1998-1999*)

In the domain of intellectual exchange 40 per cent preferred use of English followed by English & Konkani 14.54; Konkani 12.73 per cent; Marathi & English 10.91 per cent; Marathi 5.45 per cent; Marathi, Konkani & English 3.64 per cent; Marathi 7 Konkani 3.64 per cent; Hindi 1.81 per cent and Others 7.28 per cent, respectively. The majority of the legislators favoured the use of English and secondarily the regional languages in the domain of intellectual exchange.

Table-VI: Language(s) preferred (percentage) for domain of Commerce by Members of Goa Legislative Assembly:-

Language(s)	**%**
English	36.36
Marathi & English	12.73
English & Konkani	12.73
Marathi, Konkani & English	09.09
Konkani	09.09
Marathi	07.30
Hindi	03.64
Others	09.06

(*Source: Survey-II, 1998-1999*)

In the domain of commerce 36.36 per cent legislators preferred use of English followed by English & Konkani 9.09 per cent; Marathi, Konkani & English 9.09 per cent; Konkani 9.09 per cent; Marathi 7.3 per cent; Hindi 3.64 per cent; and others 9.06 per cent, respectively. The majority of the legislators favour the use of English in the domain of commerce.

Table-VII: Language(s) (per centage) preferred for domains of Legislature, Judiciary, Administration, Intellectual Exchange and Commerce in Goa by Members of Goa Legislative Assembly:-

Language(s)	**%**
English	34.54
Konkani	14.18
Konkani & English	14.18
Marathi & English	09.09
Marathi, Konkani & English	06.91
Marathi	06.18
Marathi & Konkani	05.45
Hindi	02.54
Others	06.93

(*Source: Survey-II, 1998-1999*)

The language preferred in all the five domains, viz. Legislature, judiciary, administration, intellectual exchange and commerce include, English 34.54 per cent; Konkani & English 14.18 per cent; Marathi & English 9.09 per cent; Marathi, Konkani & English 6.91 per cent; Marathi 6.18 per cent; Marathi & Konkani 5.54 per cent; Hindi 2.54 per cent and Others 6.93 per cent, respectively.

Table-VIII: Language(s) preferred (percentage) for domains of Legislature, Administration, Judiciary, Intellectual Exchange and Commerce in Goa by members of Municipal Councils:-

Language(s)	**%**
English	41.62
Konkani & English	24.07
Konkani & Marathi	06.93
Konkani	05.71
Marathi	05.30
Marathi & English	03.67
Others	12.70

(*Source: Survey-II, 1998-1999*)

As many as 41.62 per cent respondents in the municipalities in the State preferred English in the domain of legislature, judiciary, administration, intellectual exchange and commerce. 24.07 per cent respondent preferred Konkani and English. Konkani and Marathi were preferred by 6.93 percent of respondents whereas those solely favoured Konkani and Marathi included 5.71 and 5.30

per cent. Marathi and English were preferred by 3.67 per cent of the respondents and other languages were preferred by 12.70 per cent of the respondents. Thus, the members of municipalities have shown preference for the use English rather than the vernacular languages.

Table-IX: Language(s) preferred (percentage) for domains of Legislature, Judiciary, Administration, Intellectual Exchange and Commerce in Goa by members of Village Panchayats:-

Language(s)	**%**
Marathi & Konkani	42.85
Marathi & Hindi	21.42
Marathi	07.14
Konkani	07.14
English & Konkani	07.14
Others	14.31

(*Source: Survey-II, 1998-1999*)

The members of the panchayat who favour the use of Konkani and Marathi constitute 42.85 per cent, followed by Marathi and Hindi 21.42 per cent, Marathi, Konkani and Konkani & English were 7.14 per cent and others were 14.31 per cent. None opted for the use of English. Thus, the members of the gram panchayats show a marked preference for the use of regional languages and Hindi at grass root level. However, the majority of members of Goa Legislative Assembly owing allegiance to Indian National Congress and the Opposition parties including the United Goans Democratic Party, Bharatiya Janata Party, Maharashtrawadi Gomantak Party, and Independents favoured the use of English in the domain of the legislature, judiciary, administration, intellectual exchange, and commerce irrespective of party affiliations. The trend reflects that the English is entrenched in administration, commerce and education and the regional languages are relegated to the socio-cultural plane.

BIBLIOGRAPHY

Angle, Prabhakar. (1986-87). *Myth & Truth— Marathi in Goa*. Goa: Gomant Vidya Niketan.

Aiyer & Srinivasan. (1965). *Studies in Indian Democracy*. New Delhi: Allied Publishers Pvt. Ltd.

Amonkar, Suresh. (1967). *Goa Opinion Poll: Analysis & Study of Voting Pattern*. Goa: Suresh Amonkar.

Austin, Granville. (1966). *The Constitution of India— The Cornerstone of the Nation*. Oxford University Press.

Atre, P. K.(1977). *Jai Hind Jai Maharashtra*. Pune: Manorama Prakashan.

Axelvord, Paul & Fuersch M.A. (1996). *Flight of Deities: Hindu Resistance in Portuguese Goa*. UK: Modern Asian Studies.

Bapuji, B. R. (1993). *Essays on Sociology of Languages*. Hyderabad: T. R. Publications.

Basu, Durga Das (2000). *Introduction to the Constitution of India*. New Delhi: Wadhwa & Co.

Bayer, J. M. (1986) *Language, Law & National Integration*. Mysore:Central Institute of Indian Languages.

Bhembre, L V. (1979) *Purtugal Rajavatipooravichea Dharmik Vagmay*. Goa: Gomantak Marathi Parishad.

Borges, Charles, J. Feldmann (1997). *Goa: & Portugal: Their Cultural Links*. New Delhi: Concept Publishing Company.

Borges, Charles. (1994). *Goa to Me*. New Delhi: Concept Publishing Company.

Berton, Ronald. (1997). *Atlas of the Languages & Ethnic Communities of South Asia*. New Delhi: Sage Publishers.

Borges, Charles. (1994). *The Honour of Goa Jesuits: 1542-1759*. New Delhi: Concept Publishing Company.

Braganza, A. (1964). *The Discovery of Goa*. Goa: Brooks Publication.

Brass, Paul. (1974). *Language, Religion & Politics in North India*. London: Cambridge University Press.

Brass, Paul. (1991). *Ethnicity & Nationalism*. New Delhi: Sage Publications.

Brecher, Michael. (1959). *Nehru— A Political Biography.* New Delhi: Oxford University Press.

Catulo, Caetano Francisco (1951). *Historia e Evolucao Dos CTT do Estada da India.* Goa: Reparticao Central dos Services dos Correios, Telegratos e Telefones do Estada da India.

Chaudhury N. C. (1996) *The Continent of Circe.* Bombay: Publisher not mentioned.

Chavan, V. P. (1995). *The Konkan & the Konkani Language*. New Delhi: Asian Educational Services.

Chatterjee, Sunit Kumar. (1943). *Language & the Linguistic Problems*. Bombay: Oxford University Press.

Collinwood, L. (1996). *21st Century Universal Encyclopaedia*. Sydney: Vol-9 & 17, Regency Publishing Group Pvt Ltd.

Costa, Cosmo Jose. (1997). *A Missiological Conflict Between Padrado & Propagate in the East*. Goa: Pilar Publications.

Coutinho, Verssimo, (1987). *Education & Development in Goa*. Chicago: ICSS, Loyala University of Chicago.

Cunha, J. Gerson Da (1991). *The Konkani Language & the Literature.* New Delhi: Asian Educational Service.

Cunha, J. Gerson Da. (1993). *The Origin of Bombay.* New Delhi: Asian Educational Service.

Cunha, T. B. (1944). *De-nationalization of Goans.* Bombay: Massillon Almeida.

Cunha, T. B. (1961). *Goa's Freedom Struggle.* Bombay: T. B. Cunha Memorial Committee.

Desai, P. B. (1965). *Goa & Karnataka.* Dharwar: Karnataka University.

D' Mello, Rudolf. (1963). Goa: A New Deal. Bombay: Chetna Limited.

Dias, Biblial. (1991). *The Office of Speaker.* Goa: Government College of Arts, Science & Commerce.

Dantas, Norman. (1999). *The Transforming of Goa.* Goa: The Other India Press.

Dreze, Jean & Sen, Amartya. (1996). *Indian Development— Selected Regional Perspective.* Delhi: Oxford University Press.

Esteves, Sarto. (1986). *Politics & Political Leadership in Goa.* New Delhi: Sterling Publishers Pvt. Ltd.

Esteves, Sarto (1966) *Goa & Its Future.* Bombay: Markatlal & Co.

Faleiro, Eduardo. (1996). *A Voice in Parliament— Debates & Speeches in Parliament.* New Delhi: Allied Publishers.

Faleiro, Luizinho. (1999) *My Goa— An Autobiography.* Goa: Dr. Fransisco Luis Gomes Trust.

Gaitonde, P. D. (1987) *Portuguese Pioneers in India.* Bombay: Popular Prakashan.

Gaitonde, P. D. (1987) *The Liberation of Goa: A Participant's View of History.* Bombay: Oxford University Press.

Gandhi, M. K. (1960). *Thoughts on National Language.* Ahmedabad: Navjivan Publications.

Garcia, da Silva Fatima. (1997). *Kaleidoscope of Women in Goa— 1510-1961.* New Delhi: Concept Publishing Co.

George, Evagrio. (1959). *Salazar's Rule in Portugal & the Case of Goa.* New Delhi: New Age Printing Press.

Ghantkar, G. S. (1973). *An Introduction to Goan Marathi Records in Halakannada Script.* Goa: S. S. B. Caculo.

Ghatge, A. M. (1963). *Konkani of South Kanara—A Survey of Marathi Dialects.* (Part-I-V). Bombay: The State Board of Literature & Culture.

Gill, P. S. (1984). *Dismantling Democracy.* New Delhi: Lancer International.

Gokhale, Sharadchandra. (1981). *Kesari (1881 - 1991) Vaichyarik Sambandh ani Vaatchaal.* Pune: Kesari Prakashan.

Gomes, Olivinho. (1996). *Konkani Sorospaticho Itihas.* Goa: Konkani Sorospat Prakashan.

Gupta, Das Jyotindra. (1970). *Language Conflict & National Development.* England: Oxford University Press.

Hallyday, M. A. K. (1968). *Language as Social Semiotic.* London: Edward Arnold.

Harrison, Selig (1960). *India, the Most Dangerous Decades.* Princeton: Princeton University Press.

Hudson, R A. (1996). *Socio-Linguistics.* Cambridge: New York: University Press.

Hutt, Anthony. (1988). *A Travellor's History & Architectural Guide.* England: Scorpion Publishing Ltd.

Israel, Milton. (1983). *National Unity— The South Asian Experience.* New Delhi: Promilla & Co. Publishers.

Kamat, M. V. (1982). *My Mother Tongue.* Goa: Fourth Menezes Braganza Memorial Lectures.

Kamat, Pratim. (1999). *Farar Far— Local Resistance to Colonial Hegemony in Goa.* Goa: Institute Menezes Braganza.

Katre, S. M. (1966). *The Formation of Konkani.* Pune: Deccan College, Post-Graduate & Research Institute.

Kelekar, Ravindra (1965). *Nehru on Goa.* Goa: Goa Freedom Association.

Keni, Chandrakant. (1993). *Teen Dasaka.* Goa: V M Salgaonkar Pratishthan.

Keni, Chandrakant, et al. (1994). *Anna Phandse.* Mumbai: Rajiv Prakashan.

Khera, P. N. (1961). *Operation Vijay: The Liberation of Goa & other Portuguese Territories.* New Delhi: Historical Section, Defence Ministry, Government of India.

King, Robert D. (1997). *Nehru & the Language Politics of India.* New Delhi: Oxford University Press.

Kirloskar, M. S. (1952). *Swatantreachea Paanch Varshe.* Pune: Kirloskar Press.

Kishore, S. (1987). *National Integration in India.* New Delhi: Sterling Publishers.

Komarpant, Somnath. (1992). *Gomantak Marathi Sahitya Sammelan.* Goa: Gomantak Marathi Akademy.

Larsen, Karen. (1998). *Faces of Goa.* New Delhi: Gyan Publishing House.

Lohia, Rammanohar (1947). *Action in Goa.* Bombay: August Publication House.

Lohia, Rammanohar. (1986). *Language.* Hyderabad: Rammanohar Lohia Samata Nyas.

Khubchandani, L, M. (1991). *Language, Culture & Nation-building— Challenges of Modernization.* New Delhi: Manohar Publications.

Mallikarjun, B. (1986). *Language Use in Administration & National Integration.* Mysore: Central Institute of Indian Languages.

Meherwade, K. M. (1973). *Union Territories in India— A Case Study Of Goa.* Dharwar: Karnataka University Press.

Menezes, Bertha (1992). *Landmarks in My Life.* Goa: Bertha Menezes Braganza.

Menezes, Bertha. (no date) *Meet Menezes Braganza.* Bombay: Menezes Braganza Memorial Committee.

Misra, M. S. (1988). *Politics of Regionalism.* Delhi: Deep & Deep Publishers.

Mitragotri, V. R. (1999). *A Socio-cultural History of Goa from Bhojas to Vijayanagar.* Goa: Institute Menezes Braganza.

Munshi, K. M. (1967). *Indian Constitutional Development— Pilgrimage to Freedom.* (Vol-I). New Delhi: Oxford University Press.

Naik, Datta. (1987). *Laying the Ground for Communal Riots.* Goa: Saungadi Prakashan.

Nehru, Jawaharlal. (1952). *Jawaharlal Nehru's Speeches 1949-1968.* (Vol. II). New Delhi: Publications Division, Government of India.

Pai Panandikar, V. A. &*et al.* (1999). *Contemporary India.* New Delhi:Tata Mac Graw-Hill Publication Co. Ltd.

Palanithurai, G. & Thandavan, R. (1993). *Ethnic Movement in India.* New Delhi: Kanishka Publishing House.

Pearson, M. N. (1987). *The New Cambridge History Of Goa— The Portuguese in India.* Hyderabad: Cambridge University Press.

Pereira, Antonio. (1982) *The Makers of Konkani Literature.* Goa: Antonio Pereira.

Pereira, Gerald. (1973). *An Outline of Pre-Portuguese History of Goa*.Goa: Gerald Pereira.

Pereira, Jose. (1971). *Konkani: A Language*. Dharwar: Karnataka University.

Pereira, Jose. (1992). *Literary Konkani— A Brief History*. Goa: Goa Konkani Akademi.

Pereira, Rui Gomes. (1977). *Goa: Hindu Temples and Deities*, Goa: Printwell Press.

Phadke, Y. D. (1979). *Language & Politics*. Bombay: Himalaya Publishing House.

Phal, S. R. (1982). *Society in Goa*. Delhi: B R Publishing Corporation.

Pinto, Celsa (1996). *Images & Perceptions*. Goa: Rajhaunsa.

Pissurlekar, Pandurang. (1979). *Portuguese-Maratha Sambandh*. Pune: University of Pune.

Priolkar, A. K. (1958). *Printing Press in India*. Bombay: Mumbai Marathi Granth Sangrahlaya.

Priolkar, A. K., (1961). *The Goa Inquisition*. Bombay: A Quarterly Centenary Commemoration Study Of Inquisition In India, Bombay University Press.

Priolkar, A. K. (1966). *Granthik Marathi Bhashya ani Konkani Boli*. Pune: University of Pune.

Priolkar, A. K. (1967). *Goa Re-Discovered*. Bombay: Bhatkal Book International.

Rahman, Tariq (1998). *Language Politics in Pakistan*. New Delhi: Oxford University Press.

Rao, K. V. Narayan. (1973). *The Emergence of Andhra Pradesh*. Bombay: Popular Prakashan.

Rubinoff, A. G. (1998). *The Construction of a Political Community: Integration & Identity in Goa*. New Delhi: Sage Publications.

Rustow, D. A. (1967). *A World of Nations*. Washington: The Brookings Institution.

Sathe, Shanta. (1994). *Lokmanya Tilak— His Social & Political Thought*. Delhi: Ajanta Publications.

Saldanha, C. F. (1952). *A Short History of Goa*. Bombay: Anglo-Lusitano.

Saldanha, Joseph. (1907). *The Christ Purana of Thomas Stephen*. Mangaore: Joseph Saldanha.

Satoskar, B. D. (1979). *Gomantak— Prakriti ani Sanskriti*.Pune: Subhdha-Saraswat.

Sharma, G. R. (1950). *Saraswat Bhugava*. Bombay: Popular Book Depot.

Shirodkar, Prakashchandra. (1988). *Goa-Cultural Trends*. Goa: Director of Archives, Archaelogy & Museum, Government of Goa.

Shirodkar, P. P. (1995). *Itihasachya Drishtikonatoon Gomantakatil Marathi Parampareacha Udgam ani Vikas*. Goa: Gomatak Marathi Akademy.

Subrahmanyam, Sanjay. (1997). *The Career & Legend of Vasco da Gama.* (New Delhi: Cambridge University Press.

Sukhthankar, J. S. (1954). *Aicha Va Kalcha Gomantak.* Bombay: Goa Hindu Association.

Telkar, Shridhar. (1962) *Goa Yesterday & Today.* Bombay: Publisher not mentioned.

Tripathi, R. S. (1992). *History of Ancient India.* New Delhi: Motilal Banarasidass Publishers.

Varde, P, S. (1977). *History of Education in Goa from 1510 to the Present Day.* Goa: Goa Vidya Pratisthan.

Velignkar, Joseph. (1998). *India & the West— the First Encounter.* Bombay: Heras Institute of Indian History & Culture, St. Xavier's College.

Wakankar, L. S. (1986). *Devanagari Lipee, and Udgam: Vikas Va Sambhavana.* Pune: University of Pune.

Xavier, P. D. (1993). *Goa— A Social Profile.* Goa: Rajhaunsa.

Official Documents:

Government of Goa

Government of Goa. (1982). *Goa: Then & Now.* Goa: Department of Information and Public Relations.

Government of Goa. (1998). *GOA: Economy in Figures-1998.* Goa: Directorate of Planning, Statistics & Evaluation.

Government of Goa. (1997 & 1998). *Indicators of Socio-economic Development.* Goa: Directorate of Planning, Statistics and Evaluation.

Legislative Assembly of Goa, Daman & Diu Debates. (1968). Vol-V, No. 15.

Legislative Assembly of Goa, Daman & Diu Debates. (1971) Bill No. 21 of 1971.

Legislative Assembly of Goa, Daman & Diu Debates. (1983). Vol-XX, No. 2.

Legislative Assembly of Goa, Daman & Diu Debates. (1986). Vol-XXIII, No.10.

Legislative Assembly of Goa, Daman & Diu Debates. (1987).Vol-XXIV, No.1.

Official Gazette. (05/09/1987).Goa: Series-I, No. 37.

Ready Reference: Assembly Elections. (1999). Goa: Department of Information & Publicity.

Regional Plan for Goa 2000 A D, (1988). Goa: Town & Country Planning Department, 1988

Government of Goa, Daman & Diu. (1961-1967 & 1994-1995). *Statistical Pocket Book of Goa, Daman & Diu.* Goa: Department of Planning, Statistics & Evaluation.

Government of Goa, Daman & Diu. (1986). *Winds of Change.* Goa: Department of Information.

Gazetteer of the Union Territory of Goa, Daman & Diu. (1979). Part-I

Govapuri. (2000). Vol-I, January-March, No. 4. Goa: Institute Menezes Braganza,

Government of Goa. *Economic Survey— 2002-2003.* (2003). Goa: Department of Planning, Statistics, & Evaluation.

Government of Maharashtra

Goa's Freedom Struggle vis-a-vis Maharashtra-1946-61. (1978). Vol.I—III. Bombay: Publication Division.

Government of Mysore

Goa: An Integral Part of Karnataka. (1965). Bangalore, Director of Publishing and Information.

Government of India

Census of India, Goa, Daman & Diu. (1971). New Delhi: Series-28.

Census of India, (2001). Series-31, Goa, Paper-1 of 2001.

Report of Census of India. (1971, 1981, 1991). New Delhi: Census of India.

Census of India. (1991). Series-6, Paper-I of 1991.

Government of India. *Jawaharlal Nehru's Speeches.* (1952). New Delhi: Publications Division.

Government of India. (1989) *Regional Divisions of India— A Cartographic Analysis.* New Delhi: Census of India, Series-I, Vol-XXIX.

Government of India. (1964). *Techno-Economic Survey: Goa, Daman & Diu.* New Delhi: National Council of Applied Economic Research.

Government of India. *India-99.* (1999).New Delhi: Publications Division, Information & B Broadcasting Ministry.

Government of India. (1998) *Consolidated Instructions of Elections.* New Delhi: Election Commission of India.

Government of India. (1960). *The Story of Goa.* London: Information Service of India, India House.

Government of Portugal

Portugal & the anti-Colonial Campaign. (1960). Lisbon: Secretariado Nacional Da Informacao.

Private Documents

Marathi— Only Language Of Goa. (1985). Goa: Marathi Rajyabhasha Pratishthan Samiti.

KPA's Memorandum. (1985). Goa: Konkani Porjeacho Awaz.

Bhandare, B. L. (1983). *Speech.* Goa: Second Marathi Bhasha Parishad.

Katre, S. M. (1957). *Speech.* The Sixth Session of Konkani Conference. Bombay: Gomantak Printing Press.

Mallya, P. Purushothama (1997). *Selected Seminar Papers / Writings on Konkani Language & Culture (1954-97)*. Kochi, Kerala: Konkani Bhasha Prachar Sabha.

Mascarenhas, Lambert. (1989). *GUJ: In a New Era*. Goa: Goa: Union of Journalist.

Telang, M.K. (1966-1967). *The Confused Report— A Critique of the Mahajan Report on Karwar-Supa- Haliyal.* Bombay: Karwar: Karwar Citizens' Committee.

Dr. Sukhthankar, V. S., Dr. Collaco, A., Kane, P.V., Dr. Kaikini, V. M., Palekar, S. V., Priolkar, A. K., and Kagal, B. R. (1941). *Memorandum on Konkani.* Pune: Maharashtra Sahitya Parishad.

Unpublished Ph. D. / M. Phil. Dissertations

Bhat, A. R., (1980). *The Comparative Philological Study of Hindi & Konkan*i. (Ph. D. Dissertation). Bombay: University of Bombay.

Chavan, R. S. (1993). *Siddis of Janjira & the Portuguese.* (Ph. D. Dissertation). Goa: Goa University.

Dessai, Khristinanand (1993). *Trade Union Movement in Goa: 1936-1986.* (Ph. D. Dissertation). Goa: Goa University.

D'Souza, Joseph. (1975). *Conditions that Keep Gavdas Backward.* (Ph. D. dissertation). Gujarat: M. S. University.

Naik, Maya. (1993). *Maharashtrawdi Gomantak Party— Its Emergence & Functioning (1963- 84).* (M. Phil. dissertation). Bombay: University of Bombay.

Radhakrishnan, R. (1994). *Dayanand Balkrishna Bandodkar: The Architect of Modern Go*a. (Ph. D. dissertation). Goa: Goa University

Rodrigues, Maria. (1996). *Opinion Poll in Goa—An Evaluation of Method of Settlement of Controversy.* (Ph. D. Dissertation). Goa:Goa University.

Tombat, Nishta. (1995). *Tristao De Baraganza-Cunha, (1891– 1958) & the Rise of Nationalist Consciousness in Goa.* (Ph. D. dissertation).Goa: Goa University.

Newspapers/Weeklies

Harijan: 01/02/1948

Indian Express: 28/12/1999

Kesari: 09/09/1890

Kesari: 17/09/1893

Kesari: 09/01/1906

Times of India: 29/03/1999

Young India: 27/08/1925

******

Index

H

I

J

K

Q

R